Praise for Von Allan's first graphic novel

the road to god knows...

"Teenage Marie is a bit overweight and has missed too ... is her schizophrenic mother, especially since her dad - w ... isn't around much. So it's Marie who has to cope with her mother's personality changes and hospitalizations while managing her own life. Fortunately, Marie has best girlfriend Kelly, who abets Marie's obsession: TV wrestling. And when the two girls escape "reality" to watch a live match, earning ticket money through odd jobs, we know that Marie sees hope for herself. Relatively few graphic novels deal with mental illness and Allan offers an empathetic glimpse at a realistic teen who doesn't rattle cages to seek help even though we might wish she would. Instead, she just keeps going and draws on the resources she has."

- Library Journal

"Marie is the fat girl neither peers nor teachers care enough about to really know. She has a golden best friend, one whose little sister looks up to her, and for escapist heroics she follows pro wrestling, which provides relief from the reality of having a schizophrenic mother. Allan sensitively makes Marie the focus of her own story, never preaching to readers or relaying more knowledge than Marie gleans on her own. Initially, his artwork appears awkward. Allan is realistic about schizophrenia, too, including the dopey condition of a just-medicated patient. Good for those interested in mental-health issues as they relate to families, and also in girl spirit."

- Booklist Online

"The teenage years are hard, and having a schizophrenic mother does not help that. *"the road to god knows..."* is the coming of age story of one Marie, a teenage girl faced with her single mother's increasingly complex schizophrenia. Forced to grow up before her time, she learns many important lessons. *"the road to god knows..."* is an intriguing and touching graphic novel with a unique art style, highly recommended."

- The Midwest Book Review

"With *the road to god knows...* Von Allan demonstrates that he's talented as both an artist and a storyteller. The Ottawa he conjures is beautifully and lovingly detailed — on par, perhaps, with the London of Dickens or the Cleveland of Harvey Pekar's American Splendor. Stylistically, I'm also reminded of Black Hole by Charles Burns and Sloth (among other things) by Gilbert Hernandez. Regardless of his artistic influences, however, what's clear throughout this graphic novel is that Allan is an optimist who strives to explore the human heart in all of its intricate complexity."

- Small Press Reviews

Stargazer

Book One

by Von Allan

a von allan studio book

Ottawa

Library and Archives Canada Cataloguing in Publication

Allan, Von, 1974-
     Stargazer / Von Allan.

ISBN 978-0-9781237-2-7 (v. 1)

     I. Title.

PN6733.A46S83 2010   741.5'971   C2010-902254-8

Published by Von Allan Studio, P.O. Box 20520, 390 Rideau Street, Ottawa, Ontario, Canada K1N 1A3. Email: von@vonallan.com Web: http://www.vonallan.com Phone: 613-236-9957

v 1.2

For Sammy

Ever tried. Ever failed. No matter.
Try again. Fail again. Fail better.

Samuel Beckett, *Worstward Ho*

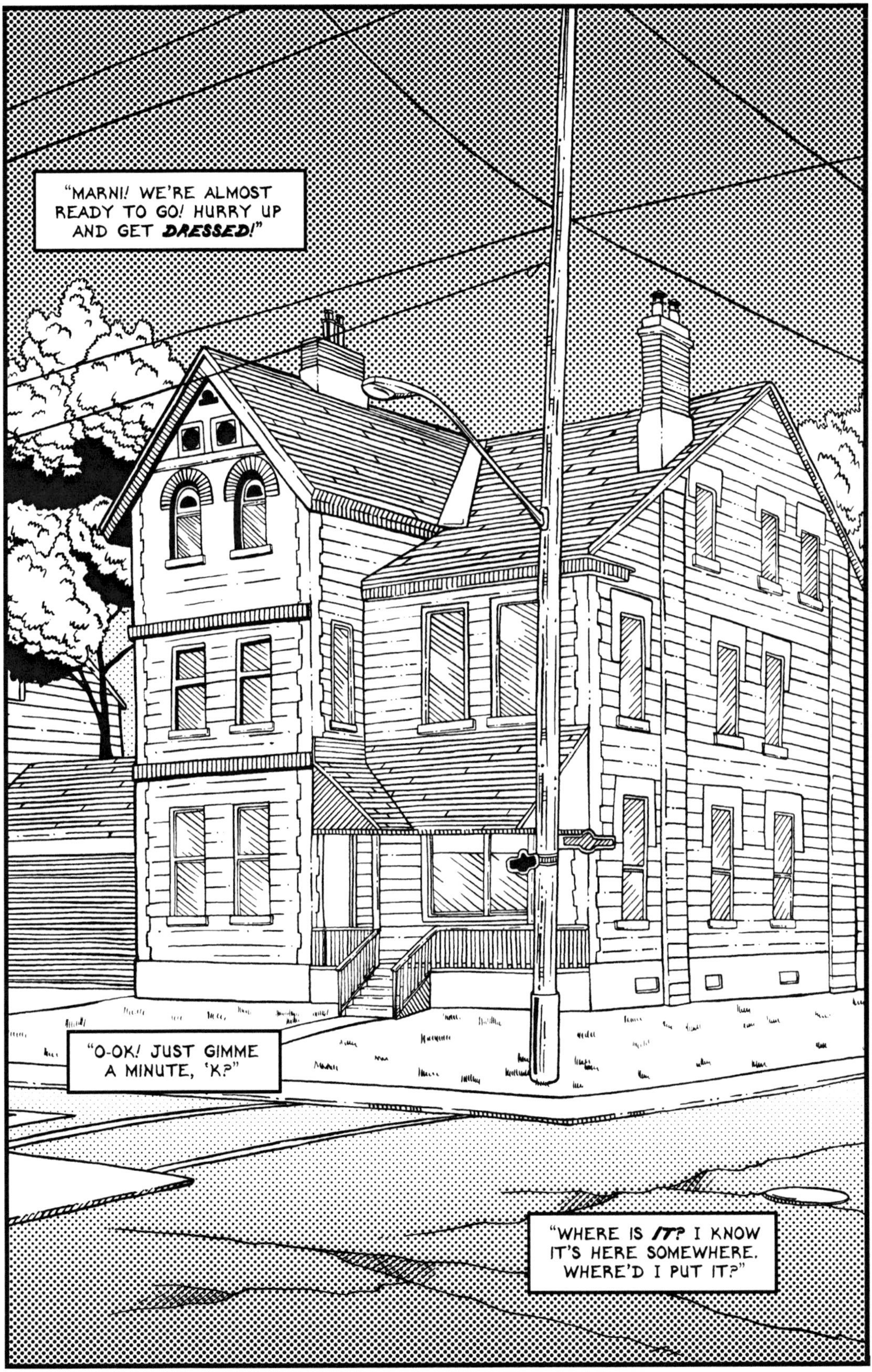
"MARNI! WE'RE ALMOST READY TO GO! HURRY UP AND GET DRESSED!"
"O-OK! JUST GIMME A MINUTE, 'K?"
"WHERE IS IT? I KNOW IT'S HERE SOMEWHERE. WHERE'D I PUT IT?"

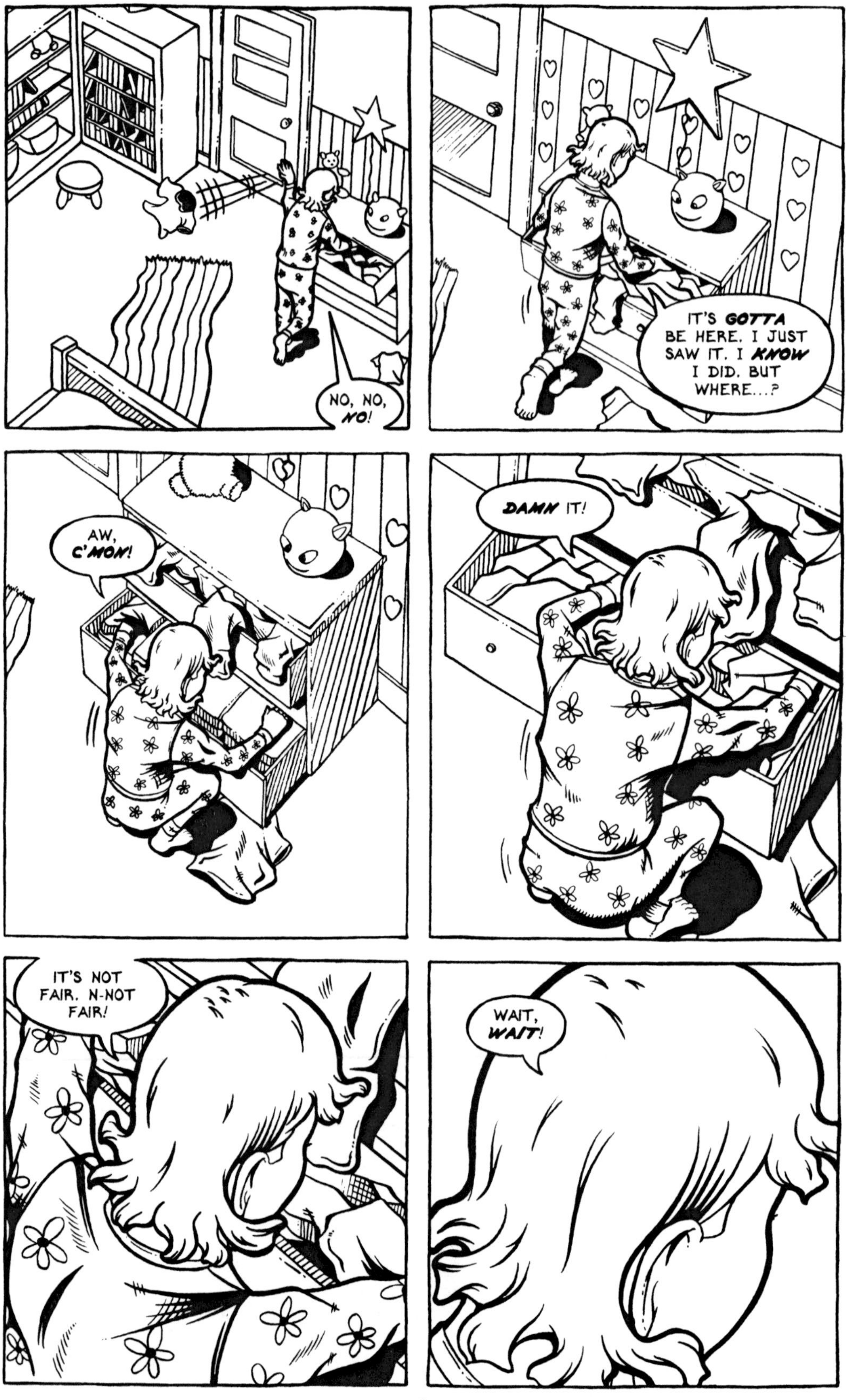
NO, NO, NO!
IT'S GOTTA BE HERE. I JUST SAW IT. I KNOW I DID. BUT WHERE...?
AW, C'MON!
DAMN IT!
IT'S NOT FAIR. N-NOT FAIR!
WAIT, WAIT!

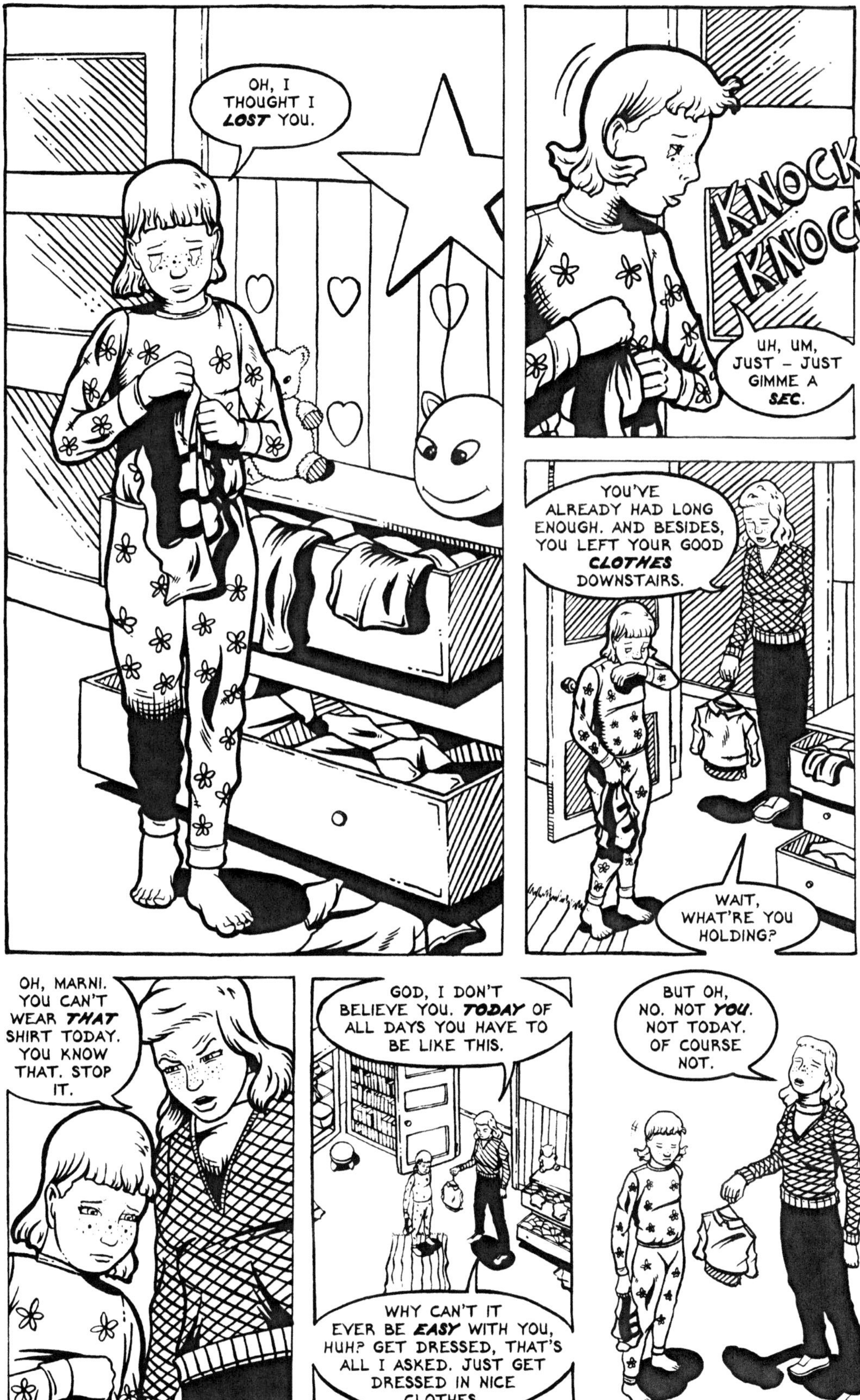
OH, I THOUGHT I LOST YOU.
KNOCK KNOCK
UH, UM, JUST – JUST GIMME A SEC.
YOU'VE ALREADY HAD LONG ENOUGH. AND BESIDES, YOU LEFT YOUR GOOD CLOTHES DOWNSTAIRS.
WAIT, WHAT'RE YOU HOLDING?
OH, MARNI. YOU CAN'T WEAR THAT SHIRT TODAY. YOU KNOW THAT. STOP IT.
GOD, I DON'T BELIEVE YOU. TODAY OF ALL DAYS YOU HAVE TO BE LIKE THIS.
WHY CAN'T IT EVER BE EASY WITH YOU, HUH? GET DRESSED, THAT'S ALL I ASKED. JUST GET DRESSED IN NICE CLOTHES.
BUT OH, NO. NOT YOU. NOT TODAY. OF COURSE NOT.

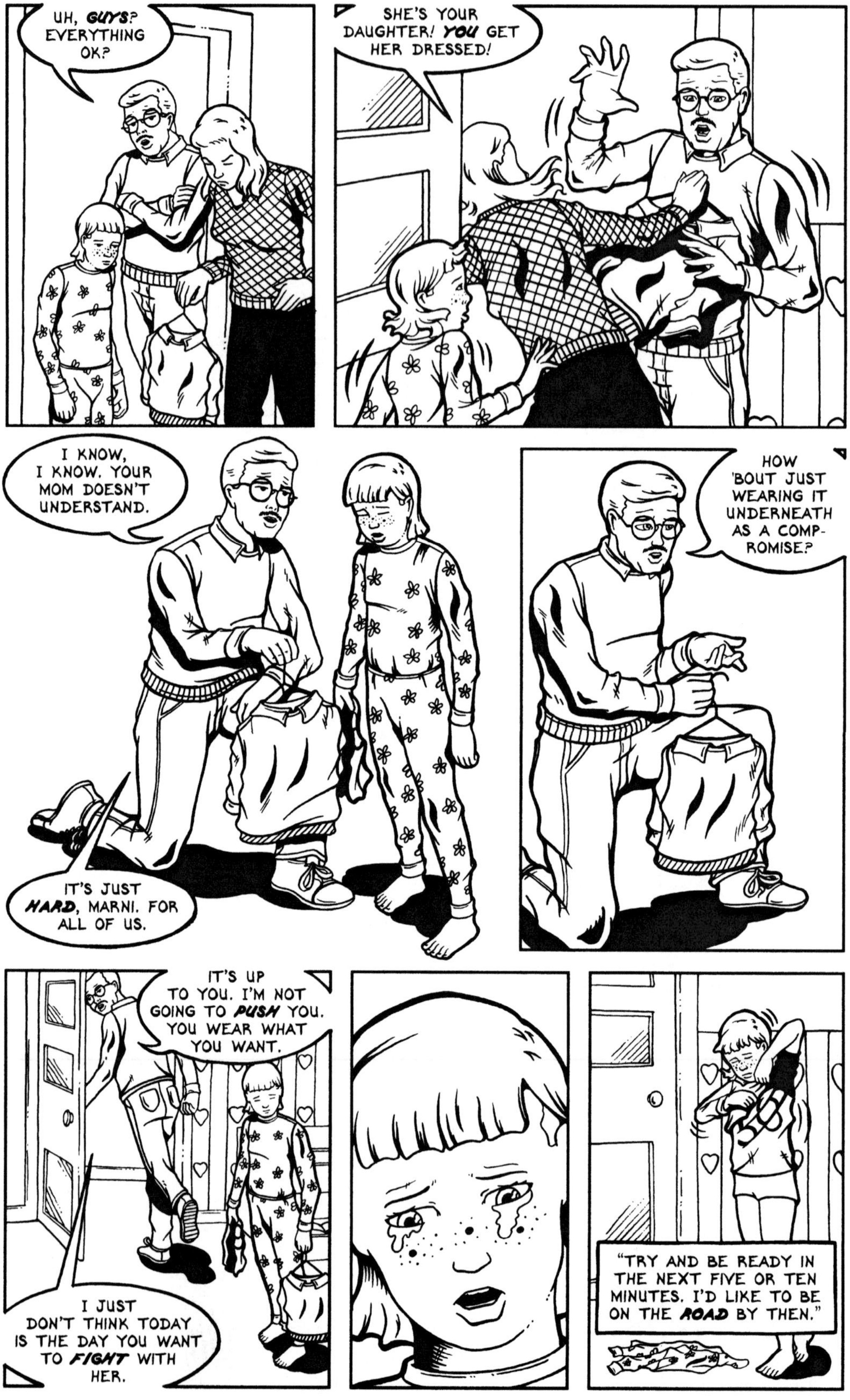
UH, GUYS? EVERYTHING OK?
SHE'S YOUR DAUGHTER! YOU GET HER DRESSED!
I KNOW, I KNOW. YOUR MOM DOESN'T UNDERSTAND.
IT'S JUST HARD, MARNI. FOR ALL OF US.
HOW 'BOUT JUST WEARING IT UNDERNEATH AS A COMP-ROMISE?
IT'S UP TO YOU. I'M NOT GOING TO PUSH YOU. YOU WEAR WHAT YOU WANT.
I JUST DON'T THINK TODAY IS THE DAY YOU WANT TO FIGHT WITH HER.
"TRY AND BE READY IN THE NEXT FIVE OR TEN MINUTES. I'D LIKE TO BE ON THE ROAD BY THEN."

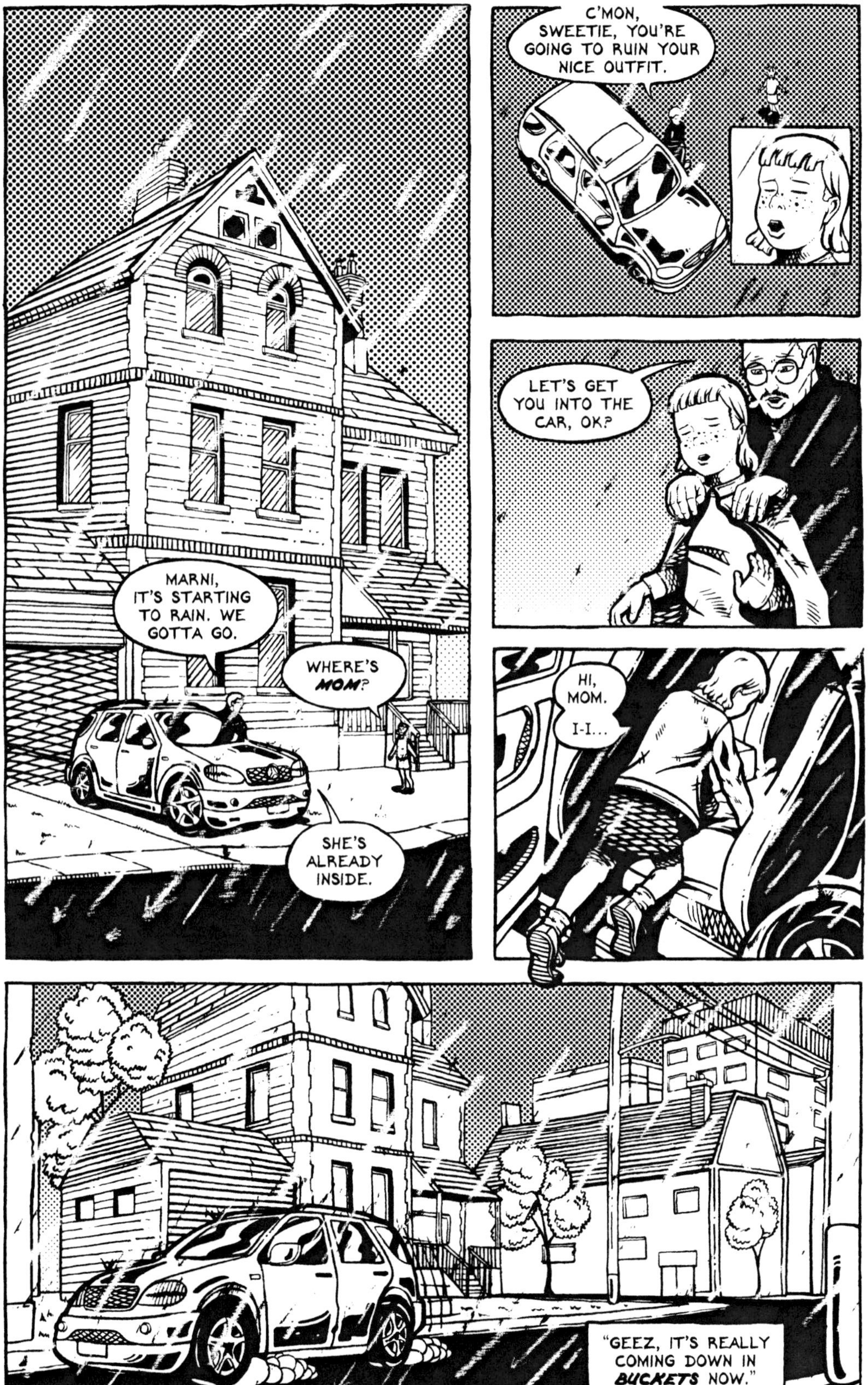
MARNI, IT'S STARTING TO RAIN. WE GOTTA GO.
WHERE'S MOM?
SHE'S ALREADY INSIDE.
C'MON, SWEETIE, YOU'RE GOING TO RUIN YOUR NICE OUTFIT.
LET'S GET YOU INTO THE CAR, OK?
HI, MOM.
I-I...
"GEEZ, IT'S REALLY COMING DOWN IN BUCKETS NOW."

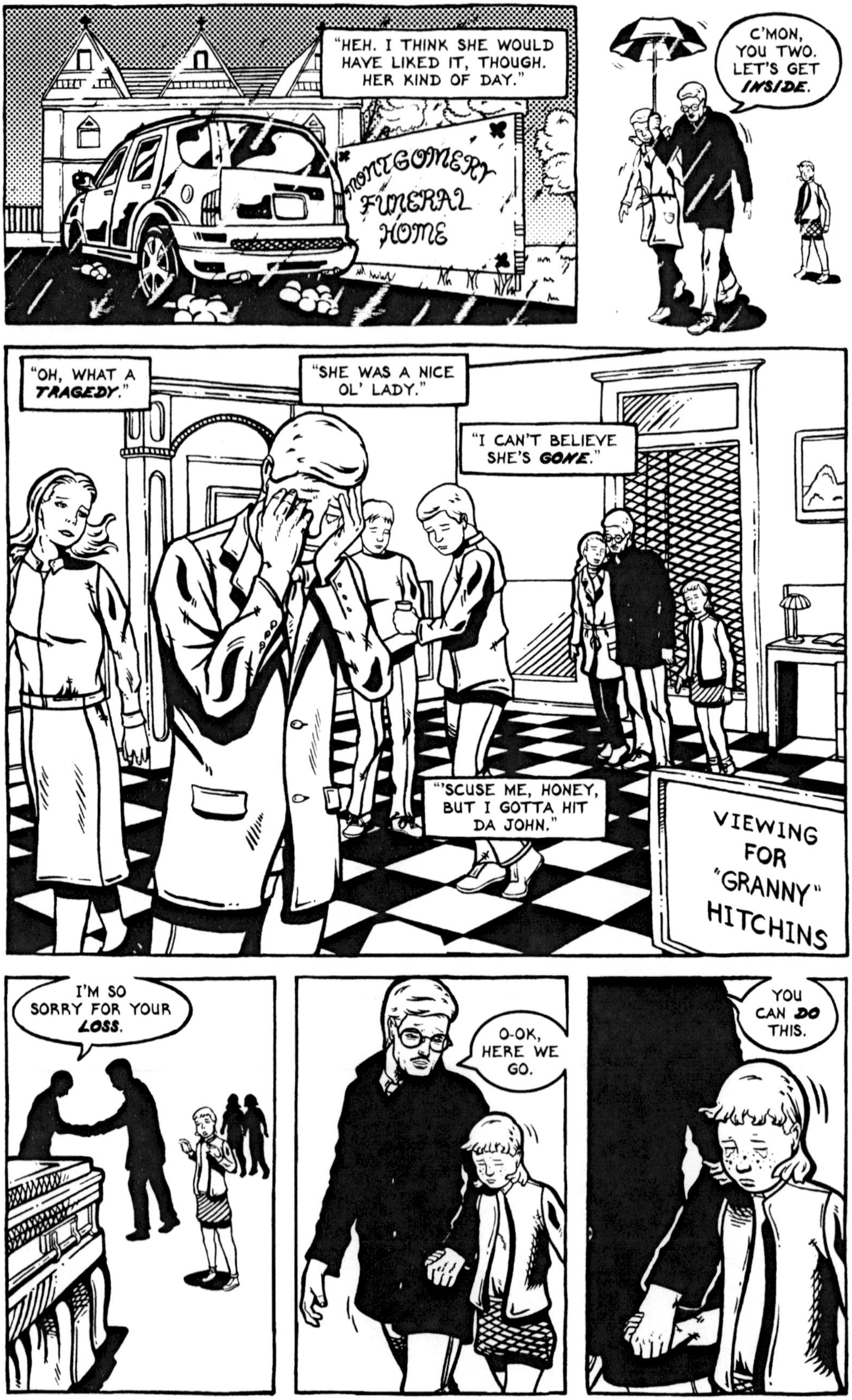
"HEH. I THINK SHE WOULD HAVE LIKED IT, THOUGH. HER KIND OF DAY."
MONTGOMERY FUNERAL HOME
C'MON, YOU TWO. LET'S GET *INSIDE*.
"OH, WHAT A *TRAGEDY*."
"SHE WAS A NICE OL' LADY."
"I CAN'T BELIEVE SHE'S *GONE*."
"'SCUSE ME, HONEY, BUT I GOTTA HIT DA JOHN."
VIEWING FOR "GRANNY" HITCHINS
I'M SO SORRY FOR YOUR *LOSS*.
O-OK, HERE WE GO.
YOU CAN *DO* THIS.

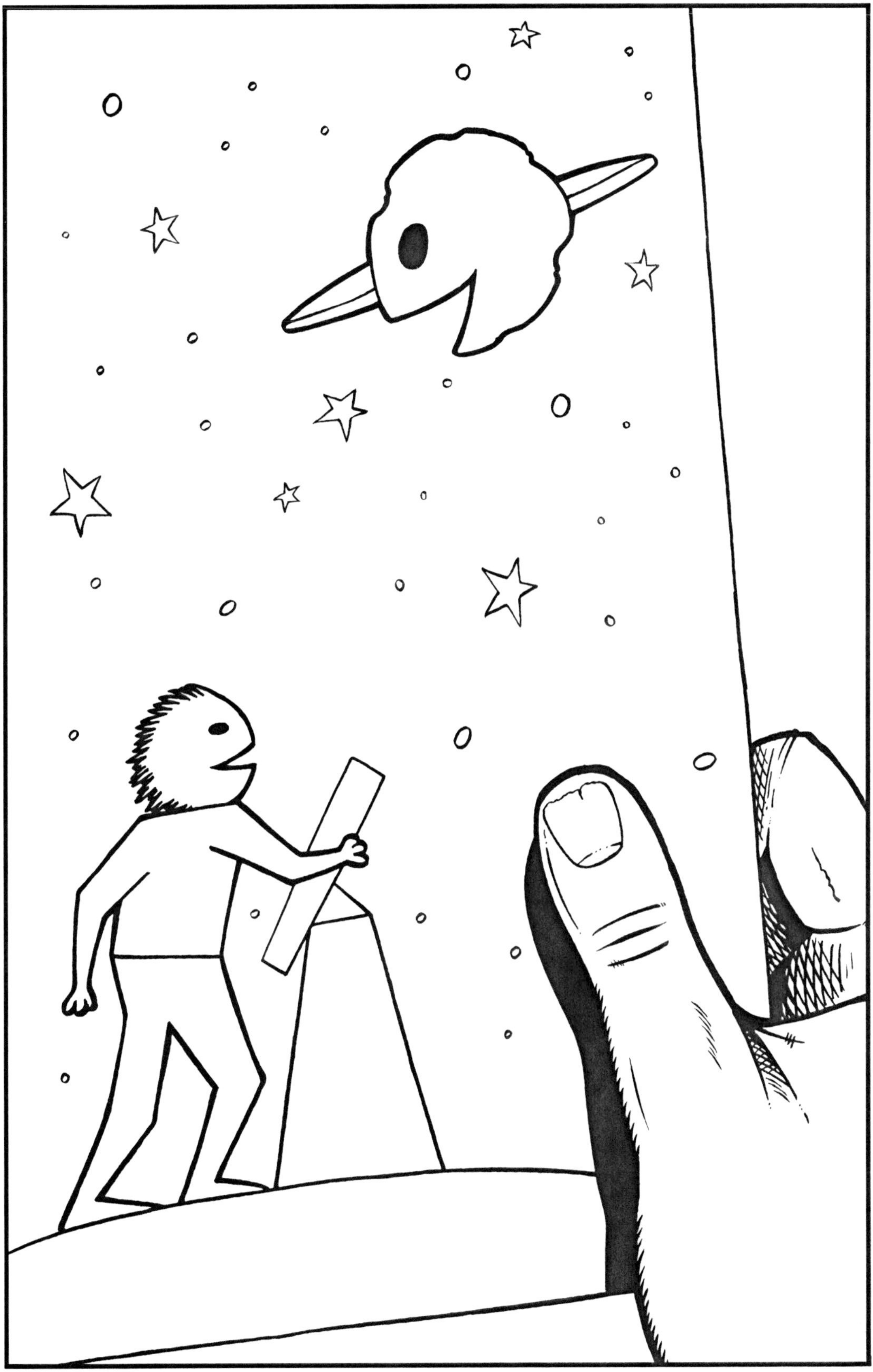

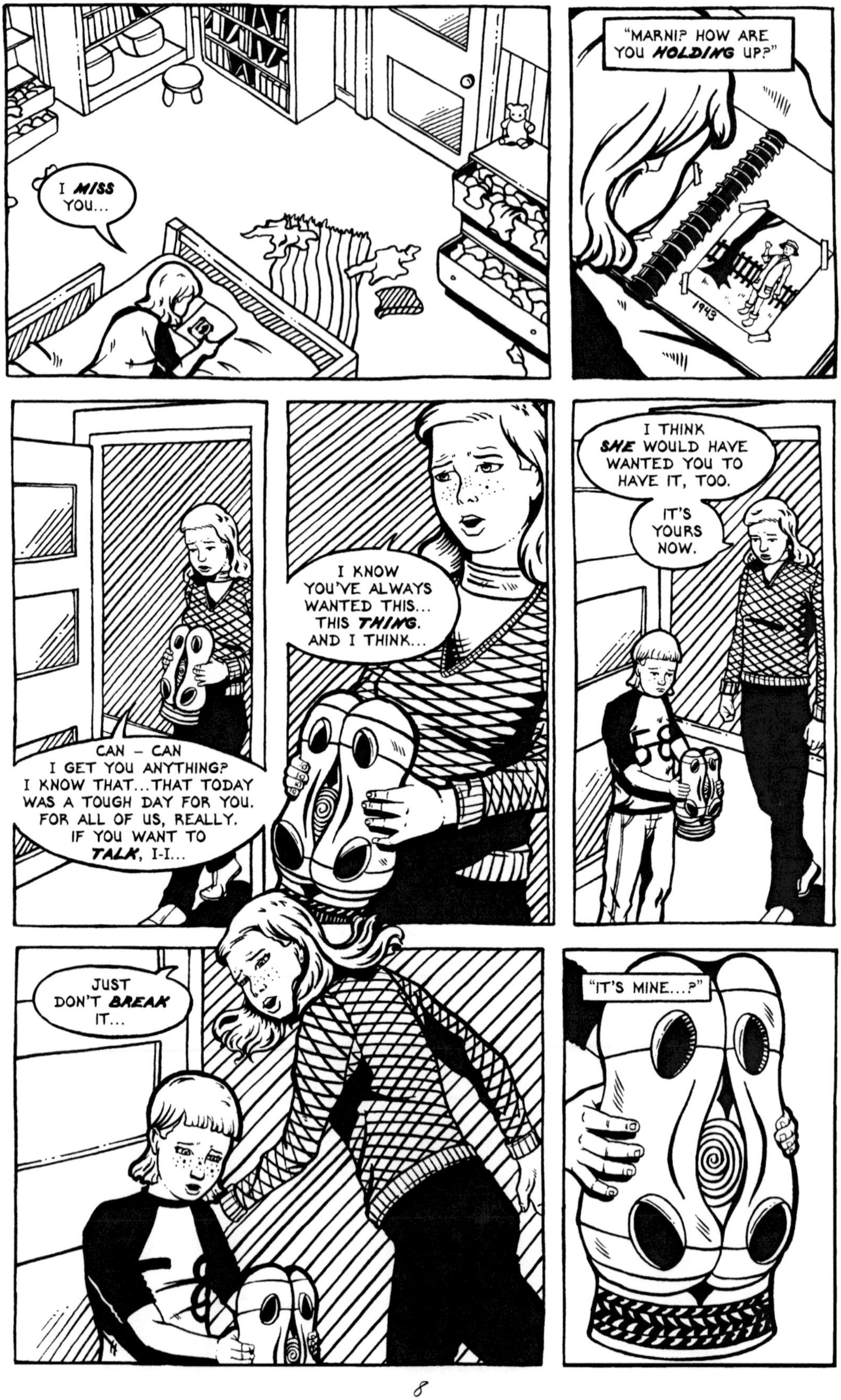
I MISS YOU...
"MARNI? HOW ARE YOU HOLDING UP?"
1943
CAN – CAN I GET YOU ANYTHING? I KNOW THAT...THAT TODAY WAS A TOUGH DAY FOR YOU. FOR ALL OF US, REALLY. IF YOU WANT TO TALK, I-I...
I KNOW YOU'VE ALWAYS WANTED THIS... THIS THING. AND I THINK...
I THINK SHE WOULD HAVE WANTED YOU TO HAVE IT, TOO.
IT'S YOURS NOW.
58
JUST DON'T BREAK IT...
"IT'S MINE...?"

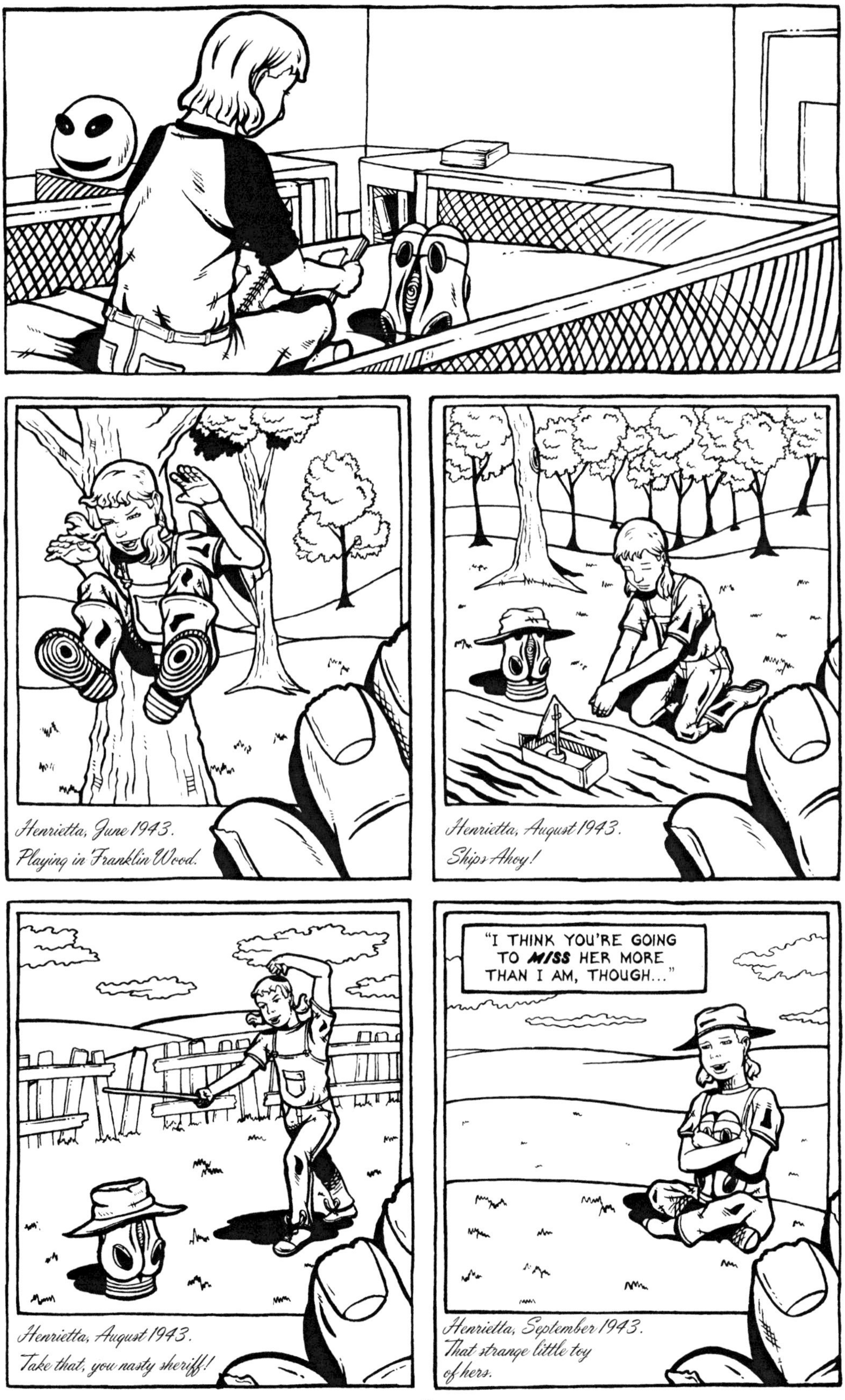
Henrietta, June 1943.
Playing in Franklin Wood.
Henrietta, August 1943.
Ships Ahoy!
Henrietta, August 1943.
Take that, you nasty sheriff!
"I THINK YOU'RE GOING TO MISS HER MORE THAN I AM, THOUGH..."
Henrietta, September 1943.
That strange little toy of hers.

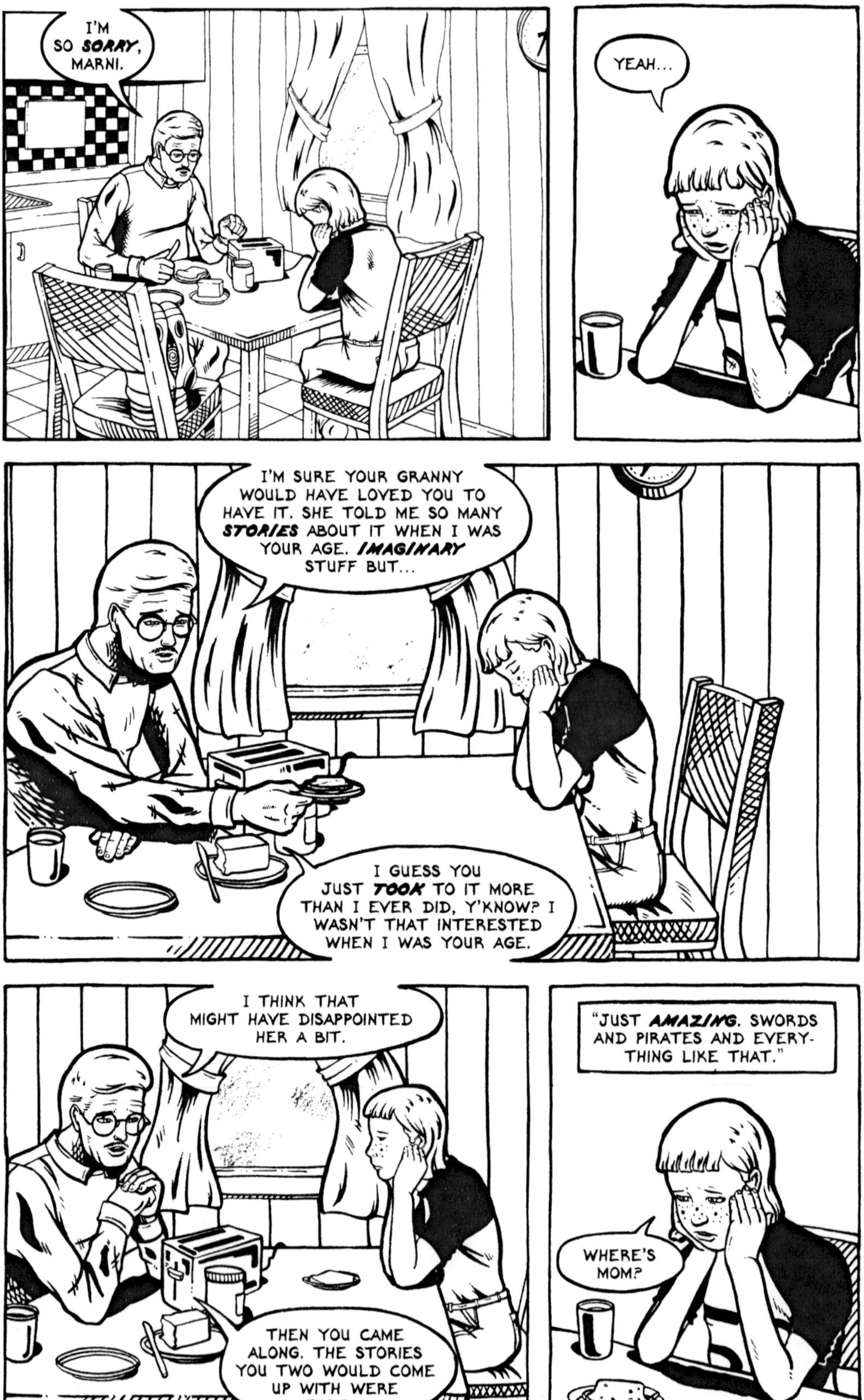
I'M SO *SORRY*, MARNI.
YEAH...
I'M SURE YOUR GRANNY WOULD HAVE LOVED YOU TO HAVE IT. SHE TOLD ME SO MANY *STORIES* ABOUT IT WHEN I WAS YOUR AGE. *IMAGINARY* STUFF BUT...
I GUESS YOU JUST *TOOK* TO IT MORE THAN I EVER DID, Y'KNOW? I WASN'T THAT INTERESTED WHEN I WAS YOUR AGE.
I THINK THAT MIGHT HAVE DISAPPOINTED HER A BIT.
THEN YOU CAME ALONG. THE STORIES YOU TWO WOULD COME UP WITH WERE JUST...
"JUST *AMAZING*. SWORDS AND PIRATES AND EVERY-THING LIKE THAT."
WHERE'S MOM?

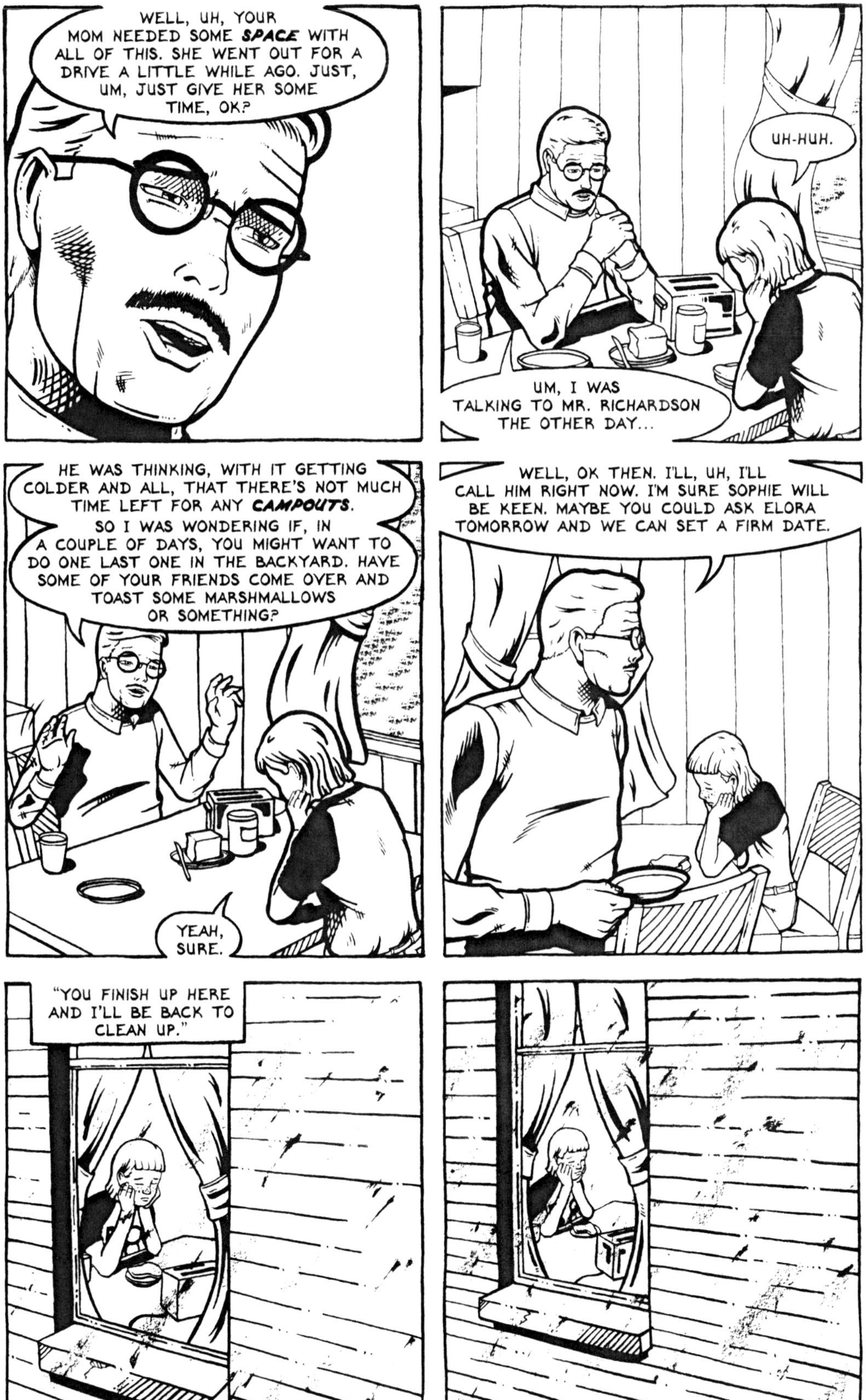
WELL, UH, YOUR MOM NEEDED SOME SPACE WITH ALL OF THIS. SHE WENT OUT FOR A DRIVE A LITTLE WHILE AGO. JUST, UM, JUST GIVE HER SOME TIME, OK?
UH-HUH.
UM, I WAS TALKING TO MR. RICHARDSON THE OTHER DAY...
HE WAS THINKING, WITH IT GETTING COLDER AND ALL, THAT THERE'S NOT MUCH TIME LEFT FOR ANY CAMPOUTS. SO I WAS WONDERING IF, IN A COUPLE OF DAYS, YOU MIGHT WANT TO DO ONE LAST ONE IN THE BACKYARD. HAVE SOME OF YOUR FRIENDS COME OVER AND TOAST SOME MARSHMALLOWS OR SOMETHING?
YEAH, SURE.
WELL, OK THEN. I'LL, UH, I'LL CALL HIM RIGHT NOW. I'M SURE SOPHIE WILL BE KEEN. MAYBE YOU COULD ASK ELORA TOMORROW AND WE CAN SET A FIRM DATE.
"YOU FINISH UP HERE AND I'LL BE BACK TO CLEAN UP."

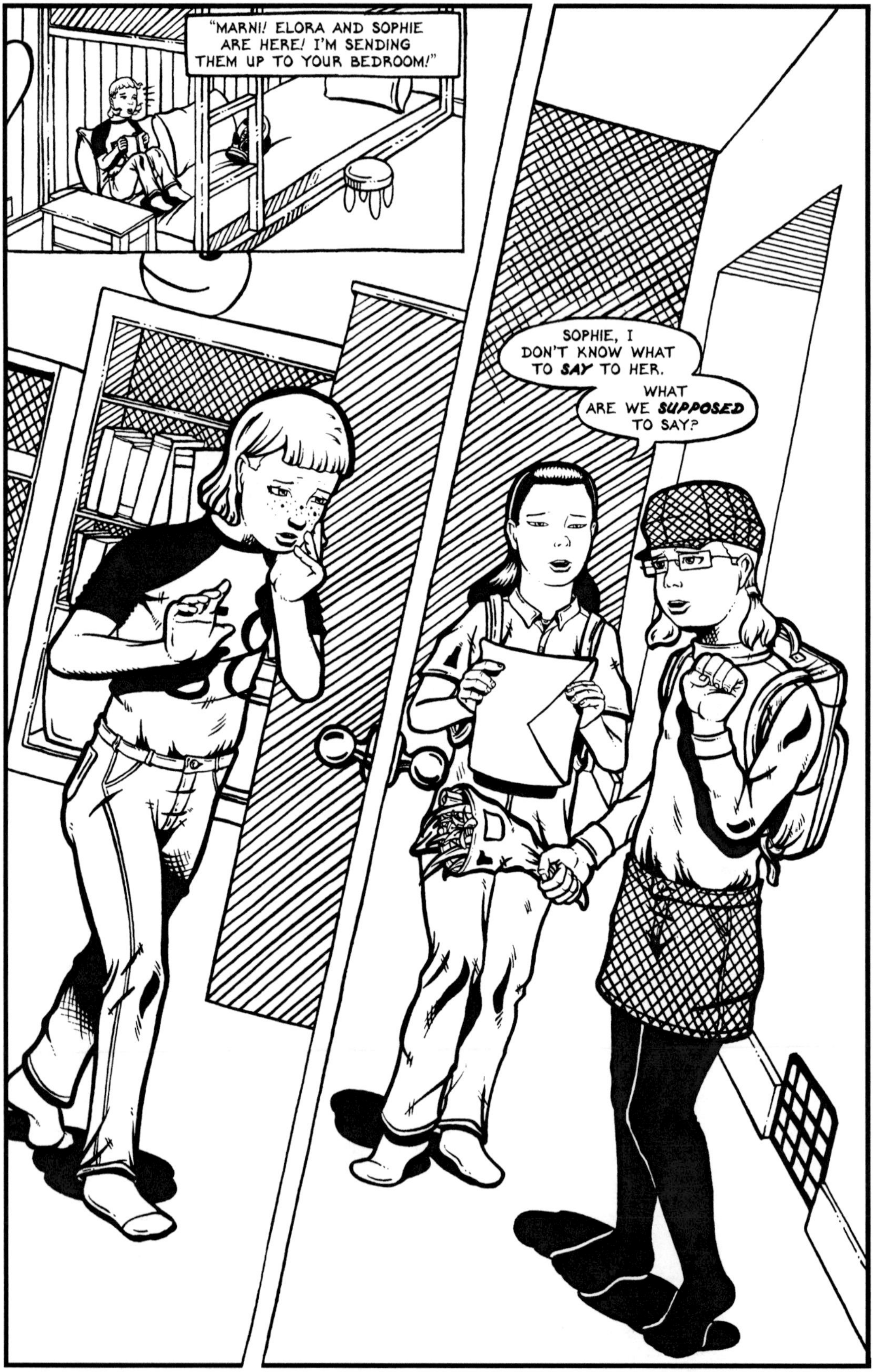
"MARNI! ELORA AND SOPHIE ARE HERE! I'M SENDING THEM UP TO YOUR BEDROOM!"
SOPHIE, I DON'T KNOW WHAT TO **SAY** TO HER.
WHAT ARE WE **SUPPOSED** TO SAY?

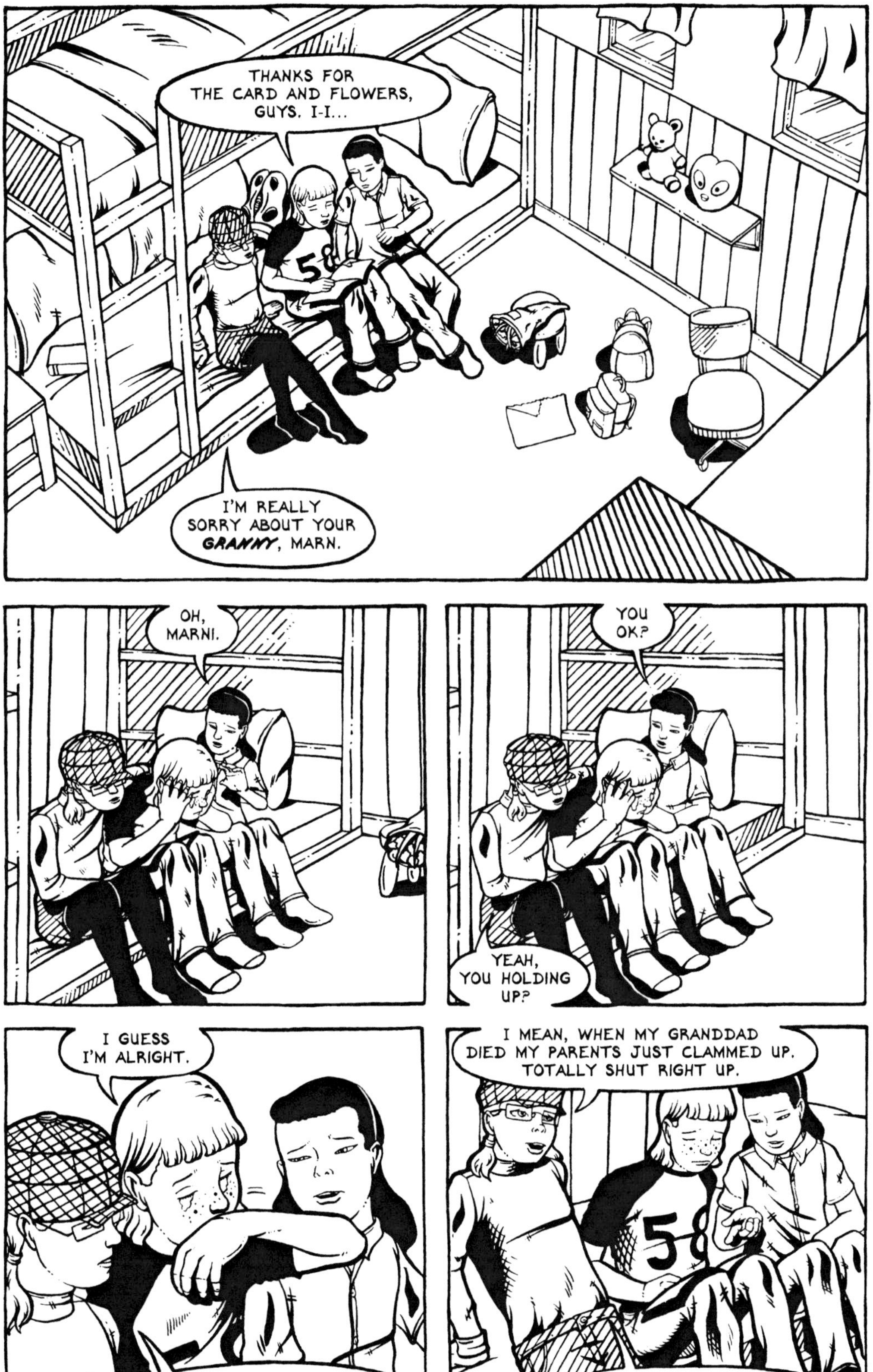
THANKS FOR THE CARD AND FLOWERS, GUYS. I-I...
I'M REALLY SORRY ABOUT YOUR *GRANNY*, MARN.
OH, MARNI.
YOU OK?
YEAH, YOU HOLDING UP?
I GUESS I'M ALRIGHT.
HOW HAVE YOUR MOM AND DAD *TREATED* YOU WITH ALL OF THIS?
I MEAN, WHEN MY GRANDDAD DIED MY PARENTS JUST CLAMMED UP. TOTALLY SHUT RIGHT UP.
THEY JUST *DROPPED* ME OFF A LOT MORE AT THE FOLKLORE CENTRE. YEESH...

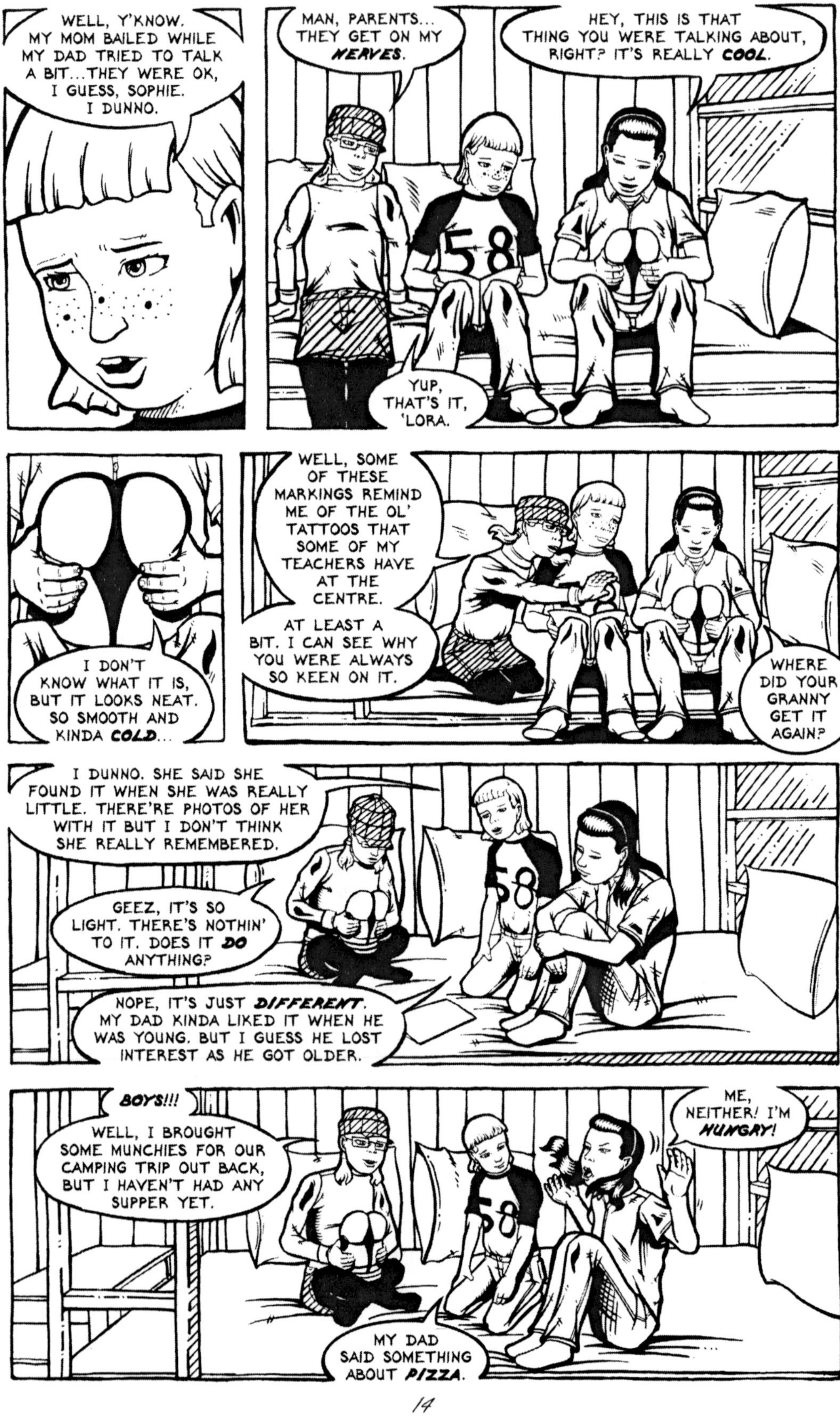
WELL, Y'KNOW. MY MOM BAILED WHILE MY DAD TRIED TO TALK A BIT...THEY WERE OK, I GUESS, SOPHIE. I DUNNO.
MAN, PARENTS... THEY GET ON MY NERVES.
HEY, THIS IS THAT THING YOU WERE TALKING ABOUT, RIGHT? IT'S REALLY COOL.
YUP, THAT'S IT, 'LORA.
I DON'T KNOW WHAT IT IS, BUT IT LOOKS NEAT. SO SMOOTH AND KINDA COLD...
WELL, SOME OF THESE MARKINGS REMIND ME OF THE OL' TATTOOS THAT SOME OF MY TEACHERS HAVE AT THE CENTRE.
AT LEAST A BIT. I CAN SEE WHY YOU WERE ALWAYS SO KEEN ON IT.
WHERE DID YOUR GRANNY GET IT AGAIN?
I DUNNO. SHE SAID SHE FOUND IT WHEN SHE WAS REALLY LITTLE. THERE'RE PHOTOS OF HER WITH IT BUT I DON'T THINK SHE REALLY REMEMBERED.
GEEZ, IT'S SO LIGHT. THERE'S NOTHIN' TO IT. DOES IT DO ANYTHING?
NOPE, IT'S JUST DIFFERENT. MY DAD KINDA LIKED IT WHEN HE WAS YOUNG. BUT I GUESS HE LOST INTEREST AS HE GOT OLDER.
BOYS!!!
WELL, I BROUGHT SOME MUNCHIES FOR OUR CAMPING TRIP OUT BACK, BUT I HAVEN'T HAD ANY SUPPER YET.
ME, NEITHER! I'M HUNGRY!
MY DAD SAID SOMETHING ABOUT PIZZA.

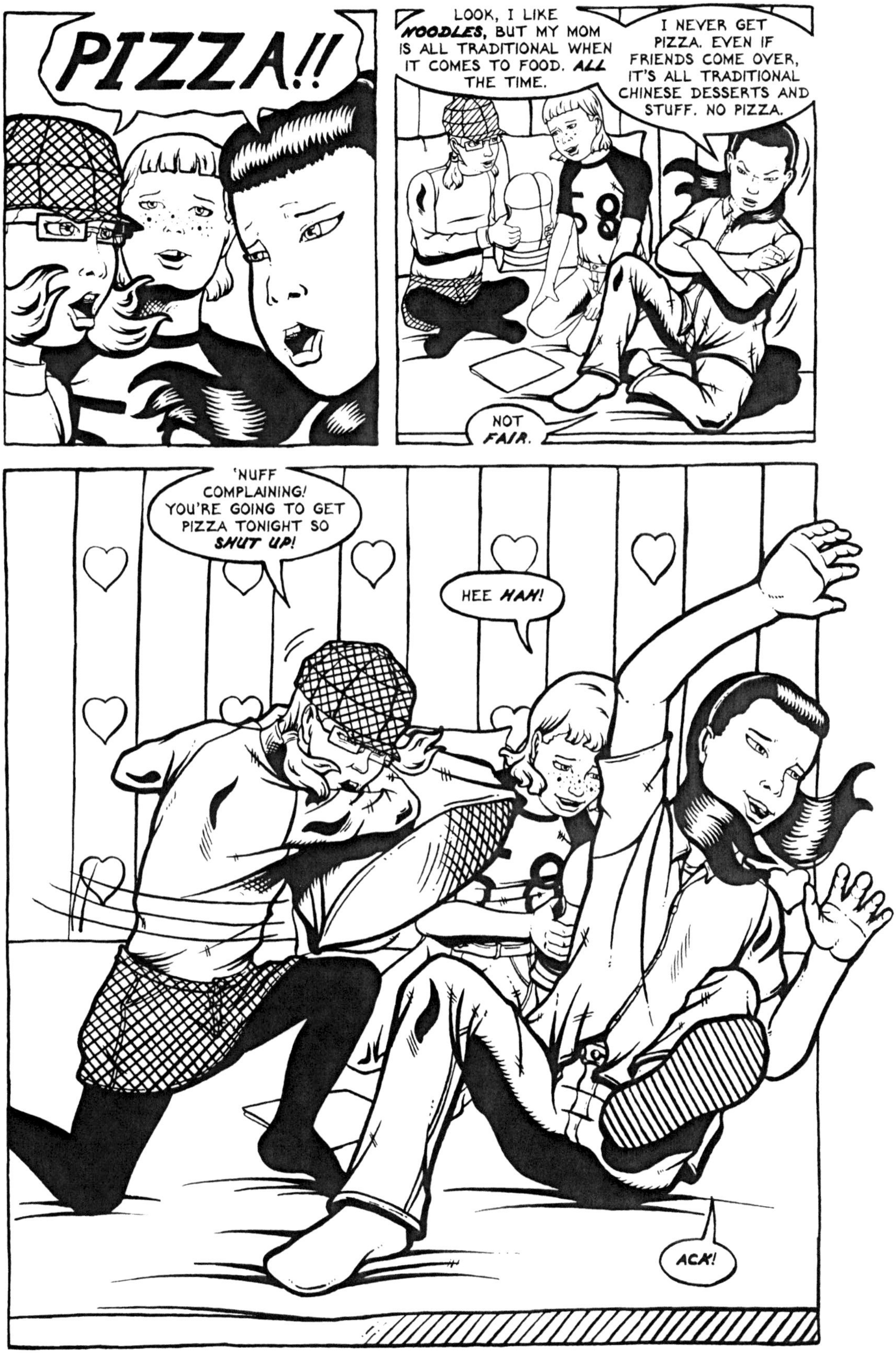
PIZZA!!
LOOK, I LIKE NOODLES, BUT MY MOM IS ALL TRADITIONAL WHEN IT COMES TO FOOD. ALL THE TIME.
I NEVER GET PIZZA. EVEN IF FRIENDS COME OVER, IT'S ALL TRADITIONAL CHINESE DESSERTS AND STUFF. NO PIZZA.
NOT FAIR.
'NUFF COMPLAINING! YOU'RE GOING TO GET PIZZA TONIGHT SO SHUT UP!
HEE HAH!
ACK!

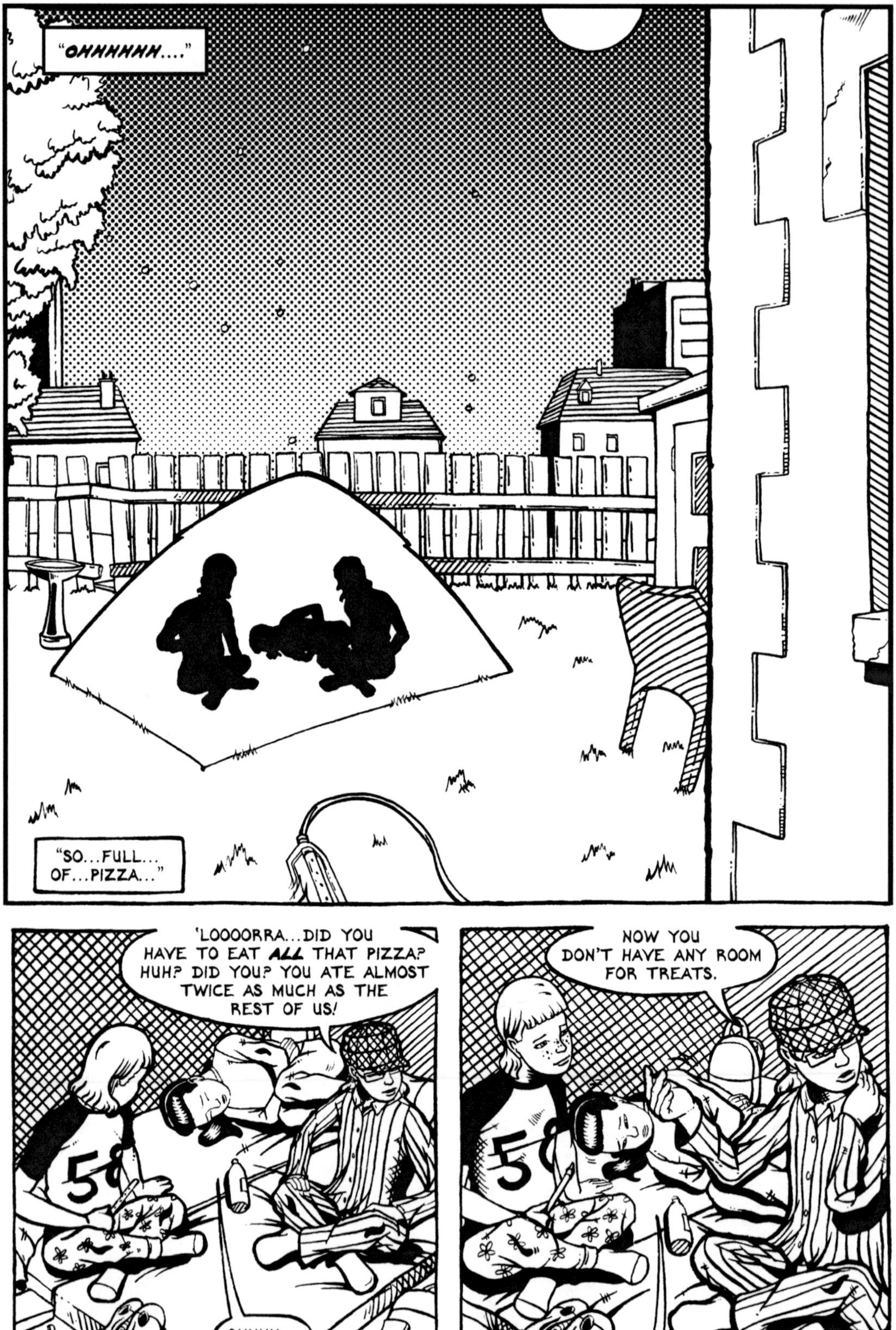
"OHHHHHH..."
"SO...FULL... OF...PIZZA..."
'LOOOORRA...DID YOU HAVE TO EAT ALL THAT PIZZA? HUH? DID YOU? YOU ATE ALMOST TWICE AS MUCH AS THE REST OF US!
OHHHH... STOP... TALKING...
NOW YOU DON'T HAVE ANY ROOM FOR TREATS.
STOP...TALKING... ABOUT...FOOD!

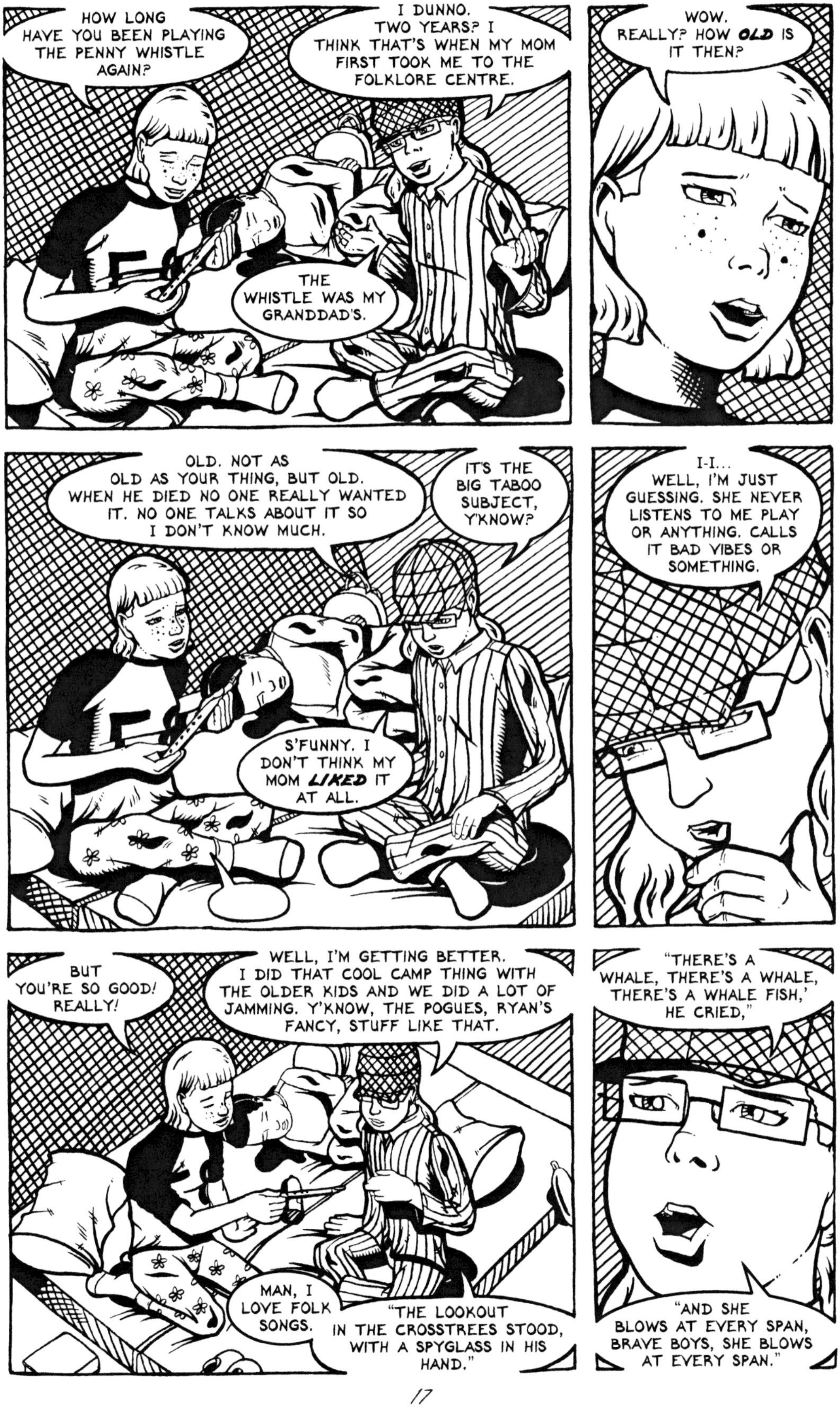
HOW LONG HAVE YOU BEEN PLAYING THE PENNY WHISTLE AGAIN?
I DUNNO. TWO YEARS? I THINK THAT'S WHEN MY MOM FIRST TOOK ME TO THE FOLKLORE CENTRE.
THE WHISTLE WAS MY GRANDDAD'S.
WOW. REALLY? HOW OLD IS IT THEN?
OLD. NOT AS OLD AS YOUR THING, BUT OLD. WHEN HE DIED NO ONE REALLY WANTED IT. NO ONE TALKS ABOUT IT SO I DON'T KNOW MUCH.
IT'S THE BIG TABOO SUBJECT, Y'KNOW?
S'FUNNY. I DON'T THINK MY MOM LIKED IT AT ALL.
I-I... WELL, I'M JUST GUESSING. SHE NEVER LISTENS TO ME PLAY OR ANYTHING. CALLS IT BAD VIBES OR SOMETHING.
BUT YOU'RE SO GOOD! REALLY!
WELL, I'M GETTING BETTER. I DID THAT COOL CAMP THING WITH THE OLDER KIDS AND WE DID A LOT OF JAMMING. Y'KNOW, THE POGUES, RYAN'S FANCY, STUFF LIKE THAT.
MAN, I LOVE FOLK SONGS.
"THE LOOKOUT IN THE CROSSTREES STOOD, WITH A SPYGLASS IN HIS HAND."
"THERE'S A WHALE, THERE'S A WHALE, THERE'S A WHALE FISH,' HE CRIED,"
"AND SHE BLOWS AT EVERY SPAN, BRAVE BOYS, SHE BLOWS AT EVERY SPAN."

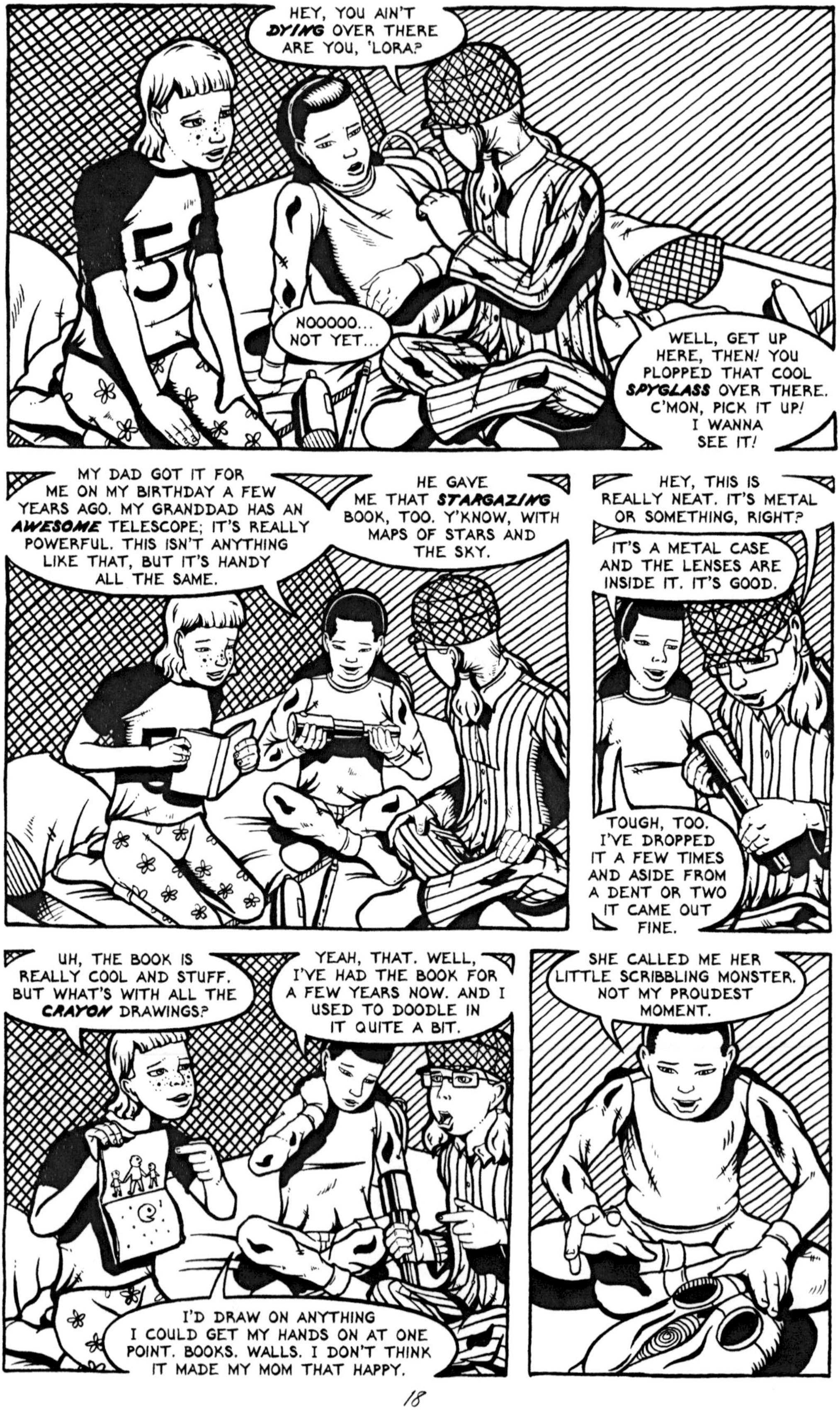
HEY, YOU AIN'T DYING OVER THERE ARE YOU, 'LORA?
NOOOOO... NOT YET...
WELL, GET UP HERE, THEN! YOU PLOPPED THAT COOL SPYGLASS OVER THERE. C'MON, PICK IT UP! I WANNA SEE IT!
MY DAD GOT IT FOR ME ON MY BIRTHDAY A FEW YEARS AGO. MY GRANDDAD HAS AN AWESOME TELESCOPE; IT'S REALLY POWERFUL. THIS ISN'T ANYTHING LIKE THAT, BUT IT'S HANDY ALL THE SAME.
HE GAVE ME THAT STARGAZING BOOK, TOO. Y'KNOW, WITH MAPS OF STARS AND THE SKY.
HEY, THIS IS REALLY NEAT. IT'S METAL OR SOMETHING, RIGHT?
IT'S A METAL CASE AND THE LENSES ARE INSIDE IT. IT'S GOOD.
TOUGH, TOO. I'VE DROPPED IT A FEW TIMES AND ASIDE FROM A DENT OR TWO IT CAME OUT FINE.
UH, THE BOOK IS REALLY COOL AND STUFF. BUT WHAT'S WITH ALL THE CRAYON DRAWINGS?
YEAH, THAT. WELL, I'VE HAD THE BOOK FOR A FEW YEARS NOW. AND I USED TO DOODLE IN IT QUITE A BIT.
I'D DRAW ON ANYTHING I COULD GET MY HANDS ON AT ONE POINT. BOOKS. WALLS. I DON'T THINK IT MADE MY MOM THAT HAPPY.
SHE CALLED ME HER LITTLE SCRIBBLING MONSTER. NOT MY PROUDEST MOMENT.

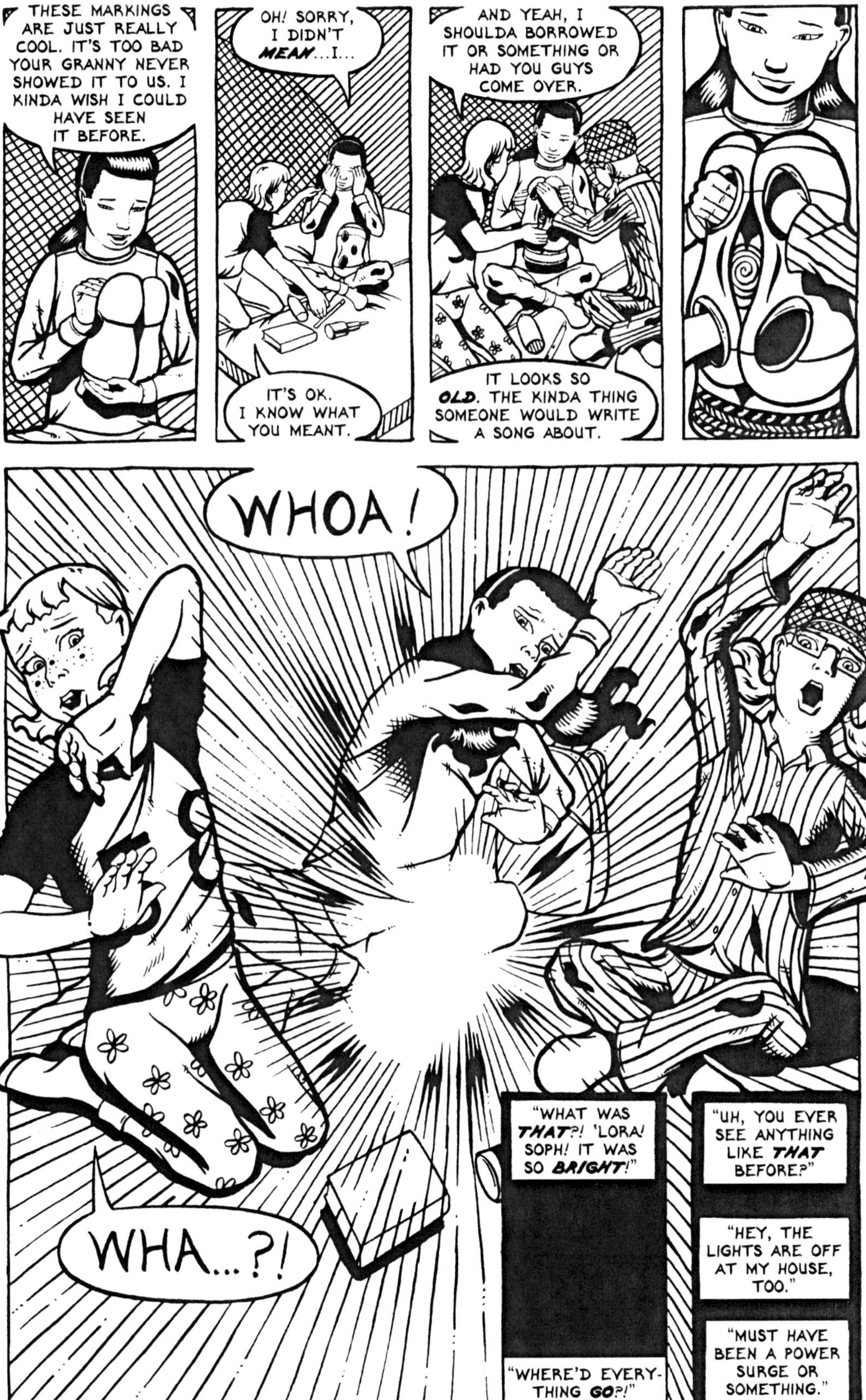
THESE MARKINGS ARE JUST REALLY COOL. IT'S TOO BAD YOUR GRANNY NEVER SHOWED IT TO US. I KINDA WISH I COULD HAVE SEEN IT BEFORE.
OH! SORRY, I DIDN'T *MEAN*...I...
IT'S OK. I KNOW WHAT YOU MEANT.
AND YEAH, I SHOULDA BORROWED IT OR SOMETHING OR HAD YOU GUYS COME OVER.
IT LOOKS SO ***OLD***. THE KINDA THING SOMEONE WOULD WRITE A SONG ABOUT.
WHOA!
WHA...?!
"WHAT WAS ***THAT***?! 'LORA! SOPH! IT WAS SO ***BRIGHT***!"
"WHERE'D EVERYTHING ***GO***?!"
"UH, YOU EVER SEE ANYTHING LIKE ***THAT*** BEFORE?"
"HEY, THE LIGHTS ARE OFF AT MY HOUSE, TOO."
"MUST HAVE BEEN A POWER SURGE OR SOMETHING."

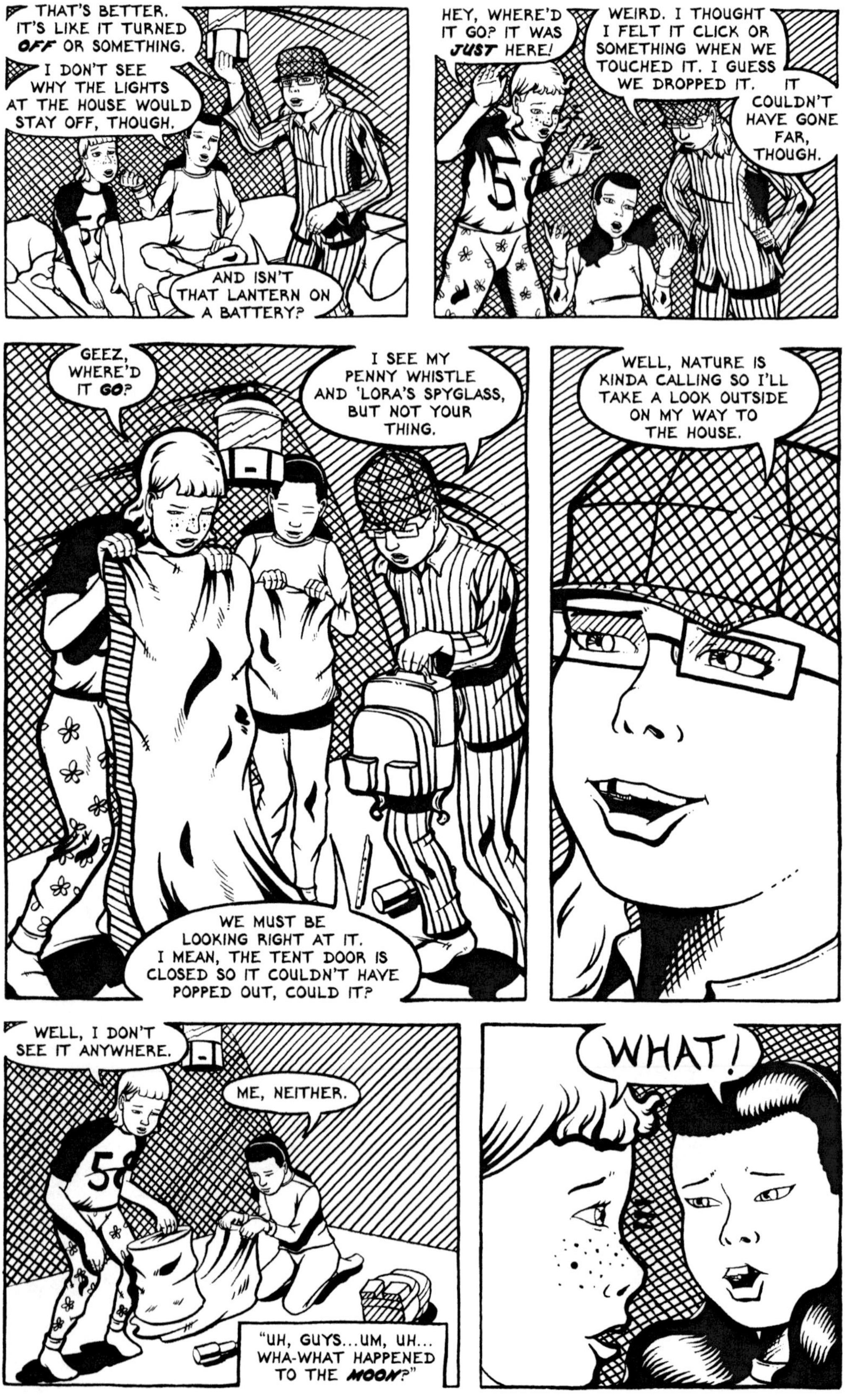

THAT'S BETTER. IT'S LIKE IT TURNED OFF OR SOMETHING.
I DON'T SEE WHY THE LIGHTS AT THE HOUSE WOULD STAY OFF, THOUGH.
AND ISN'T THAT LANTERN ON A BATTERY?
HEY, WHERE'D IT GO? IT WAS JUST HERE!
WEIRD. I THOUGHT I FELT IT CLICK OR SOMETHING WHEN WE TOUCHED IT. I GUESS WE DROPPED IT.
IT COULDN'T HAVE GONE FAR, THOUGH.
GEEZ, WHERE'D IT GO?
I SEE MY PENNY WHISTLE AND 'LORA'S SPYGLASS, BUT NOT YOUR THING.
WE MUST BE LOOKING RIGHT AT IT. I MEAN, THE TENT DOOR IS CLOSED SO IT COULDN'T HAVE POPPED OUT, COULD IT?
WELL, NATURE IS KINDA CALLING SO I'LL TAKE A LOOK OUTSIDE ON MY WAY TO THE HOUSE.
WELL, I DON'T SEE IT ANYWHERE.
ME, NEITHER.
"UH, GUYS...UM, UH... WHA-WHAT HAPPENED TO THE MOON?"
WHAT!

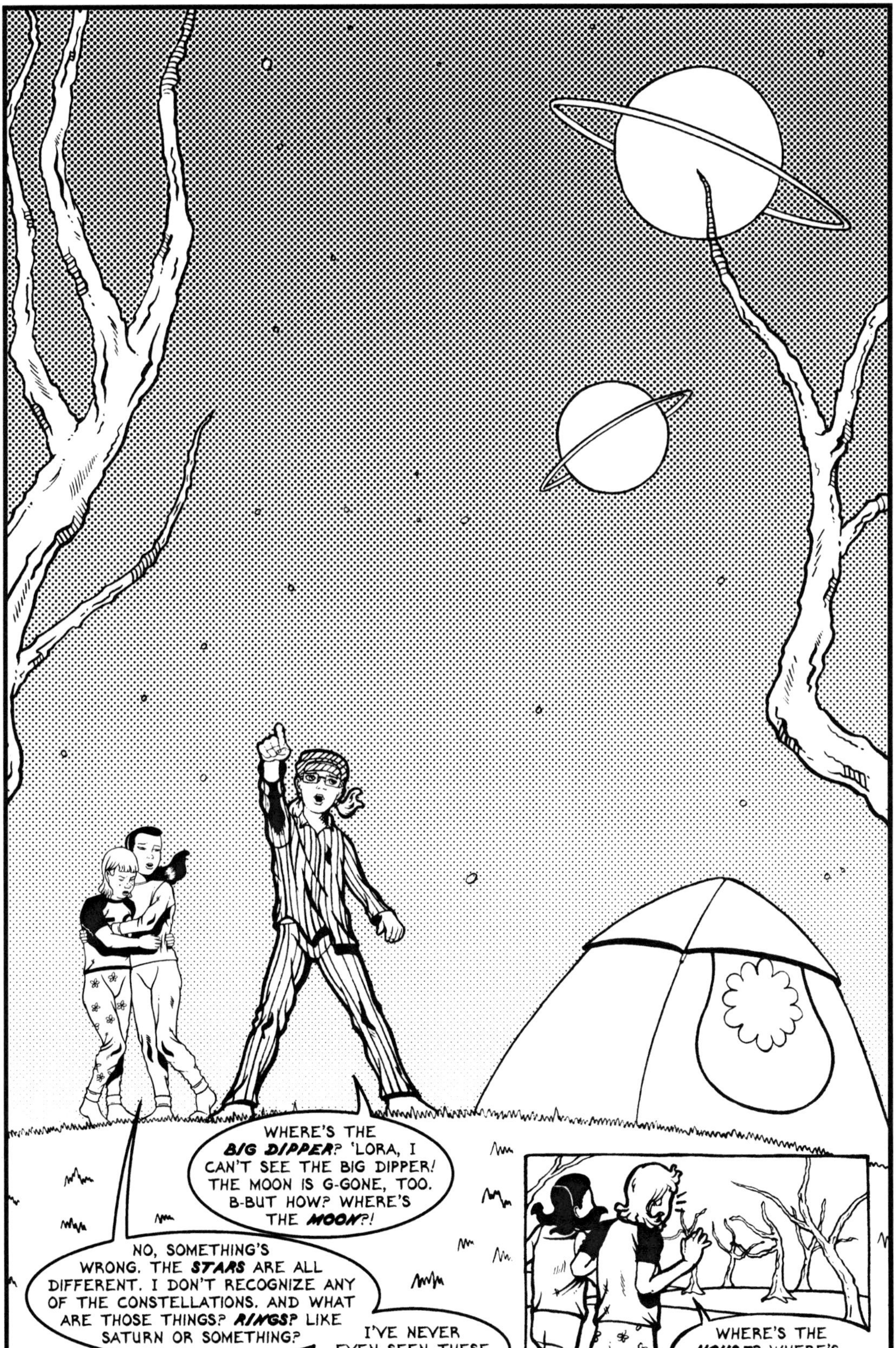
WHERE'S THE BIG DIPPER? 'LORA, I CAN'T SEE THE BIG DIPPER! THE MOON IS G-GONE, TOO. B-BUT HOW? WHERE'S THE MOON?!
NO, SOMETHING'S WRONG. THE STARS ARE ALL DIFFERENT. I DON'T RECOGNIZE ANY OF THE CONSTELLATIONS. AND WHAT ARE THOSE THINGS? RINGS? LIKE SATURN OR SOMETHING?
I'VE NEVER EVEN SEEN THESE IN PICTURES...
WHERE'S THE HOUSE? WHERE'S MY HOUSE?!!

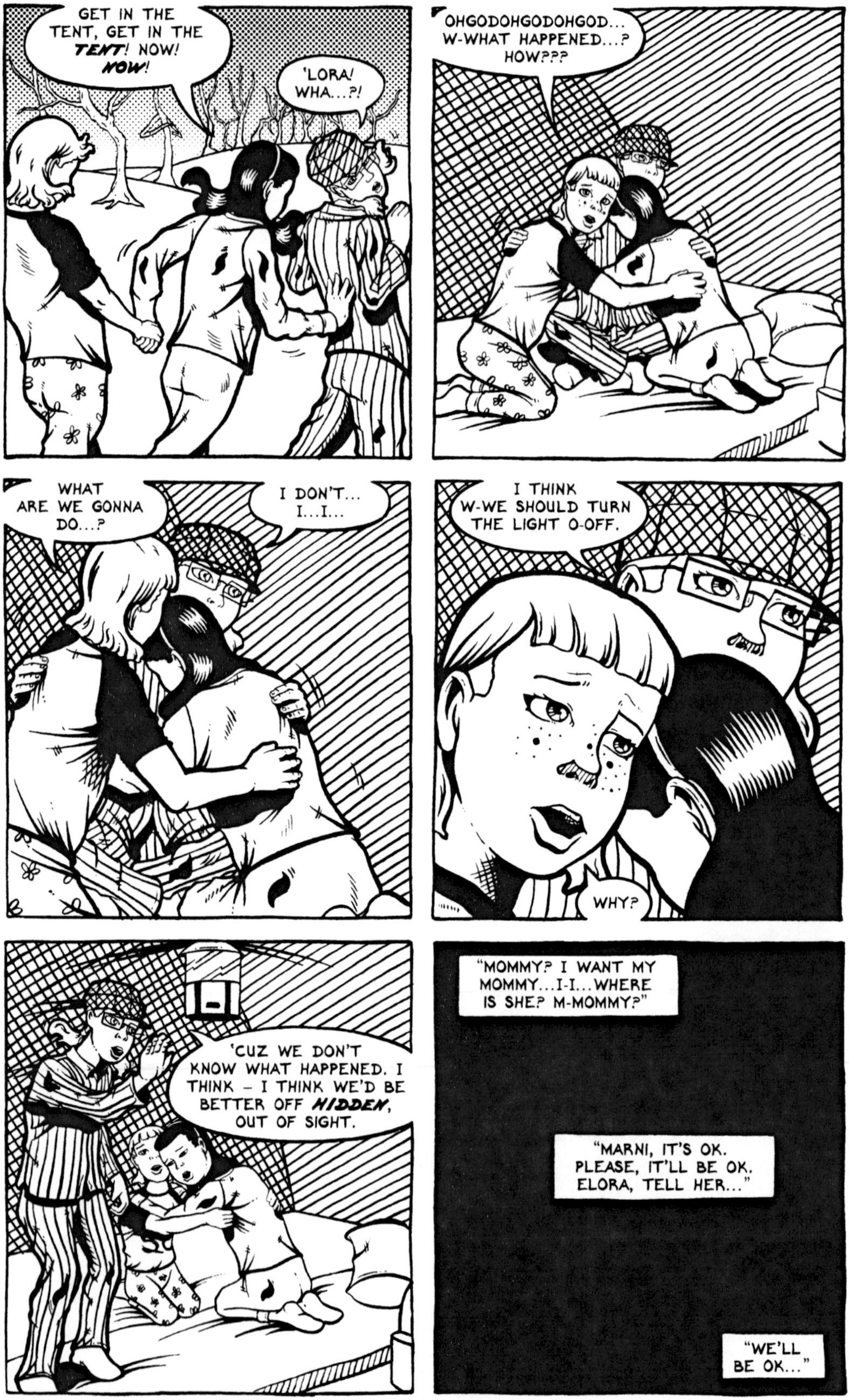
GET IN THE TENT, GET IN THE TENT! NOW! NOW!
'LORA! WHA...?!
OHGODOHGODOHGOD... W-WHAT HAPPENED...? HOW???
WHAT ARE WE GONNA DO...?
I DON'T... I...I...
I THINK W-WE SHOULD TURN THE LIGHT O-OFF.
WHY?
'CUZ WE DON'T KNOW WHAT HAPPENED. I THINK – I THINK WE'D BE BETTER OFF HIDDEN, OUT OF SIGHT.
"MOMMY? I WANT MY MOMMY...I-I...WHERE IS SHE? M-MOMMY?"
"MARNI, IT'S OK. PLEASE, IT'LL BE OK. ELORA, TELL HER..."
"WE'LL BE OK..."

HOW *LONG*...?

IT'S BEEN HOURS...

YEAH. GUYS, I...

I REALLY HAVE TO *PEE*. I CAN'T STAY IN HERE ANYMORE.

PLEASE, SOMEONE COME WITH ME?

"OK, SOPHIE...C'MON, 'LORA. WE'LL ALL GO OUTSIDE *TOGETHER*."

WHERE ARE WE....? HOW'D WE GET *HERE*? AND HOW'D THIS HAPPEN? HOW DO WE GET *BACK*?

SOMEONE HAS TO COME AND FIND US. SOMEONE WILL LOOK. SOMEONE *HAS* TO LOOK!

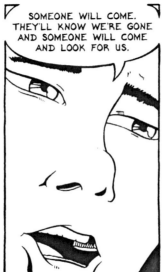

SOMEONE WILL COME. THEY'LL KNOW WE'RE GONE AND SOMEONE WILL COME AND LOOK FOR US.

HOW!? WHERE ARE WE? HUH? *WHERE*? THEY WON'T EVEN KNOW WHERE TO LOOK, ELORA.

WE DIDN'T RUN AWAY OR SOMETHING.

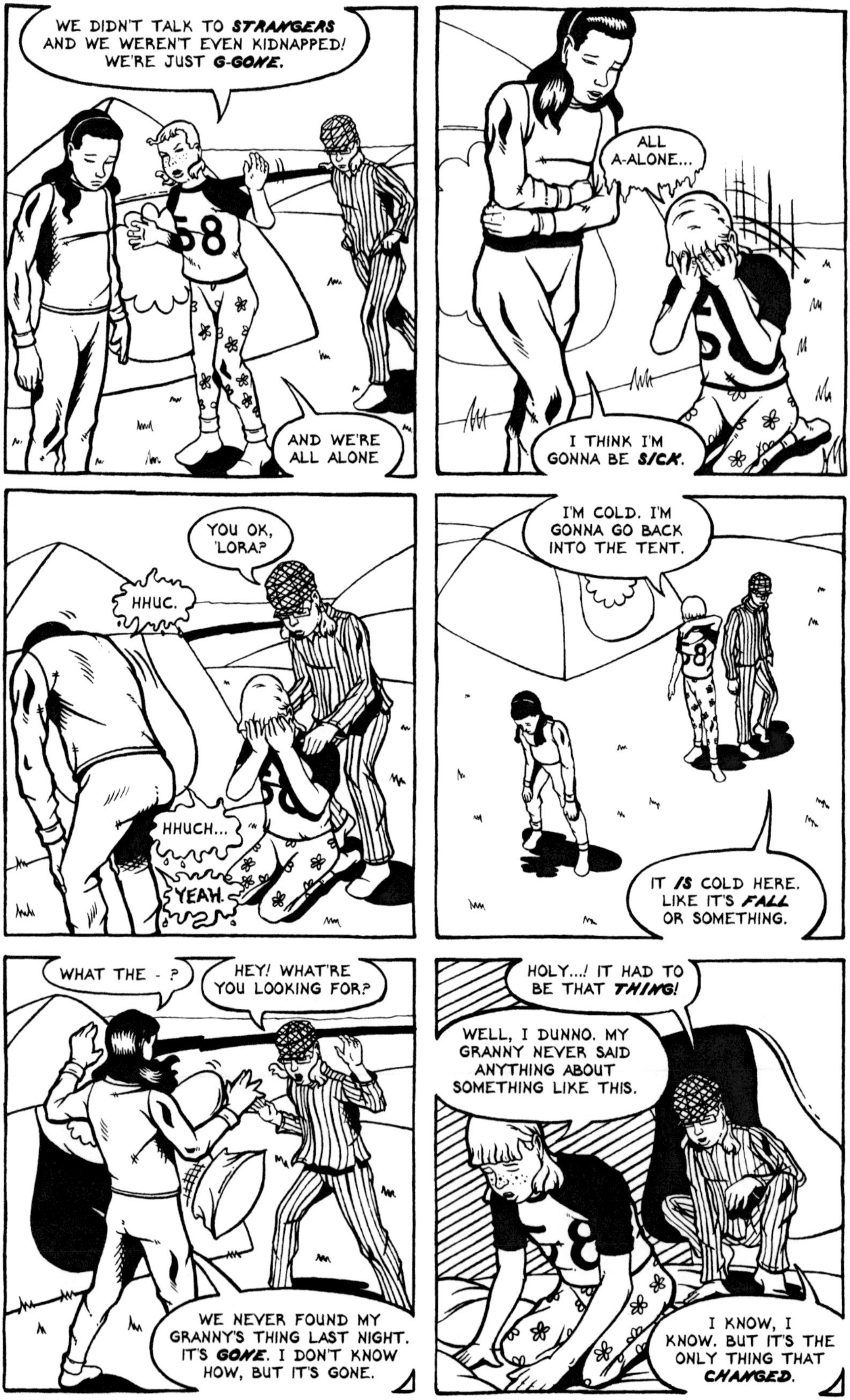
WE DIDN'T TALK TO STRANGERS AND WE WEREN'T EVEN KIDNAPPED! WE'RE JUST G-GONE.
AND WE'RE ALL ALONE
ALL A-ALONE...
I THINK I'M GONNA BE SICK.
YOU OK, 'LORA?
HHUC.
HHUCH...
YEAH.
I'M COLD. I'M GONNA GO BACK INTO THE TENT.
IT IS COLD HERE. LIKE IT'S FALL OR SOMETHING.
WHAT THE - ?
HEY! WHAT'RE YOU LOOKING FOR?
WE NEVER FOUND MY GRANNY'S THING LAST NIGHT. IT'S GONE. I DON'T KNOW HOW, BUT IT'S GONE.
HOLY...! IT HAD TO BE THAT THING!
WELL, I DUNNO. MY GRANNY NEVER SAID ANYTHING ABOUT SOMETHING LIKE THIS.
I KNOW, I KNOW. BUT IT'S THE ONLY THING THAT CHANGED.

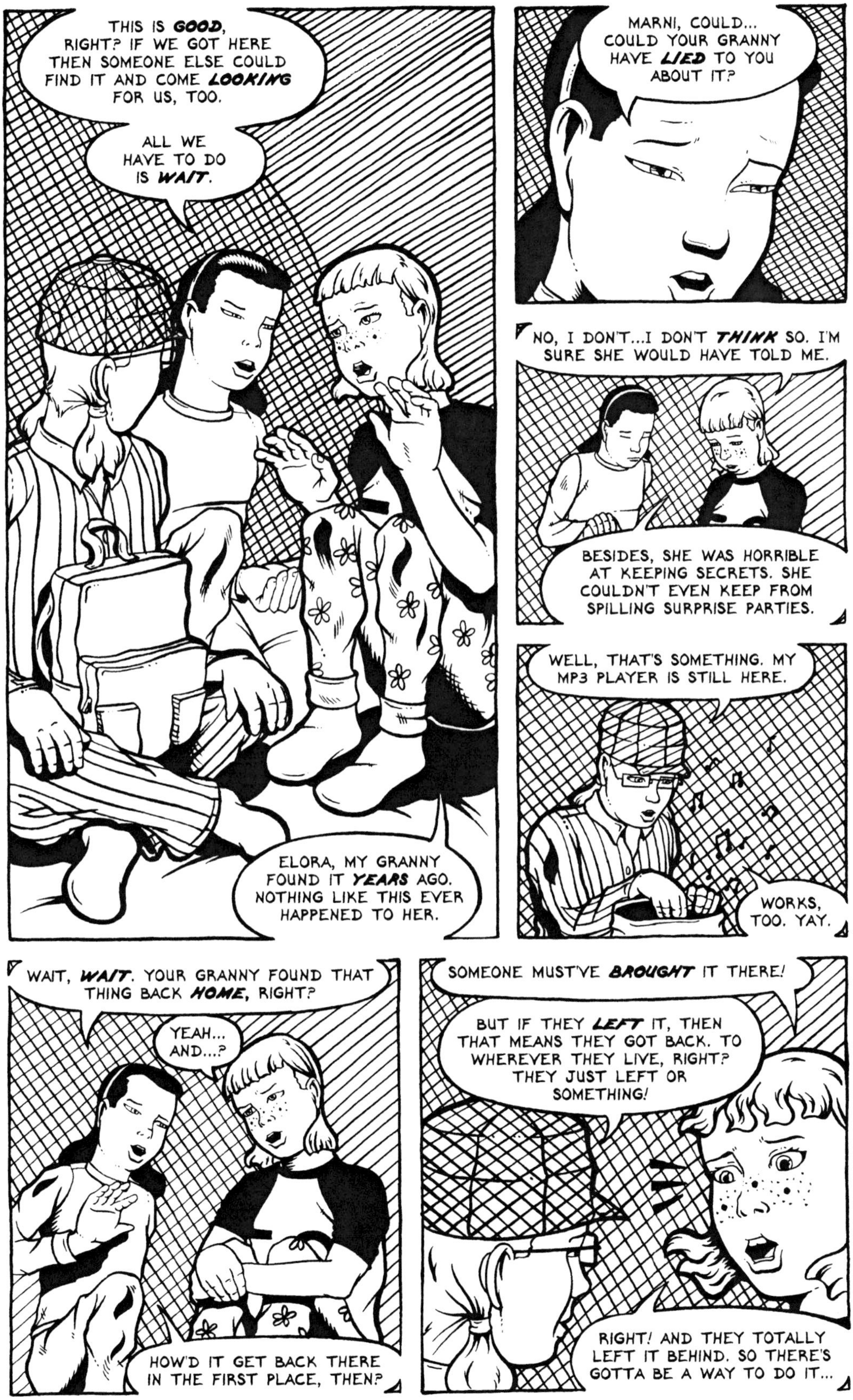
THIS IS GOOD, RIGHT? IF WE GOT HERE THEN SOMEONE ELSE COULD FIND IT AND COME LOOKING FOR US, TOO.
ALL WE HAVE TO DO IS WAIT.
ELORA, MY GRANNY FOUND IT YEARS AGO. NOTHING LIKE THIS EVER HAPPENED TO HER.
MARNI, COULD... COULD YOUR GRANNY HAVE LIED TO YOU ABOUT IT?
NO, I DON'T...I DON'T THINK SO. I'M SURE SHE WOULD HAVE TOLD ME.
BESIDES, SHE WAS HORRIBLE AT KEEPING SECRETS. SHE COULDN'T EVEN KEEP FROM SPILLING SURPRISE PARTIES.
WELL, THAT'S SOMETHING. MY MP3 PLAYER IS STILL HERE.
WORKS, TOO. YAY.
WAIT, WAIT. YOUR GRANNY FOUND THAT THING BACK HOME, RIGHT?
YEAH... AND...?
HOW'D IT GET BACK THERE IN THE FIRST PLACE, THEN?
SOMEONE MUST'VE BROUGHT IT THERE!
BUT IF THEY LEFT IT, THEN THAT MEANS THEY GOT BACK. TO WHEREVER THEY LIVE, RIGHT? THEY JUST LEFT OR SOMETHING!
RIGHT! AND THEY TOTALLY LEFT IT BEHIND. SO THERE'S GOTTA BE A WAY TO DO IT...

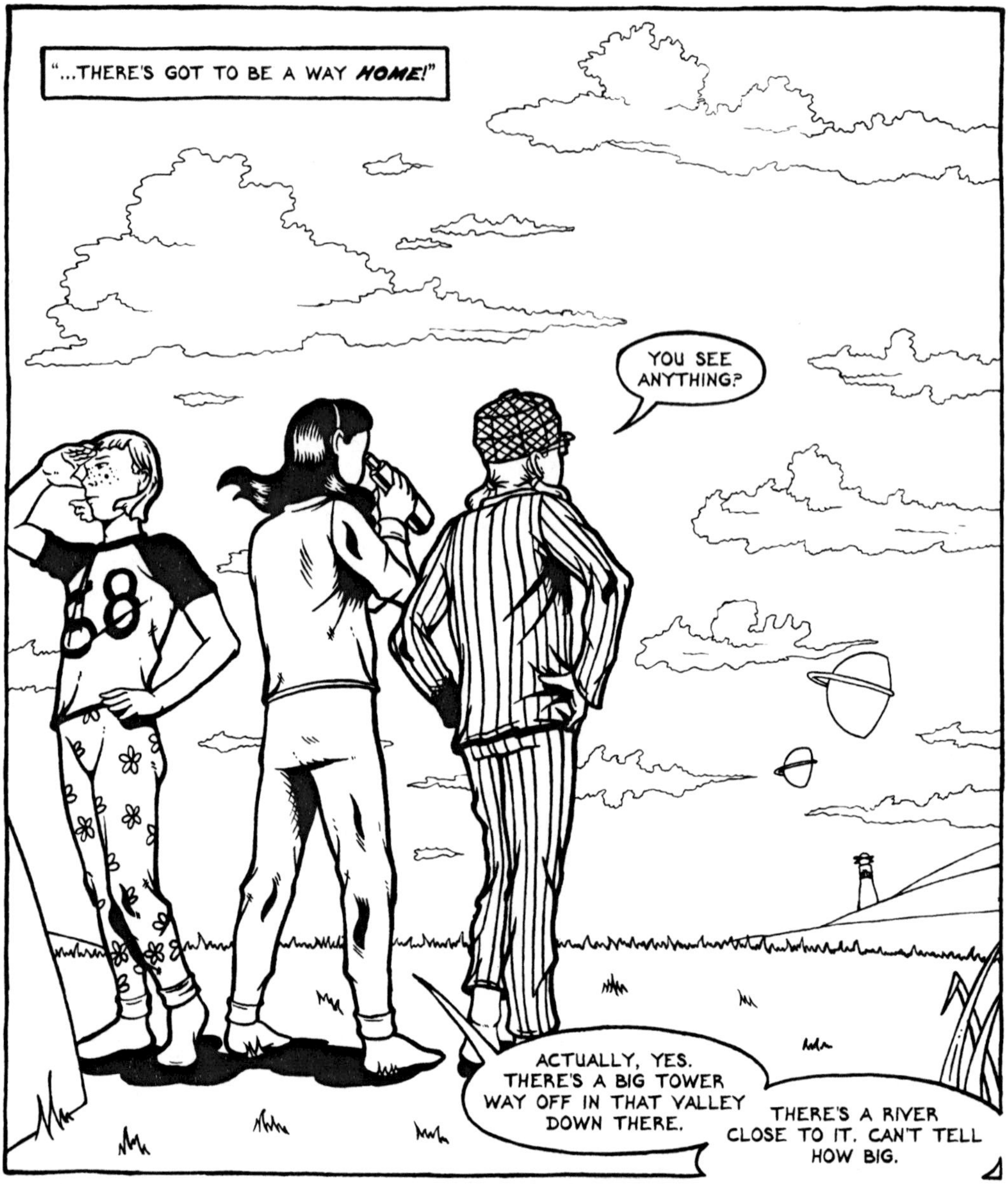
"...THERE'S GOT TO BE A WAY **HOME!**"
YOU SEE ANYTHING?
ACTUALLY, YES. THERE'S A BIG TOWER WAY OFF IN THAT VALLEY DOWN THERE.
THERE'S A RIVER CLOSE TO IT. CAN'T TELL HOW BIG.

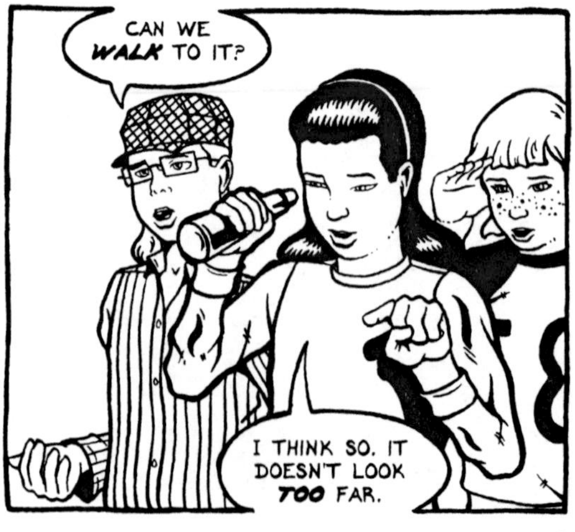
CAN WE **WALK** TO IT?
I THINK SO. IT DOESN'T LOOK **TOO** FAR.

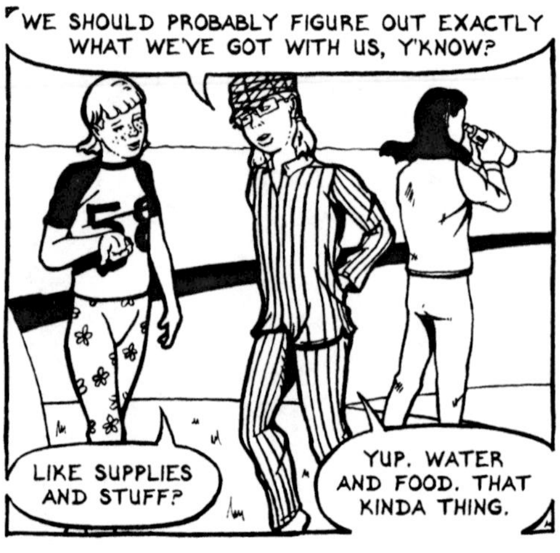
WE SHOULD PROBABLY FIGURE OUT EXACTLY WHAT WE'VE GOT WITH US, Y'KNOW?
LIKE SUPPLIES AND STUFF?
YUP. WATER AND FOOD. THAT KINDA THING.

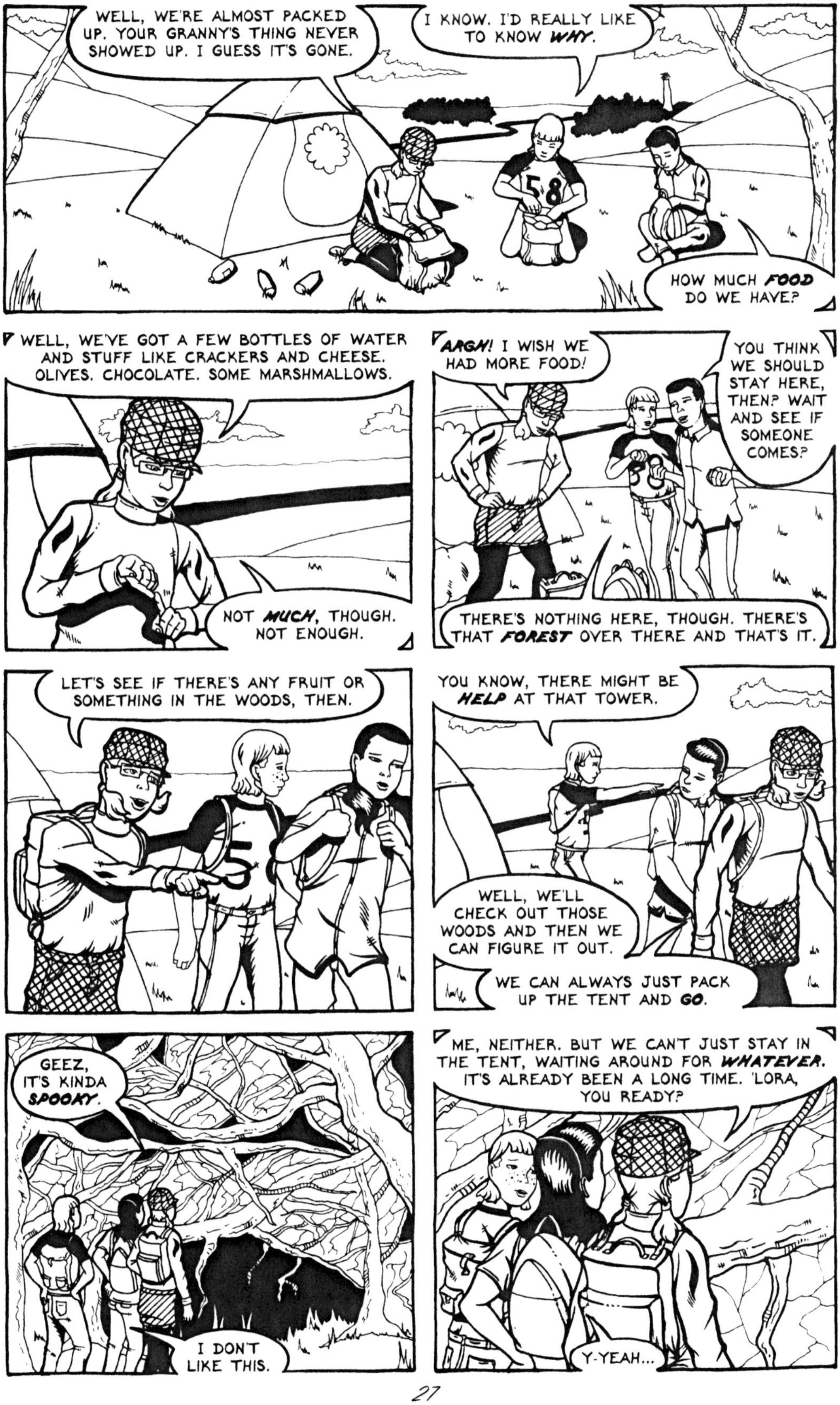
WELL, WE'RE ALMOST PACKED UP. YOUR GRANNY'S THING NEVER SHOWED UP. I GUESS IT'S GONE.
I KNOW. I'D REALLY LIKE TO KNOW WHY.
HOW MUCH FOOD DO WE HAVE?
WELL, WE'VE GOT A FEW BOTTLES OF WATER AND STUFF LIKE CRACKERS AND CHEESE. OLIVES. CHOCOLATE. SOME MARSHMALLOWS.
NOT MUCH, THOUGH. NOT ENOUGH.
ARGH! I WISH WE HAD MORE FOOD!
YOU THINK WE SHOULD STAY HERE, THEN? WAIT AND SEE IF SOMEONE COMES?
THERE'S NOTHING HERE, THOUGH. THERE'S THAT FOREST OVER THERE AND THAT'S IT.
LET'S SEE IF THERE'S ANY FRUIT OR SOMETHING IN THE WOODS, THEN.
YOU KNOW, THERE MIGHT BE HELP AT THAT TOWER.
WELL, WE'LL CHECK OUT THOSE WOODS AND THEN WE CAN FIGURE IT OUT.
WE CAN ALWAYS JUST PACK UP THE TENT AND GO.
GEEZ, IT'S KINDA SPOOKY.
I DON'T LIKE THIS.
ME, NEITHER. BUT WE CAN'T JUST STAY IN THE TENT, WAITING AROUND FOR WHATEVER. IT'S ALREADY BEEN A LONG TIME. 'LORA, YOU READY?
Y-YEAH...

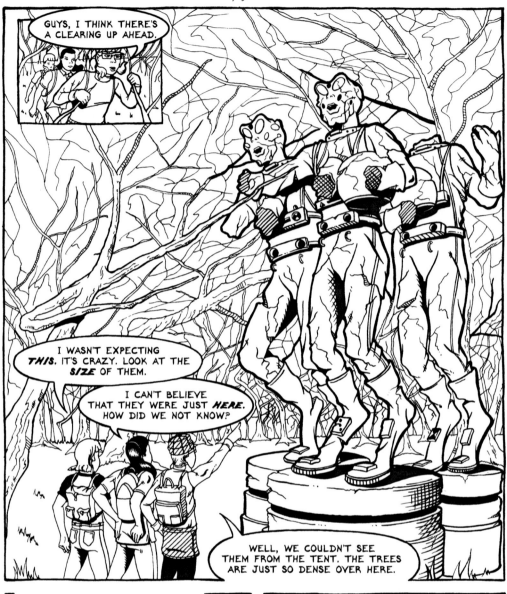

GUYS, I THINK THERE'S A CLEARING UP AHEAD.

I WASN'T EXPECTING *THIS.* IT'S CRAZY. LOOK AT THE *SIZE* OF THEM.

I CAN'T BELIEVE THAT THEY WERE JUST *HERE.* HOW DID WE NOT KNOW?

WELL, WE COULDN'T SEE THEM FROM THE TENT. THE TREES ARE JUST SO DENSE OVER HERE.

THIS...THIS IS *UNBELIEVABLE.* WHAT ARE THEY? WHAT *IS* THIS PLACE?

RUINS? MAYBE? SOME TYPE OF OLD MONUMENT OR SOMETHING?

WOW...

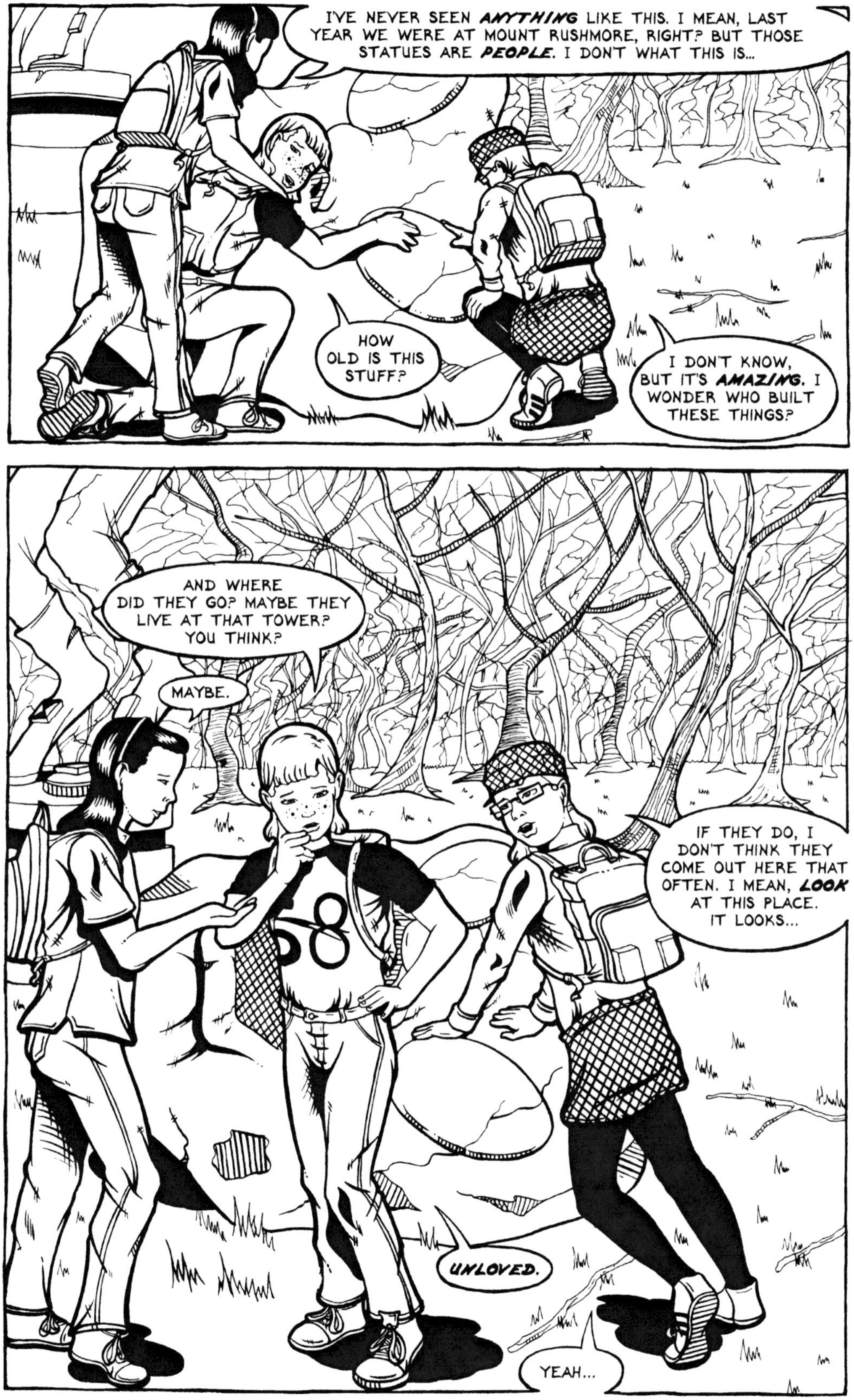
I'VE NEVER SEEN ANYTHING LIKE THIS. I MEAN, LAST YEAR WE WERE AT MOUNT RUSHMORE, RIGHT? BUT THOSE STATUES ARE PEOPLE. I DON'T WHAT THIS IS...
HOW OLD IS THIS STUFF?
I DON'T KNOW, BUT IT'S AMAZING. I WONDER WHO BUILT THESE THINGS?
AND WHERE DID THEY GO? MAYBE THEY LIVE AT THAT TOWER? YOU THINK?
MAYBE.
IF THEY DO, I DON'T THINK THEY COME OUT HERE THAT OFTEN. I MEAN, LOOK AT THIS PLACE. IT LOOKS...
UNLOVED.
YEAH...

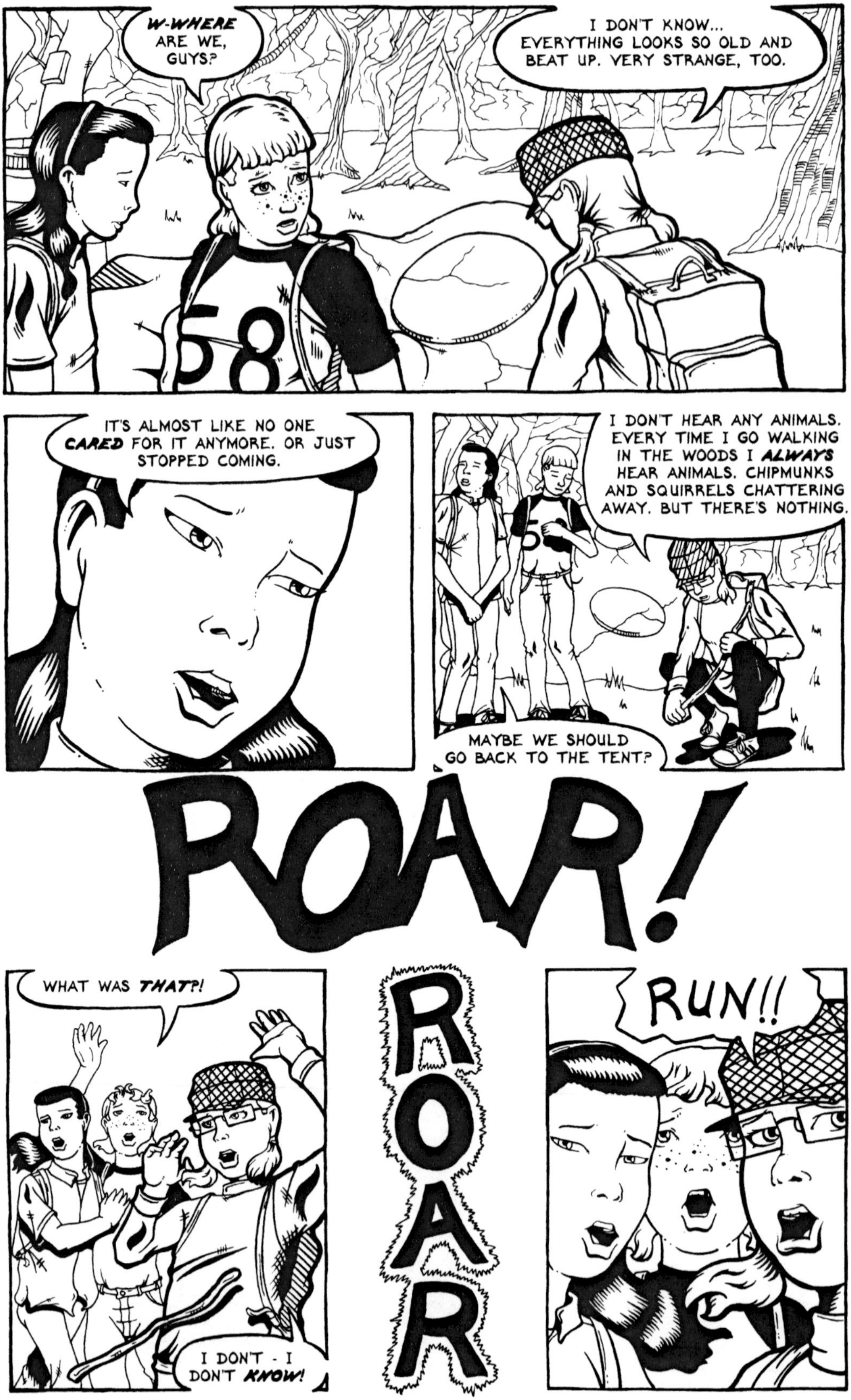
W-WHERE ARE WE, GUYS?
I DON'T KNOW... EVERYTHING LOOKS SO OLD AND BEAT UP. VERY STRANGE, TOO.
IT'S ALMOST LIKE NO ONE CARED FOR IT ANYMORE. OR JUST STOPPED COMING.
I DON'T HEAR ANY ANIMALS. EVERY TIME I GO WALKING IN THE WOODS I ALWAYS HEAR ANIMALS. CHIPMUNKS AND SQUIRRELS CHATTERING AWAY. BUT THERE'S NOTHING.
MAYBE WE SHOULD GO BACK TO THE TENT?
ROAR!
WHAT WAS THAT?!
I DON'T - I DON'T KNOW!
ROAR
RUN!!

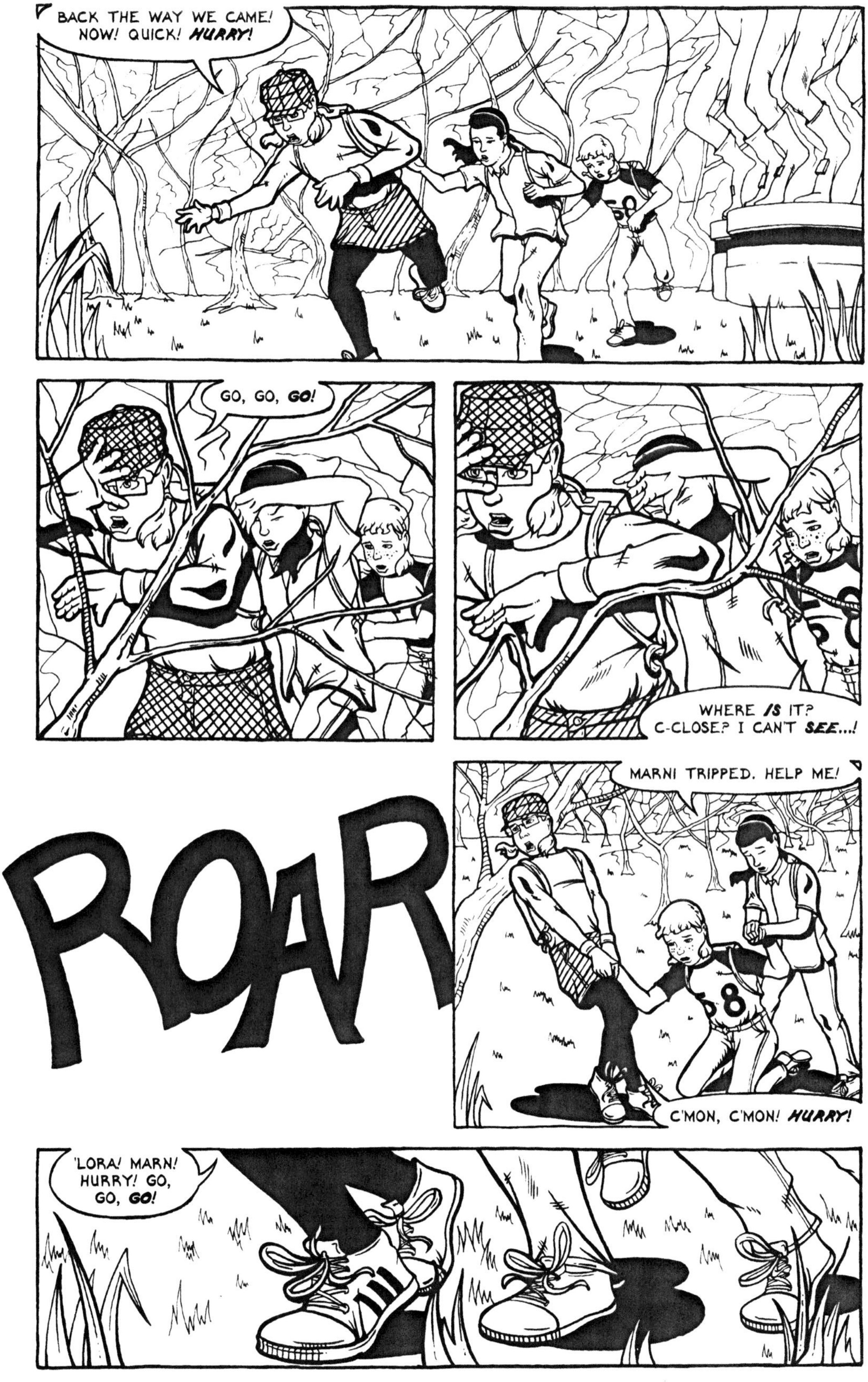
BACK THE WAY WE CAME! NOW! QUICK! **HURRY!**
GO, GO, **GO!**
WHERE ***IS*** IT? C-CLOSE? I CAN'T ***SEE...!***
ROAR
MARNI TRIPPED. HELP ME!
C'MON, C'MON! ***HURRY!***
'LORA! MARN! HURRY! GO, GO, **GO!**

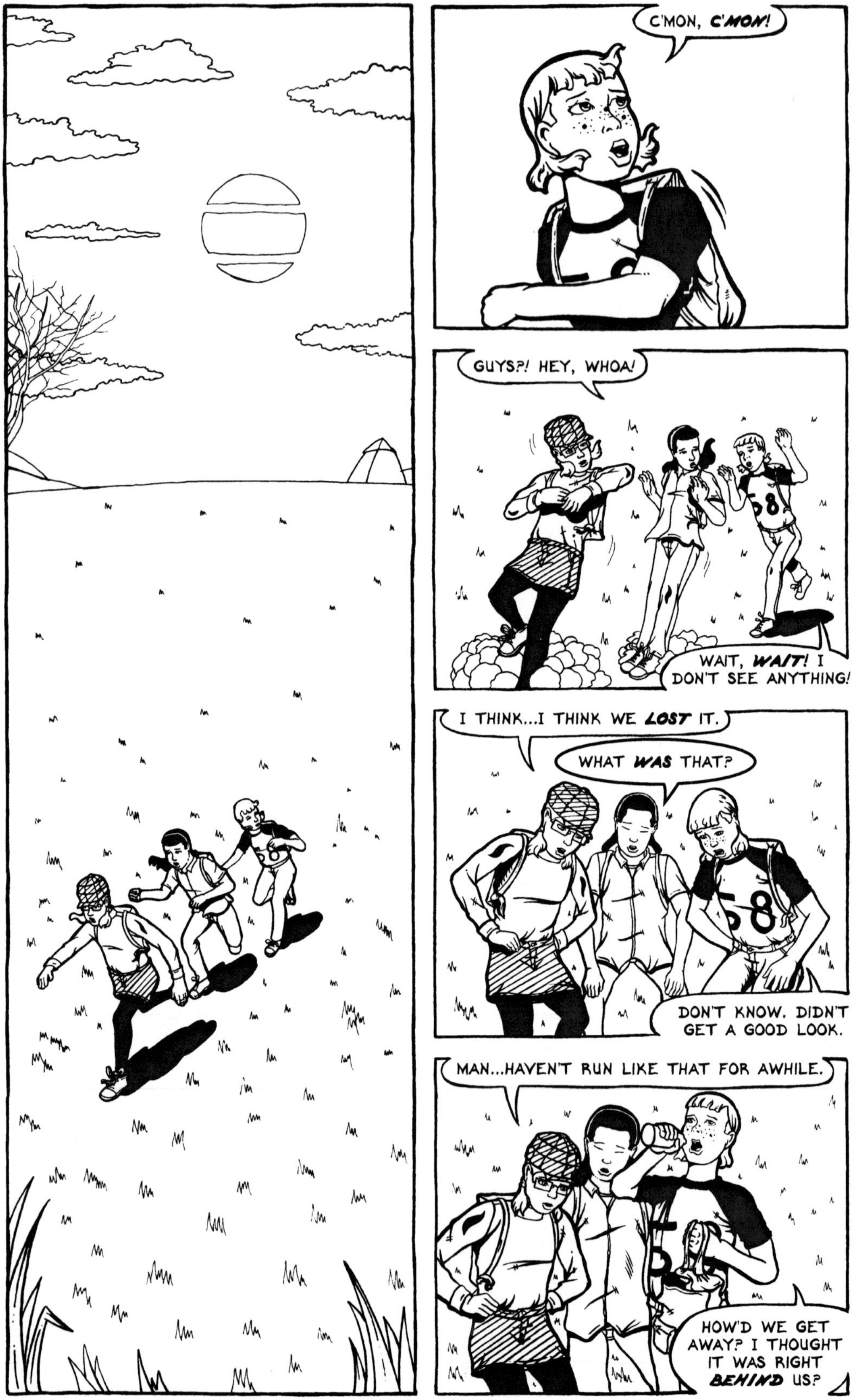
C'MON, **C'MON!**
GUYS?! HEY, WHOA!
WAIT, **WAIT!** I DON'T SEE ANYTHING!
I THINK...I THINK WE **LOST** IT.
WHAT **WAS** THAT?
DON'T KNOW. DIDN'T GET A GOOD LOOK.
MAN...HAVEN'T RUN LIKE THAT FOR AWHILE.
HOW'D WE GET AWAY? I THOUGHT IT WAS RIGHT **BEHIND** US?

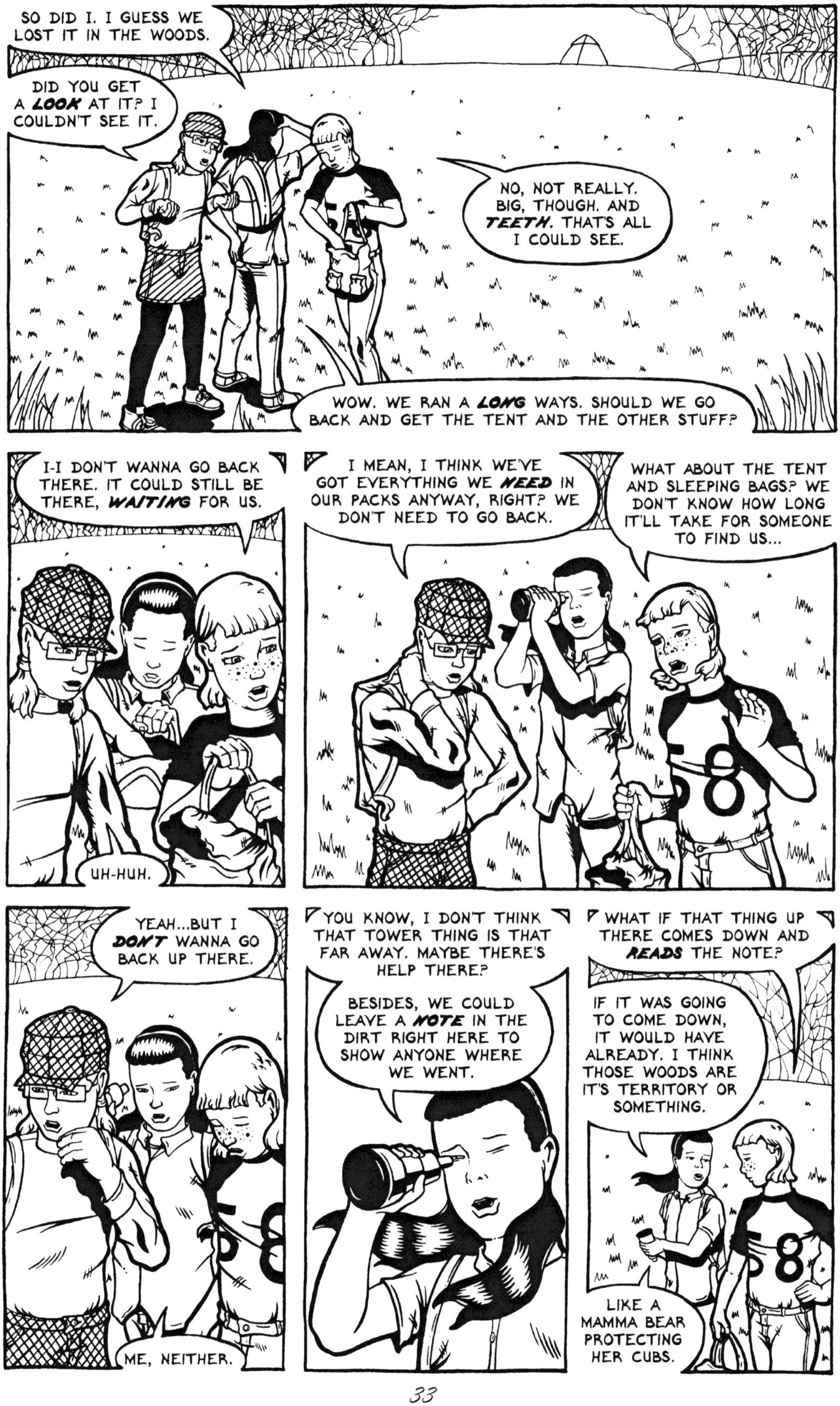
SO DID I. I GUESS WE LOST IT IN THE WOODS.
DID YOU GET A *LOOK* AT IT? I COULDN'T SEE IT.
NO, NOT REALLY. BIG, THOUGH. AND *TEETH*. THAT'S ALL I COULD SEE.
WOW. WE RAN A *LONG* WAYS. SHOULD WE GO BACK AND GET THE TENT AND THE OTHER STUFF?
I-I DON'T WANNA GO BACK THERE. IT COULD STILL BE THERE, *WAITING* FOR US.
UH-HUH.
I MEAN, I THINK WE'VE GOT EVERYTHING WE *NEED* IN OUR PACKS ANYWAY, RIGHT? WE DON'T NEED TO GO BACK.
WHAT ABOUT THE TENT AND SLEEPING BAGS? WE DON'T KNOW HOW LONG IT'LL TAKE FOR SOMEONE TO FIND US...
YEAH...BUT I *DON'T* WANNA GO BACK UP THERE.
ME, NEITHER.
YOU KNOW, I DON'T THINK THAT TOWER THING IS THAT FAR AWAY. MAYBE THERE'S HELP THERE?
BESIDES, WE COULD LEAVE A *NOTE* IN THE DIRT RIGHT HERE TO SHOW ANYONE WHERE WE WENT.
WHAT IF THAT THING UP THERE COMES DOWN AND *READS* THE NOTE?
IF IT WAS GOING TO COME DOWN, IT WOULD HAVE ALREADY. I THINK THOSE WOODS ARE IT'S TERRITORY OR SOMETHING.
LIKE A MAMMA BEAR PROTECTING HER CUBS.

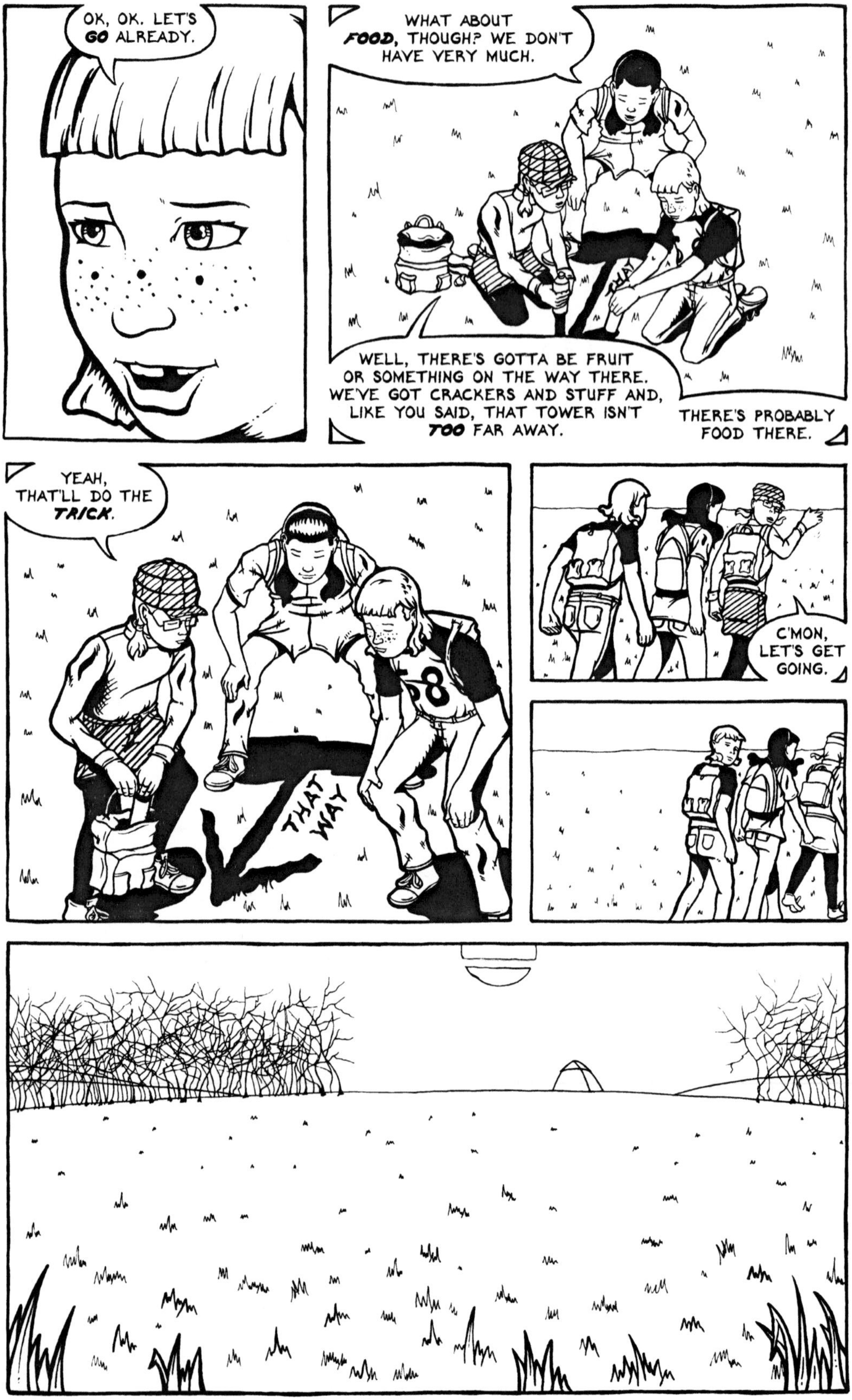
OK, OK. LET'S GO ALREADY.
WHAT ABOUT FOOD, THOUGH? WE DON'T HAVE VERY MUCH.
WELL, THERE'S GOTTA BE FRUIT OR SOMETHING ON THE WAY THERE. WE'VE GOT CRACKERS AND STUFF AND, LIKE YOU SAID, THAT TOWER ISN'T TOO FAR AWAY.
THERE'S PROBABLY FOOD THERE.
YEAH, THAT'LL DO THE TRICK.
THAT WAY
C'MON, LET'S GET GOING.

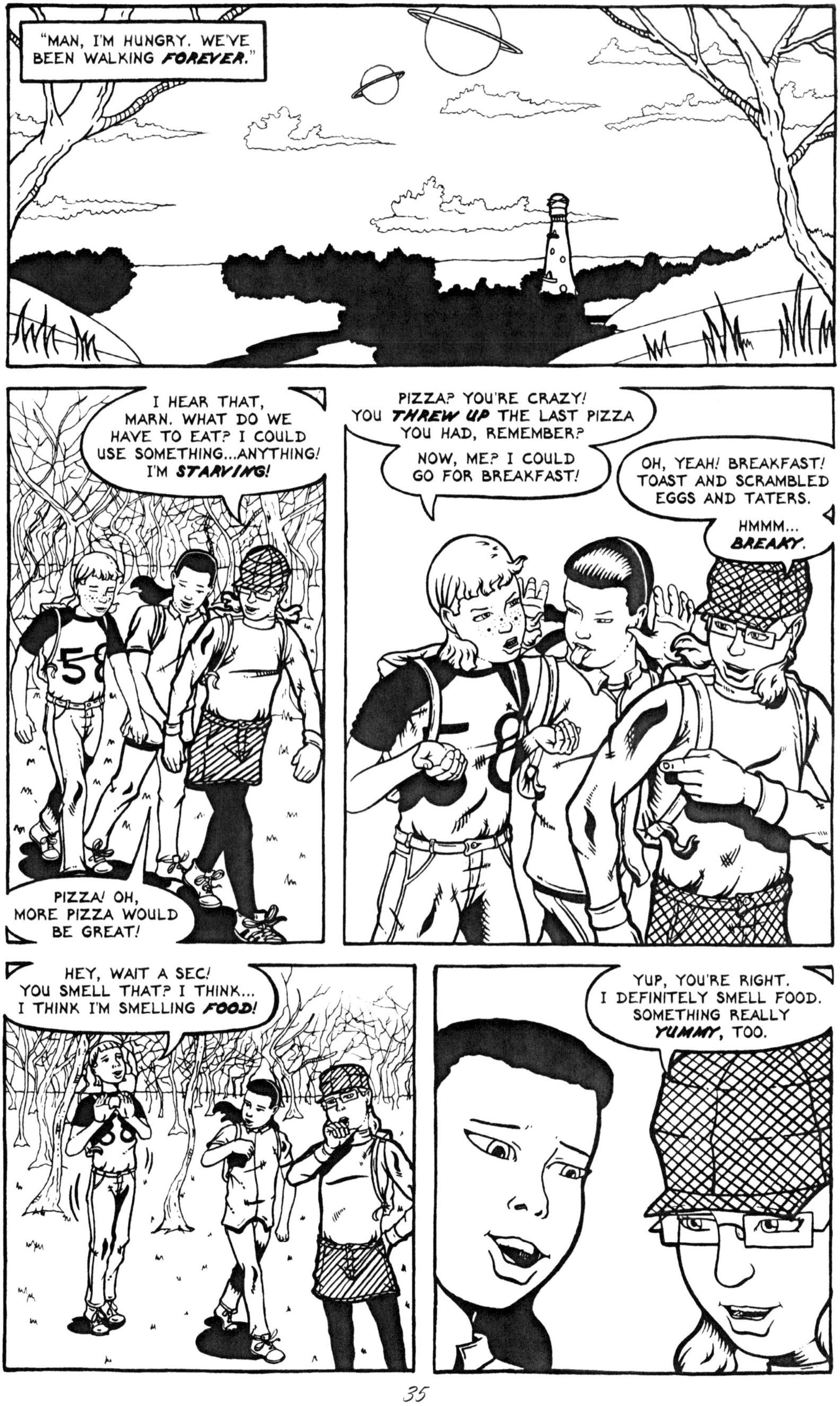
"MAN, I'M HUNGRY. WE'VE BEEN WALKING FOREVER."
I HEAR THAT, MARN. WHAT DO WE HAVE TO EAT? I COULD USE SOMETHING...ANYTHING! I'M STARVING!
PIZZA! OH, MORE PIZZA WOULD BE GREAT!
PIZZA? YOU'RE CRAZY! YOU THREW UP THE LAST PIZZA YOU HAD, REMEMBER?
NOW, ME? I COULD GO FOR BREAKFAST!
OH, YEAH! BREAKFAST! TOAST AND SCRAMBLED EGGS AND TATERS.
HMMM... BREAKY.
HEY, WAIT A SEC! YOU SMELL THAT? I THINK... I THINK I'M SMELLING FOOD!
YUP, YOU'RE RIGHT. I DEFINITELY SMELL FOOD. SOMETHING REALLY YUMMY, TOO.

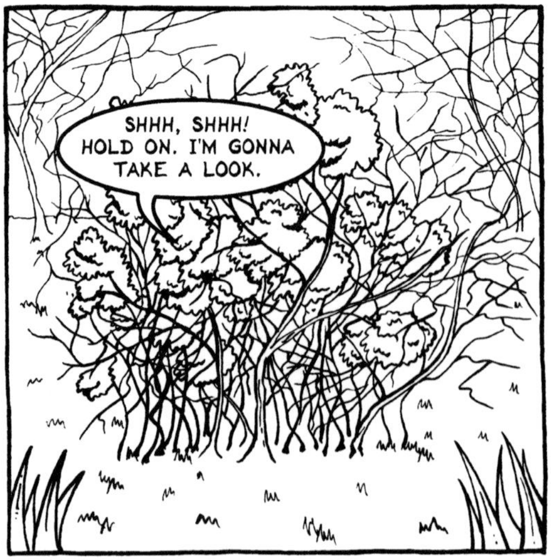
SHHH, SHHH! HOLD ON. I'M GONNA TAKE A LOOK.

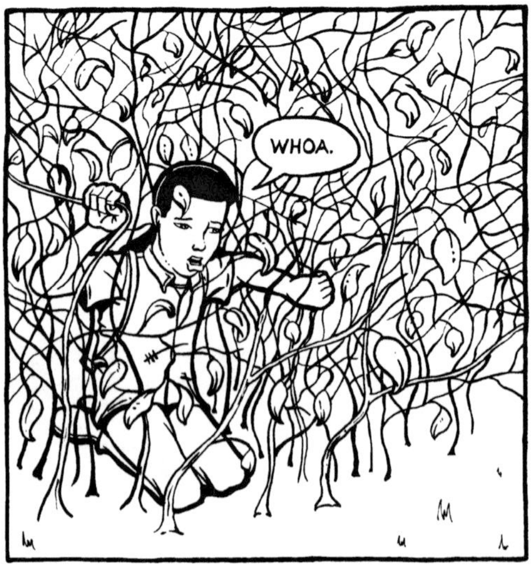
WHOA.

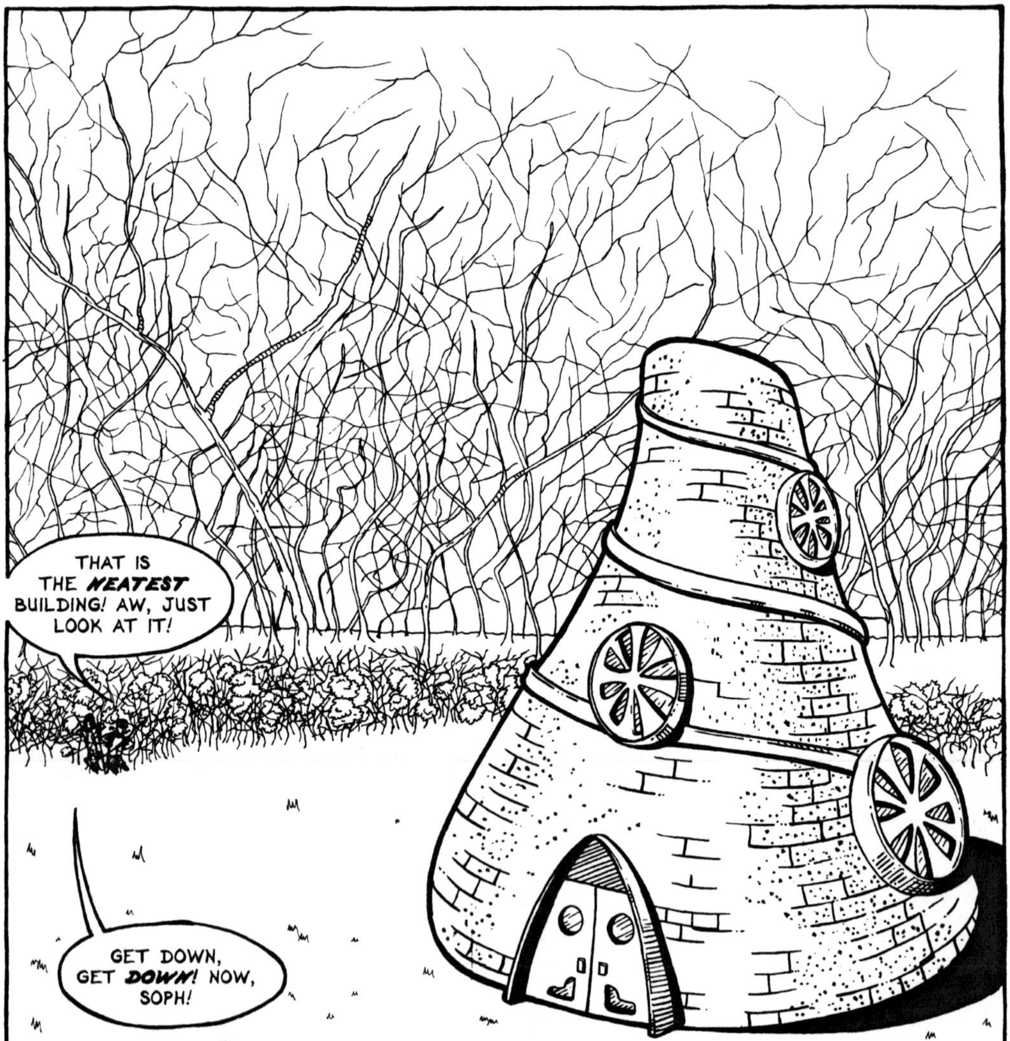
THAT IS THE ***NEATEST*** BUILDING! AW, JUST LOOK AT IT!
GET DOWN, GET ***DOWN***! NOW, SOPH!

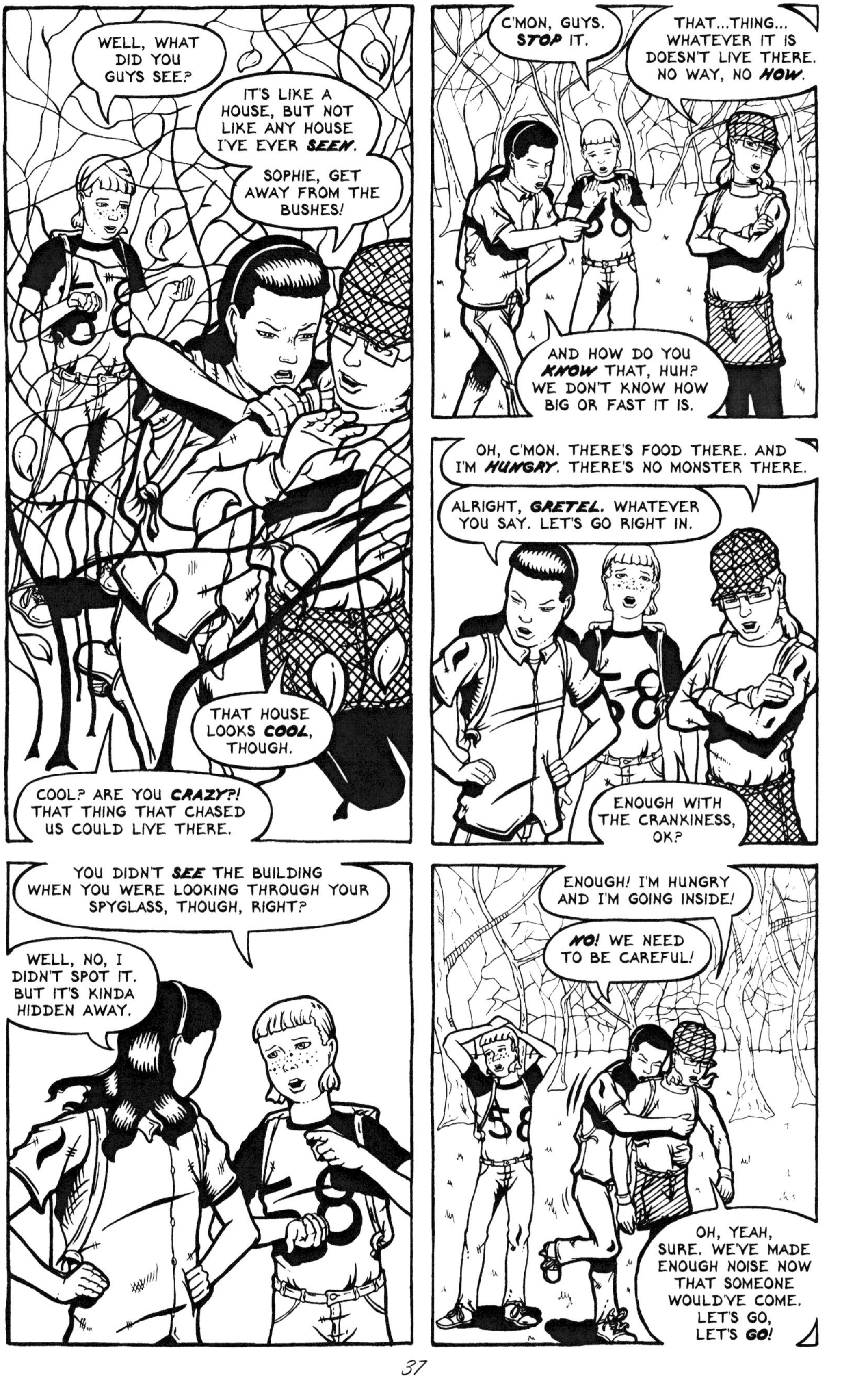
WELL, WHAT DID YOU GUYS SEE?
IT'S LIKE A HOUSE, BUT NOT LIKE ANY HOUSE I'VE EVER SEEN.
SOPHIE, GET AWAY FROM THE BUSHES!
THAT HOUSE LOOKS COOL, THOUGH.
COOL? ARE YOU CRAZY?! THAT THING THAT CHASED US COULD LIVE THERE.
C'MON, GUYS. STOP IT.
THAT...THING... WHATEVER IT IS DOESN'T LIVE THERE. NO WAY, NO HOW.
AND HOW DO YOU KNOW THAT, HUH? WE DON'T KNOW HOW BIG OR FAST IT IS.
OH, C'MON. THERE'S FOOD THERE. AND I'M HUNGRY. THERE'S NO MONSTER THERE.
ALRIGHT, GRETEL. WHATEVER YOU SAY. LET'S GO RIGHT IN.
ENOUGH WITH THE CRANKINESS, OK?
YOU DIDN'T SEE THE BUILDING WHEN YOU WERE LOOKING THROUGH YOUR SPYGLASS, THOUGH, RIGHT?
WELL, NO, I DIDN'T SPOT IT. BUT IT'S KINDA HIDDEN AWAY.
ENOUGH! I'M HUNGRY AND I'M GOING INSIDE!
NO! WE NEED TO BE CAREFUL!
OH, YEAH, SURE. WE'VE MADE ENOUGH NOISE NOW THAT SOMEONE WOULD'VE COME. LET'S GO, LET'S GO!

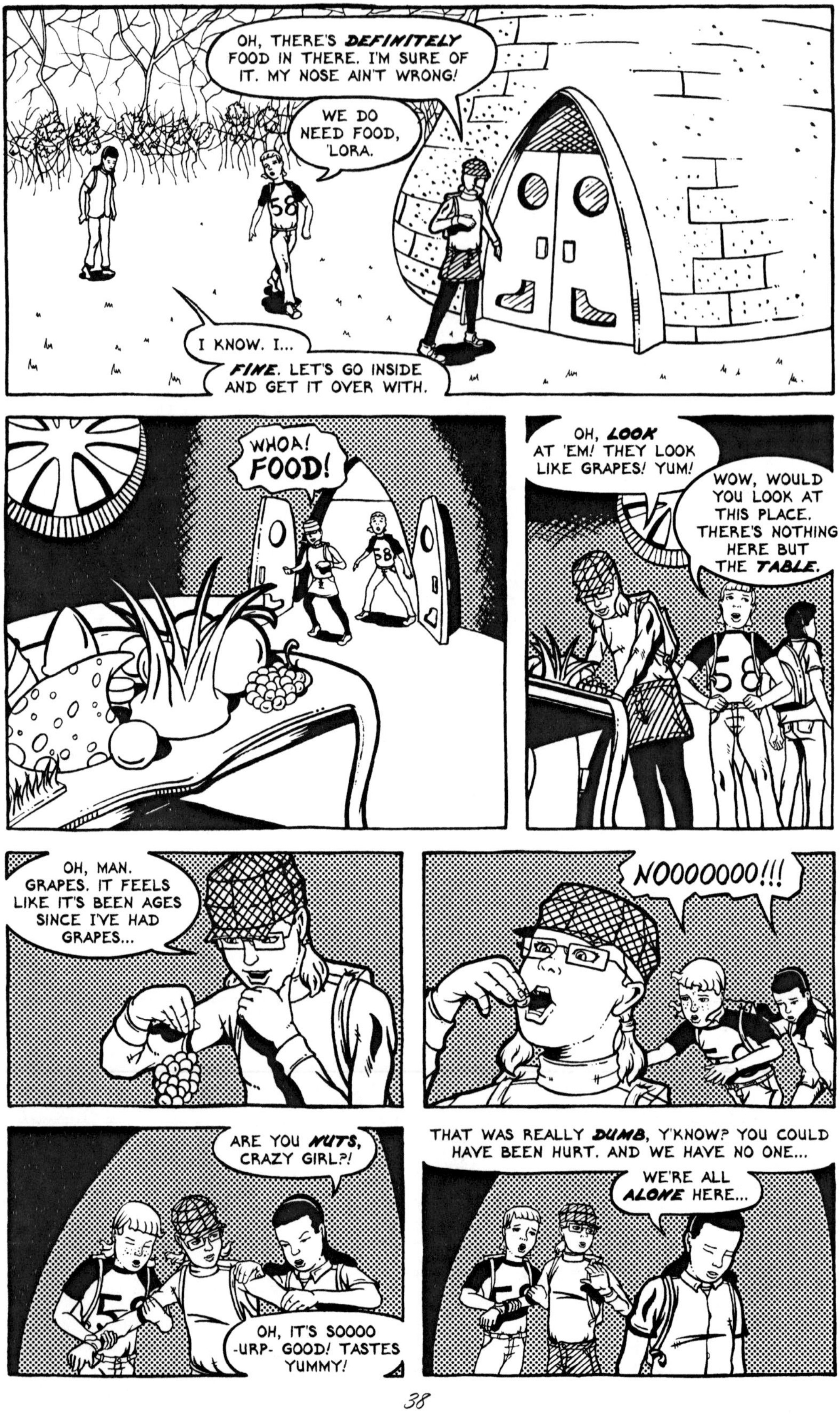
OH, THERE'S DEFINITELY FOOD IN THERE. I'M SURE OF IT. MY NOSE AIN'T WRONG!
WE DO NEED FOOD, 'LORA.
I KNOW. I...
FINE. LET'S GO INSIDE AND GET IT OVER WITH.
WHOA! FOOD!
OH, LOOK AT 'EM! THEY LOOK LIKE GRAPES! YUM!
WOW, WOULD YOU LOOK AT THIS PLACE. THERE'S NOTHING HERE BUT THE TABLE.
OH, MAN. GRAPES. IT FEELS LIKE IT'S BEEN AGES SINCE I'VE HAD GRAPES...
NOOOOOOO!!!
ARE YOU NUTS, CRAZY GIRL?!
OH, IT'S SOOOO -URP- GOOD! TASTES YUMMY!
THAT WAS REALLY DUMB, Y'KNOW? YOU COULD HAVE BEEN HURT. AND WE HAVE NO ONE...
WE'RE ALL ALONE HERE...

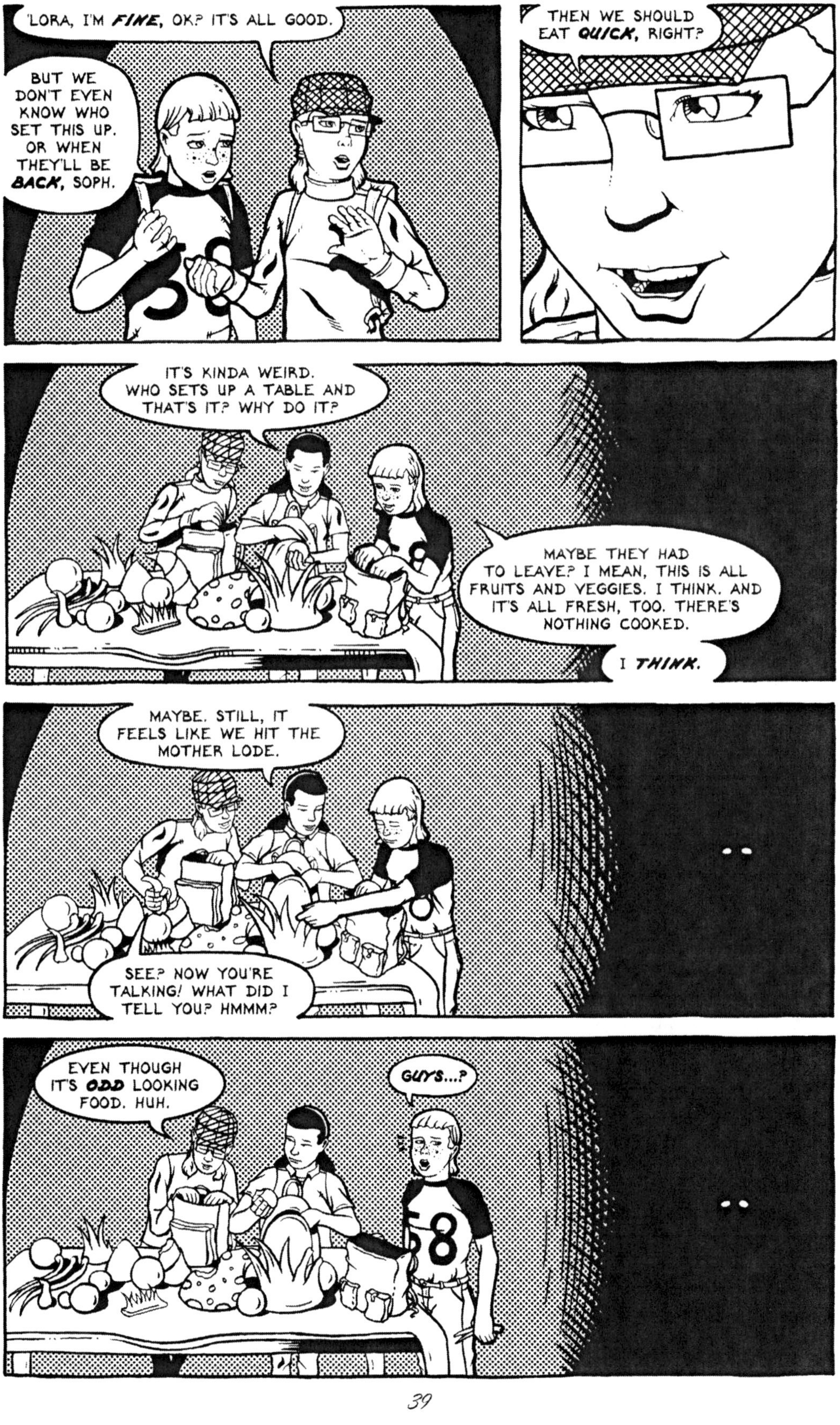
'LORA, I'M FINE, OK? IT'S ALL GOOD.
BUT WE DON'T EVEN KNOW WHO SET THIS UP. OR WHEN THEY'LL BE BACK, SOPH.
THEN WE SHOULD EAT QUICK, RIGHT?
IT'S KINDA WEIRD. WHO SETS UP A TABLE AND THAT'S IT? WHY DO IT?
MAYBE THEY HAD TO LEAVE? I MEAN, THIS IS ALL FRUITS AND VEGGIES. I THINK. AND IT'S ALL FRESH, TOO. THERE'S NOTHING COOKED.
I THINK.
MAYBE. STILL, IT FEELS LIKE WE HIT THE MOTHER LODE.
SEE? NOW YOU'RE TALKING! WHAT DID I TELL YOU? HMMM?
EVEN THOUGH IT'S ODD LOOKING FOOD. HUH.
GUYS...?

I THINK WE'RE BEING **WATCHED**. SOMETHING'S BACK THERE.

WHAT'S THE **MATTER?**

I THINK...

REALLY? I CAN'T SEE ANYTHING. ARE YOU **SURE?**

YES.

I DON'T KNOW, MARN. I DON'T SEE ANYTHING, EITHER.

WELL, THERE'S ONE WAY TO FIND OUT!

ACK!

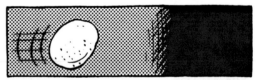

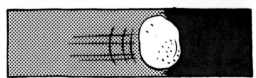

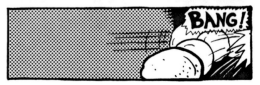

BANG!

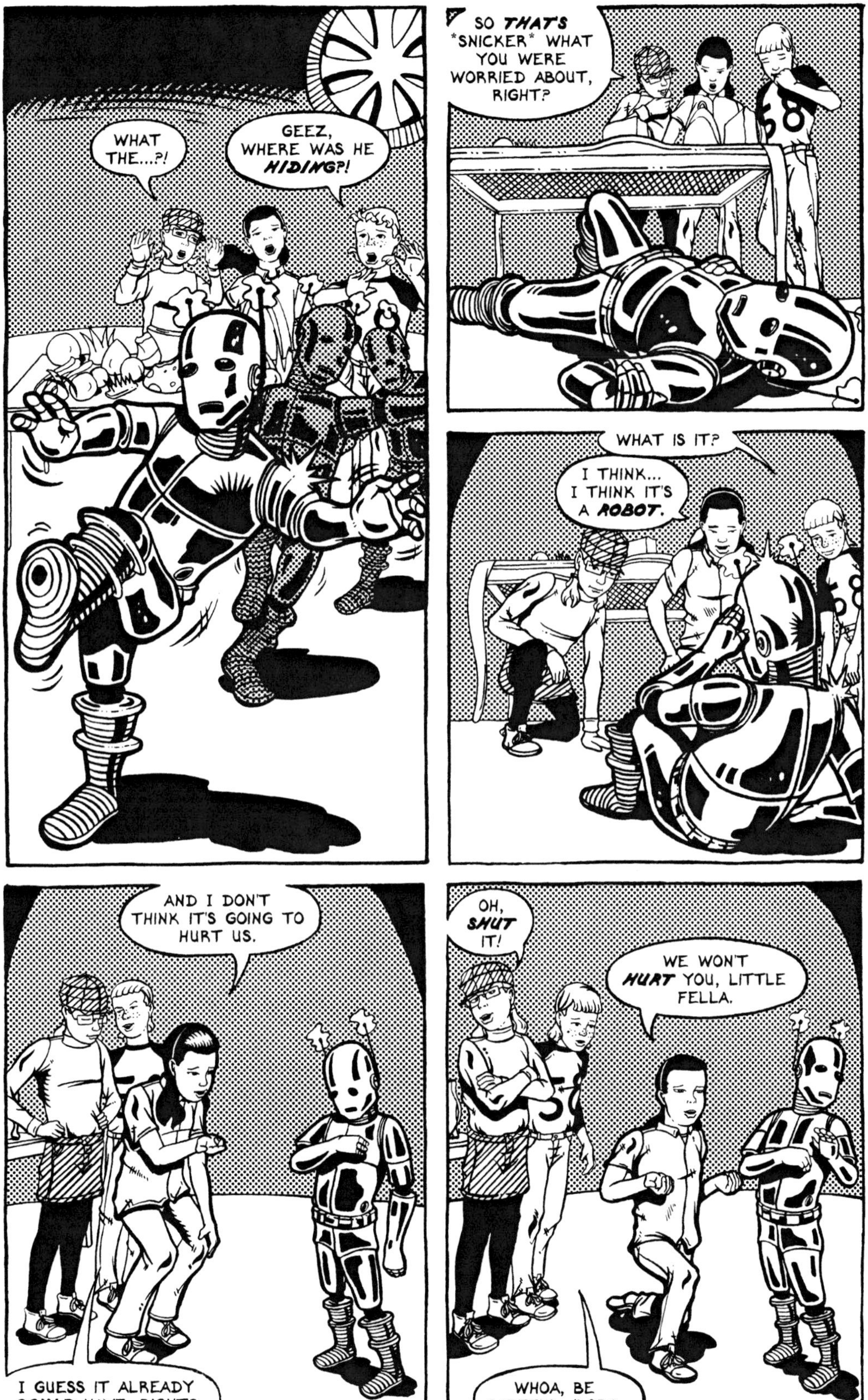
WHAT THE...?!
GEEZ, WHERE WAS HE HIDING?!
SO THAT'S *SNICKER* WHAT YOU WERE WORRIED ABOUT, RIGHT?
WHAT IS IT?
I THINK... I THINK IT'S A ROBOT.
AND I DON'T THINK IT'S GOING TO HURT US.
I GUESS IT ALREADY COULD HAVE, RIGHT?
OH, SHUT IT!
WE WON'T HURT YOU, LITTLE FELLA.
WHOA, BE CAREFUL, 'LORA.

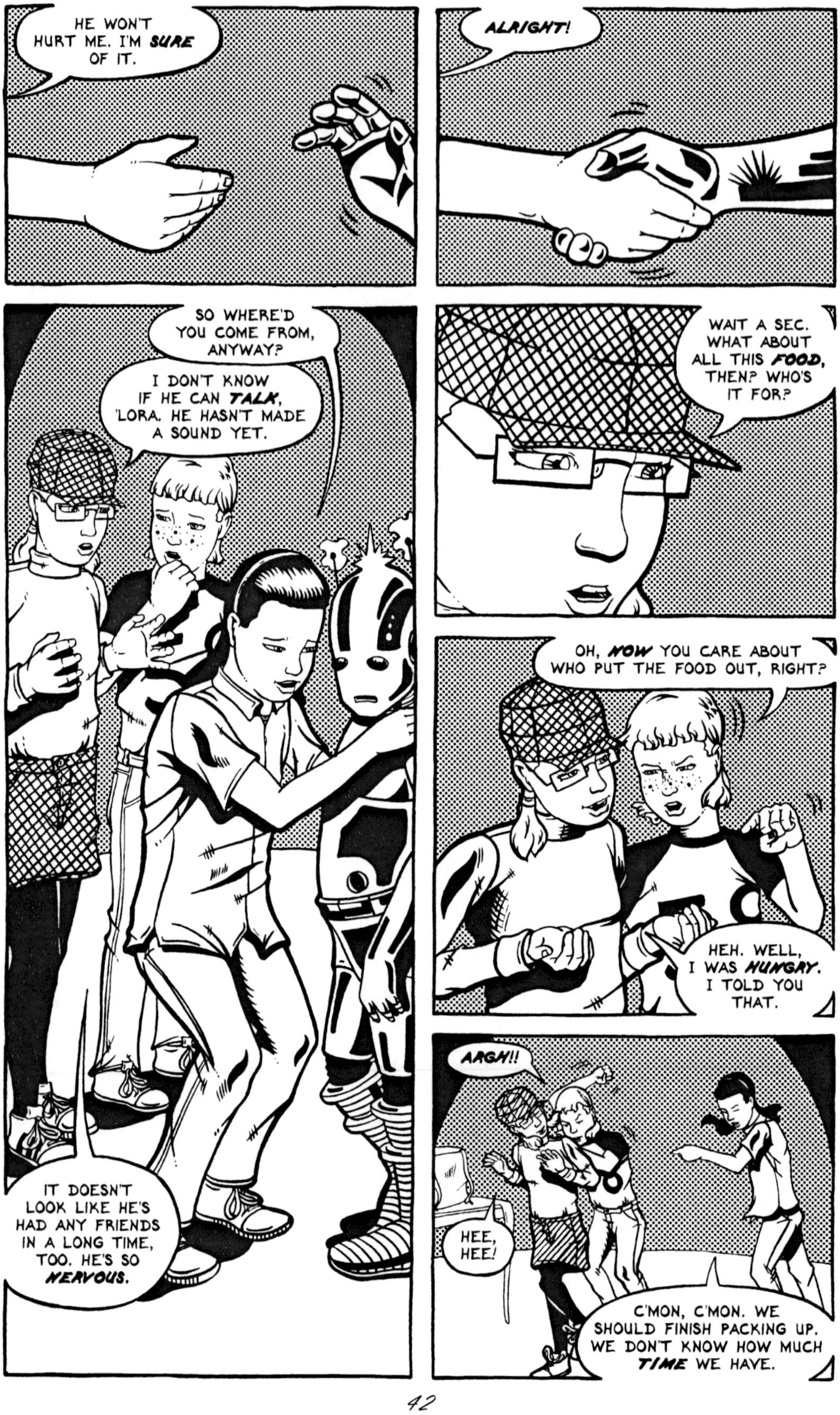
HE WON'T HURT ME. I'M SURE OF IT.
ALRIGHT!
SO WHERE'D YOU COME FROM, ANYWAY?
I DON'T KNOW IF HE CAN TALK, 'LORA. HE HASN'T MADE A SOUND YET.
IT DOESN'T LOOK LIKE HE'S HAD ANY FRIENDS IN A LONG TIME, TOO. HE'S SO NERVOUS.
WAIT A SEC. WHAT ABOUT ALL THIS FOOD, THEN? WHO'S IT FOR?
OH, NOW YOU CARE ABOUT WHO PUT THE FOOD OUT, RIGHT?
HEH. WELL, I WAS HUNGRY. I TOLD YOU THAT.
ARGH!!
HEE, HEE!
C'MON, C'MON. WE SHOULD FINISH PACKING UP. WE DON'T KNOW HOW MUCH TIME WE HAVE.

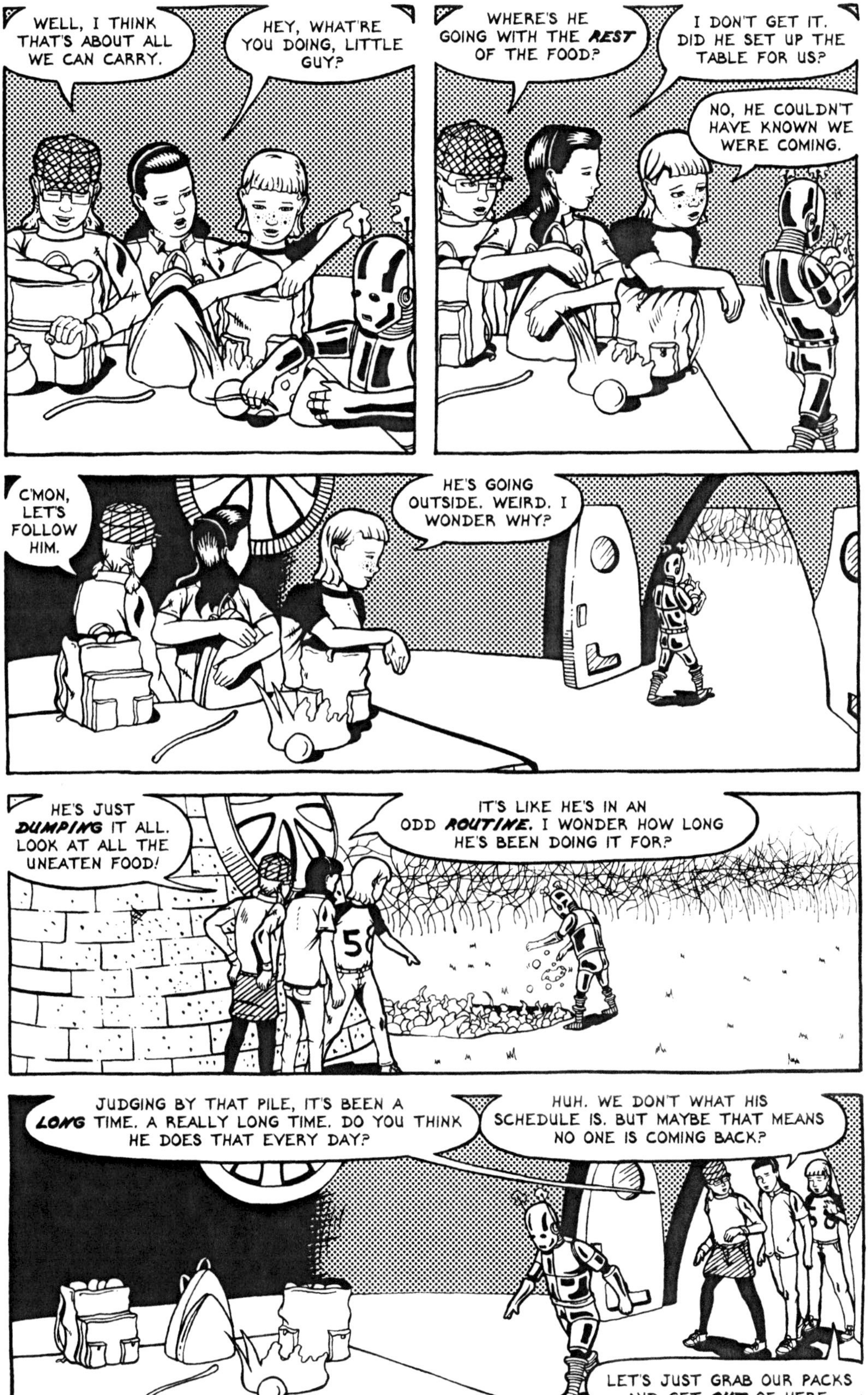
WELL, I THINK THAT'S ABOUT ALL WE CAN CARRY.
HEY, WHAT'RE YOU DOING, LITTLE GUY?
WHERE'S HE GOING WITH THE *REST* OF THE FOOD?
I DON'T GET IT. DID HE SET UP THE TABLE FOR US?
NO, HE COULDN'T HAVE KNOWN WE WERE COMING.
C'MON, LET'S FOLLOW HIM.
HE'S GOING OUTSIDE. WEIRD. I WONDER WHY?
HE'S JUST *DUMPING* IT ALL. LOOK AT ALL THE UNEATEN FOOD!
IT'S LIKE HE'S IN AN ODD *ROUTINE*. I WONDER HOW LONG HE'S BEEN DOING IT FOR?
JUDGING BY THAT PILE, IT'S BEEN A *LONG* TIME. A REALLY LONG TIME. DO YOU THINK HE DOES THAT EVERY DAY?
HUH. WE DON'T WHAT HIS SCHEDULE IS. BUT MAYBE THAT MEANS NO ONE IS COMING BACK?
LET'S JUST GRAB OUR PACKS AND GET *OUT* OF HERE.

WHAT DO YOU WANNA DO THEN? WHERE ARE WE GONNA *SLEEP*? THE SLEEPING BAGS ARE BACK AT THE TENT.

I DON'T THINK ANYONE'S COMING BACK HERE. SO WHY DON'T WE JUST STAY RIGHT HERE?

WELL, WE WON'T BE GETTING TO THE TOWER TONIGHT, THAT'S FOR SURE.

YOU THINK WE'LL BE OK HERE?

DUNNO. BUT THE ROBOT COULD HAVE HURT US ALREADY IF HE WANTED TO. BESIDES, I KINDA FEEL SAFE HERE.

REALLY?

YEAH.

I DON'T KNOW ABOUT YOU TWO, BUT I REALLY *DON'T* WANT TO SLEEP IN THE WOODS.

AND WHO KNOWS WHERE THAT *MONSTER* IS.

THAT, TOO.

OK, OK. I'M GAME IF YOU GUYS ARE.

YAY! LET'S GET UN-PACKED.

I'M GONNA GET MY PJS ON.

YEAH, ME, TOO.

"GOODNIGHT, SOPH."

"GOODNIGHT, MARN."

"OH, AND GOODNIGHT, 'BOT!"

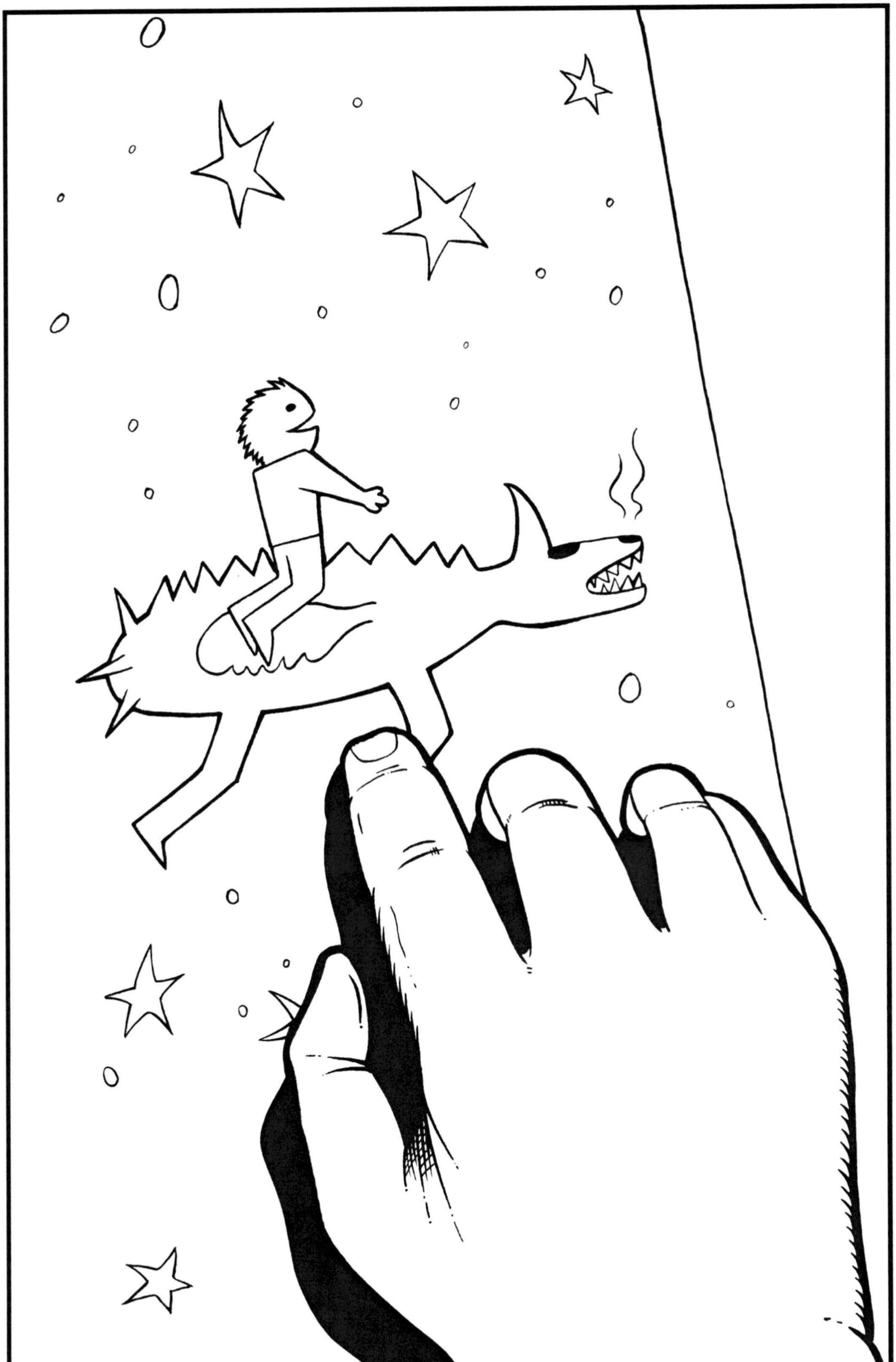

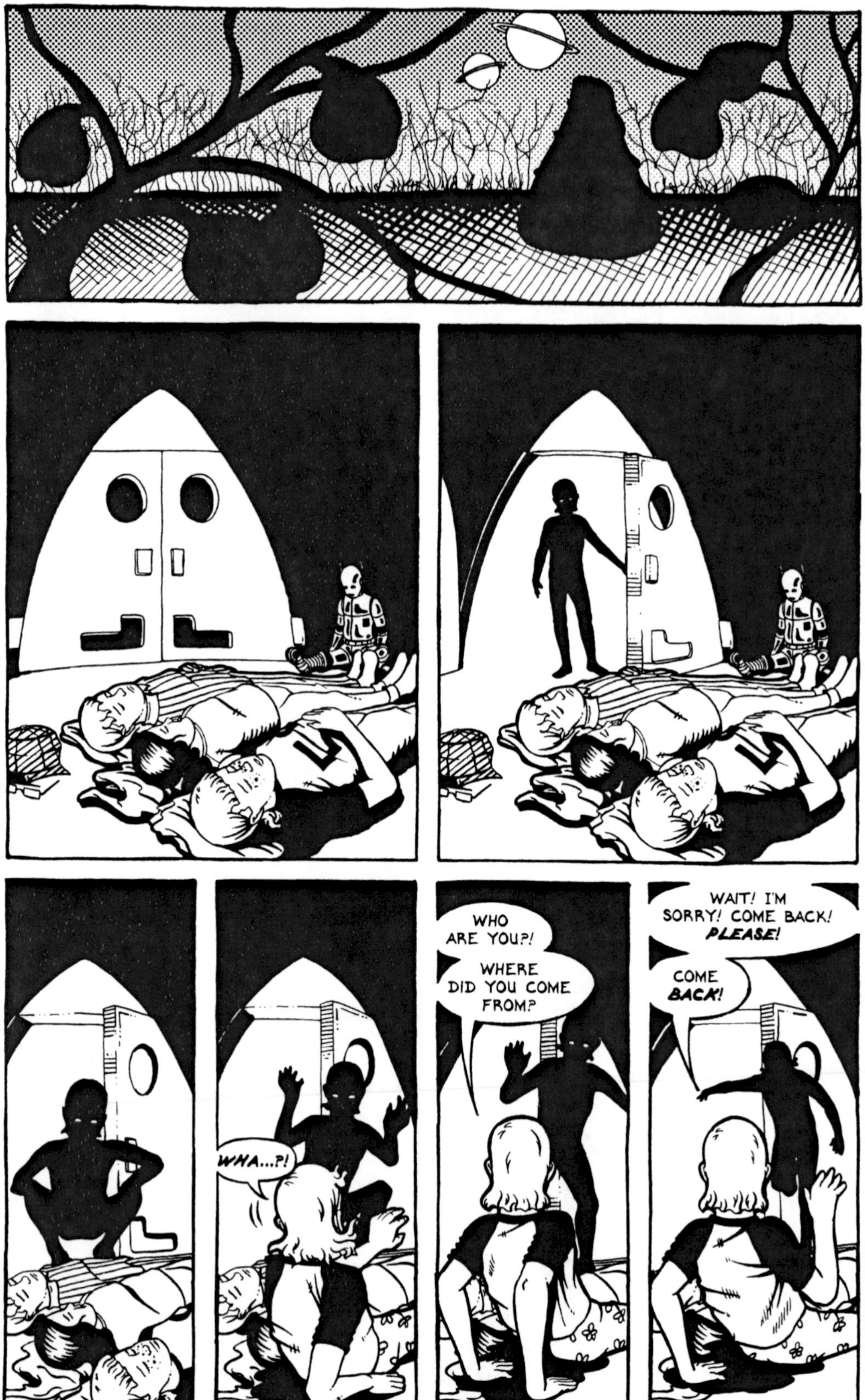
WHA...?!
WHO ARE YOU?!
WHERE DID YOU COME FROM?
WAIT! I'M SORRY! COME BACK! **PLEASE!**
COME **BACK!**

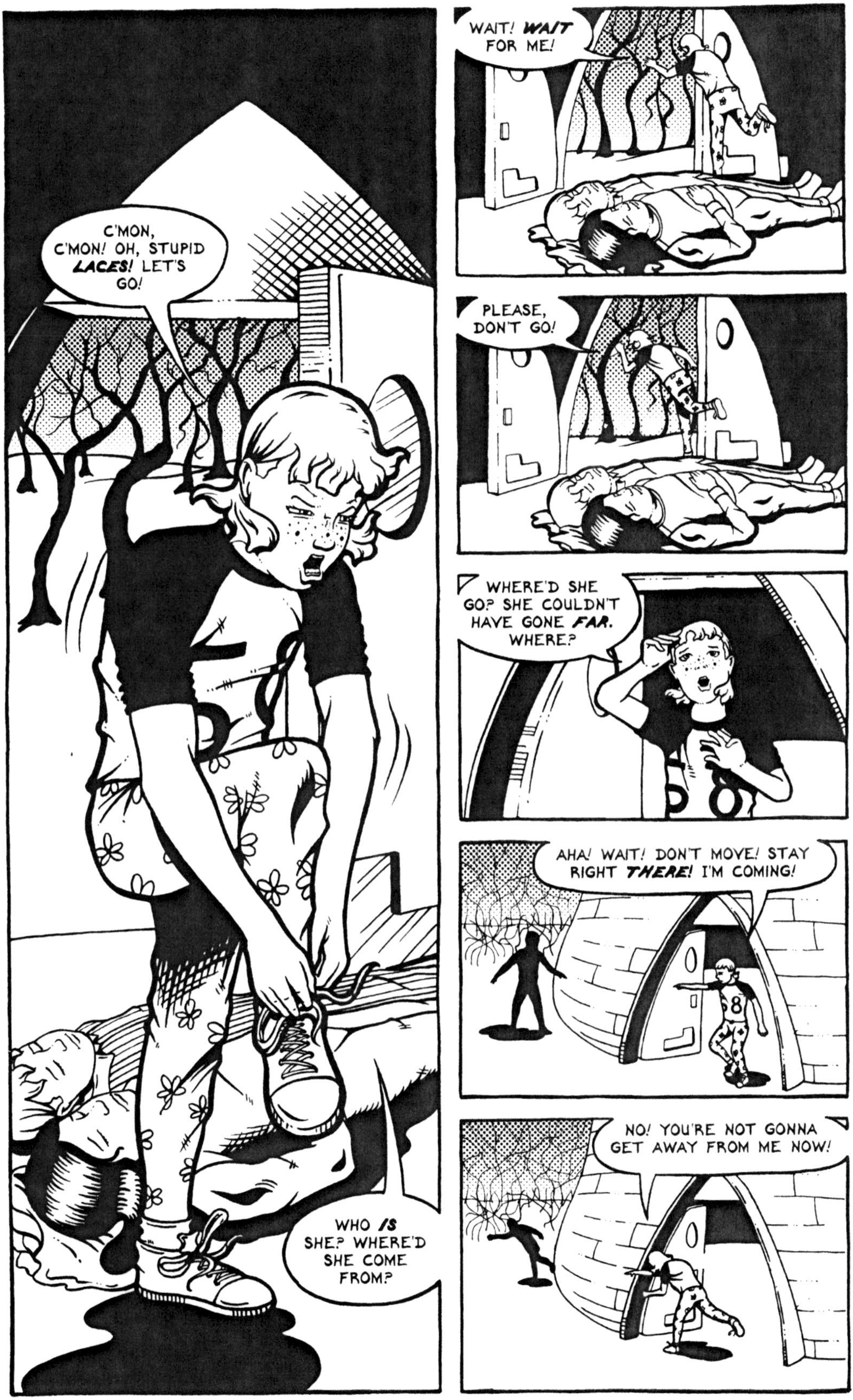
C'MON, C'MON! OH, STUPID LACES! LET'S GO!
WHO IS SHE? WHERE'D SHE COME FROM?
WAIT! WAIT FOR ME!
PLEASE, DON'T GO!
WHERE'D SHE GO? SHE COULDN'T HAVE GONE FAR. WHERE?
AHA! WAIT! DON'T MOVE! STAY RIGHT THERE! I'M COMING!
NO! YOU'RE NOT GONNA GET AWAY FROM ME NOW!

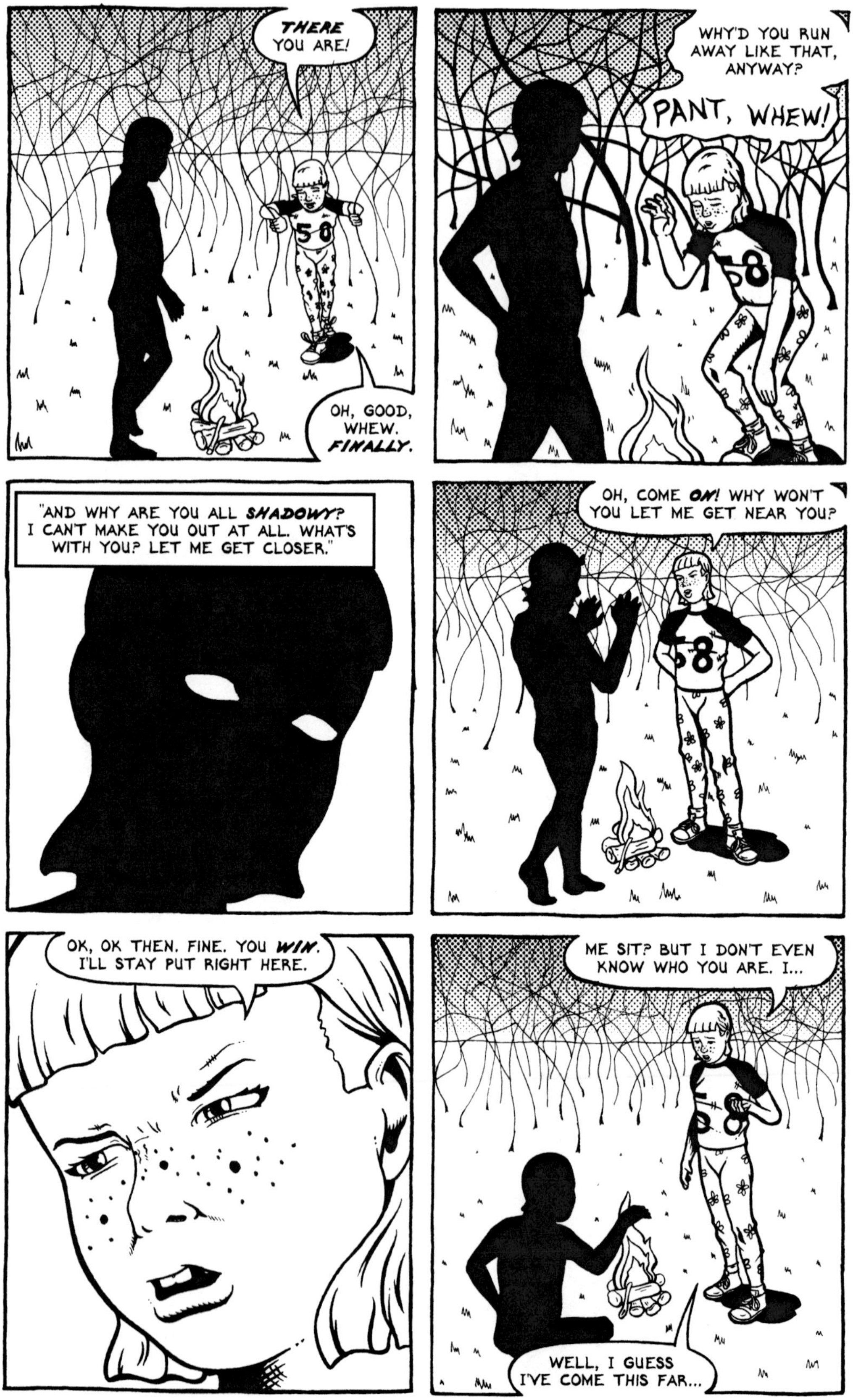
THERE YOU ARE!
OH, GOOD, WHEW. FINALLY.
WHY'D YOU RUN AWAY LIKE THAT, ANYWAY?
PANT, WHEW!
"AND WHY ARE YOU ALL SHADOWY? I CAN'T MAKE YOU OUT AT ALL. WHAT'S WITH YOU? LET ME GET CLOSER."
OH, COME ON! WHY WON'T YOU LET ME GET NEAR YOU?
OK, OK THEN. FINE. YOU WIN. I'LL STAY PUT RIGHT HERE.
ME SIT? BUT I DON'T EVEN KNOW WHO YOU ARE. I...
WELL, I GUESS I'VE COME THIS FAR...

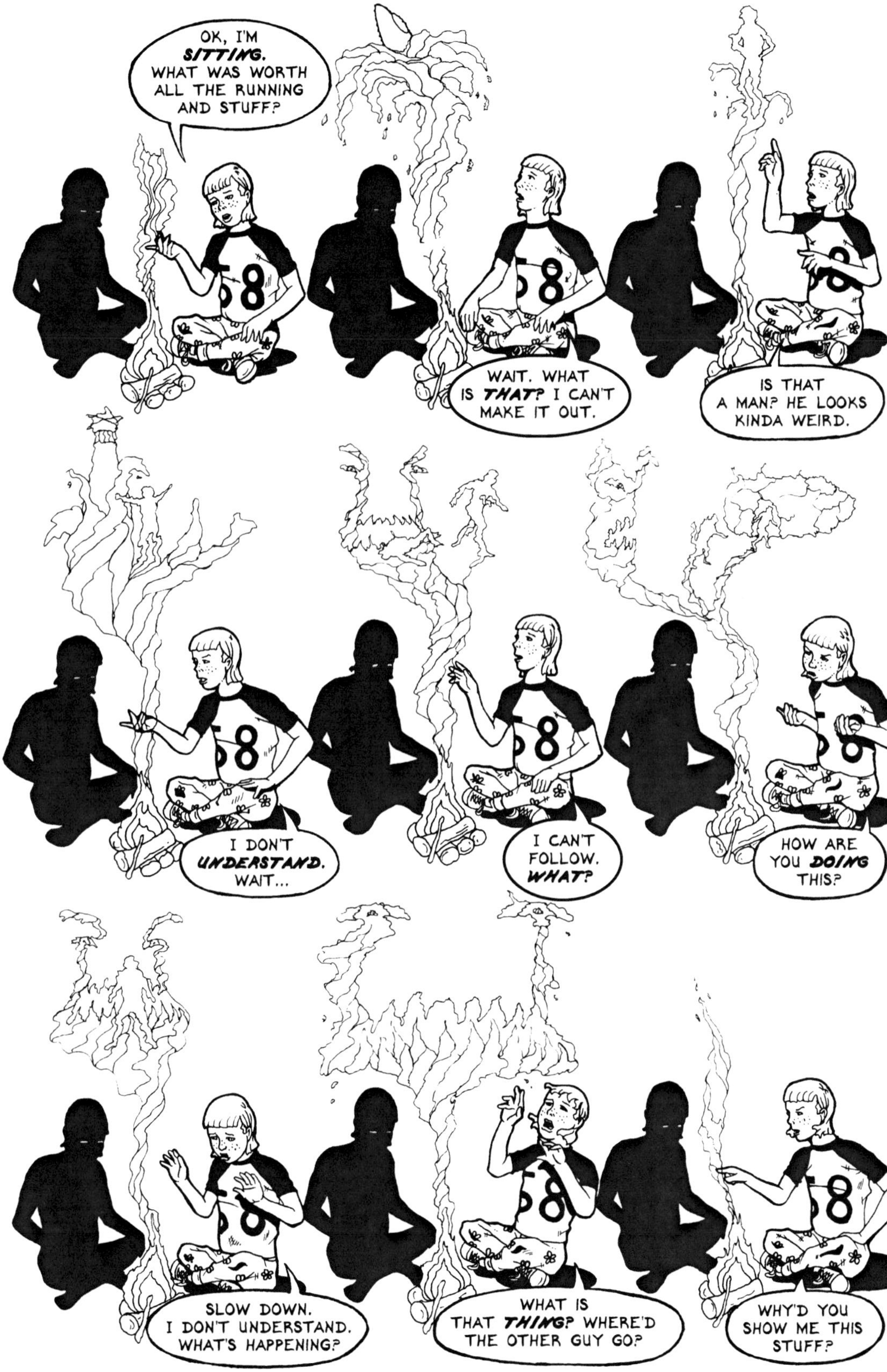
OK, I'M *SITTING.* WHAT WAS WORTH ALL THE RUNNING AND STUFF?
WAIT. WHAT IS *THAT?* I CAN'T MAKE IT OUT.
IS THAT A MAN? HE LOOKS KINDA WEIRD.
I DON'T *UNDERSTAND.* WAIT...
I CAN'T FOLLOW. *WHAT?*
HOW ARE YOU *DOING* THIS?
SLOW DOWN. I DON'T UNDERSTAND. WHAT'S HAPPENING?
WHAT IS THAT *THING?* WHERE'D THE OTHER GUY GO?
WHY'D YOU SHOW ME THIS STUFF?

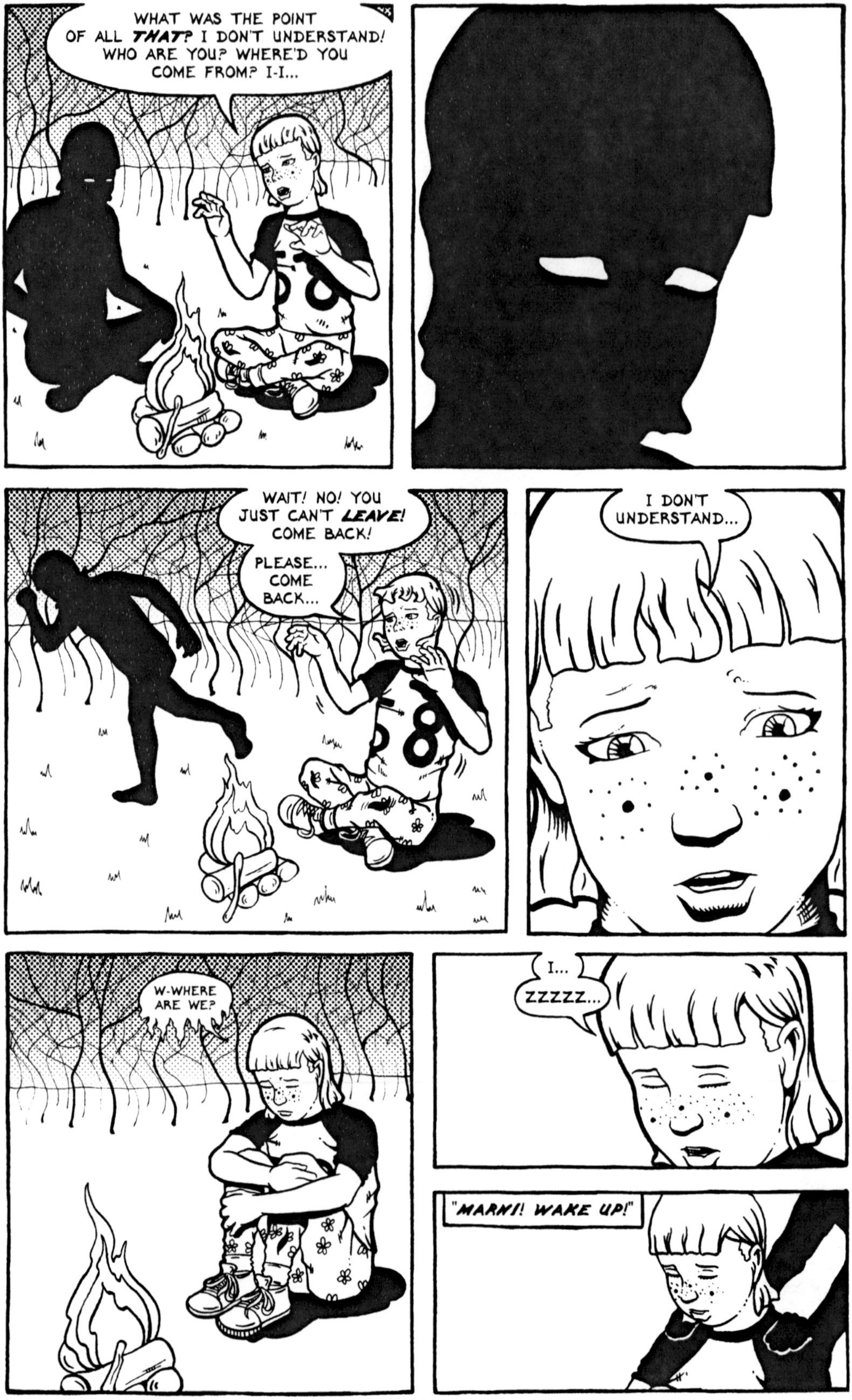
WHAT WAS THE POINT OF ALL THAT? I DON'T UNDERSTAND! WHO ARE YOU? WHERE'D YOU COME FROM? I-I...
WAIT! NO! YOU JUST CAN'T LEAVE! COME BACK!
PLEASE... COME BACK...
I DON'T UNDERSTAND...
W-WHERE ARE WE?
I...
ZZZZZ...
"MARNI! WAKE UP!"

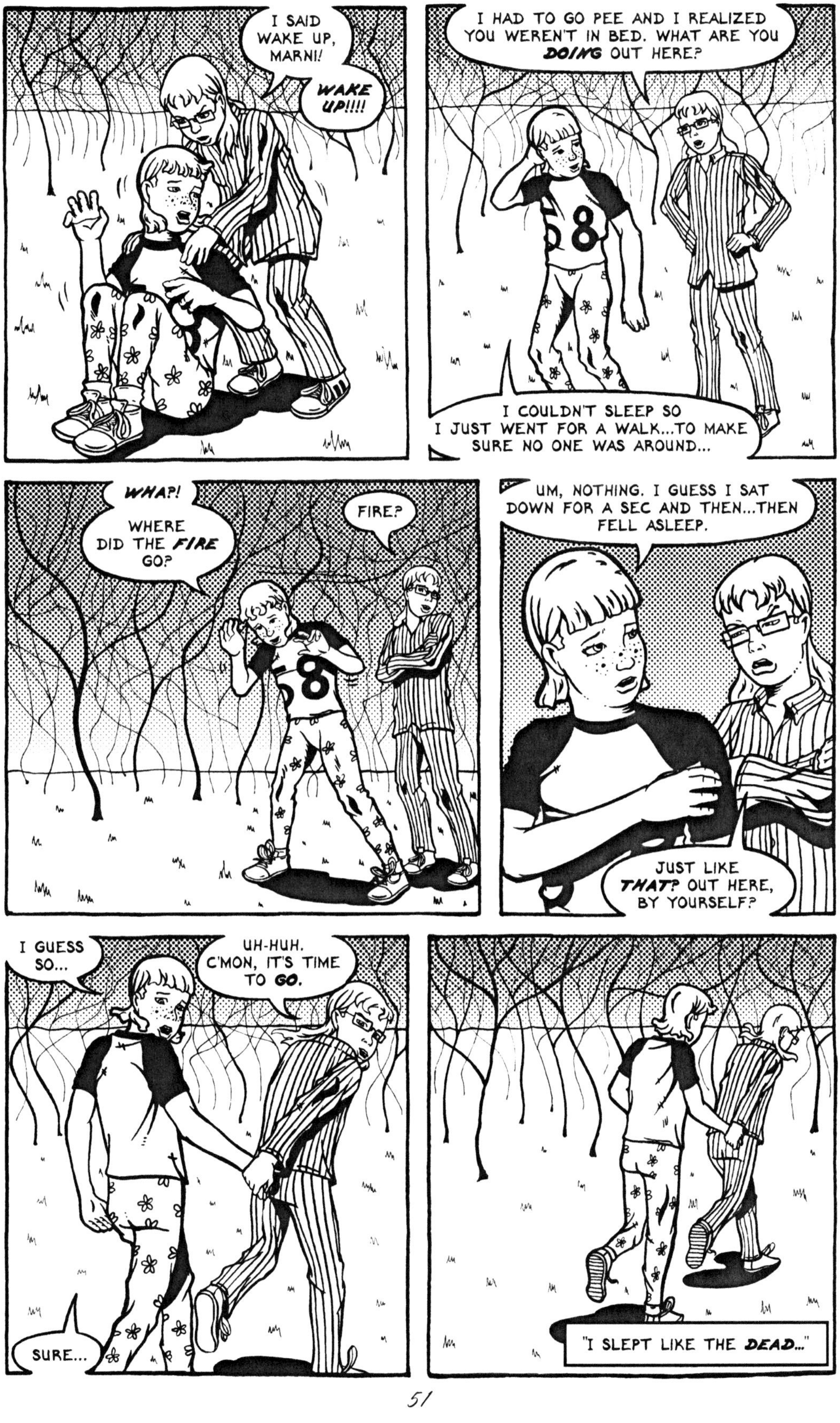
I SAID WAKE UP, MARNI!
WAKE UP!!!!
I HAD TO GO PEE AND I REALIZED YOU WEREN'T IN BED. WHAT ARE YOU *DOING* OUT HERE?
I COULDN'T SLEEP SO I JUST WENT FOR A WALK...TO MAKE SURE NO ONE WAS AROUND...
WHA?! WHERE DID THE *FIRE* GO?
FIRE?
UM, NOTHING. I GUESS I SAT DOWN FOR A SEC AND THEN...THEN FELL ASLEEP.
JUST LIKE *THAT?* OUT HERE, BY YOURSELF?
I GUESS SO...
UH-HUH. C'MON, IT'S TIME TO *GO*.
SURE...
"I SLEPT LIKE THE *DEAD*..."

YUP, I'M SURE THE DEAD SLEEP JUST LIKE *THAT.* I WAS OUT LIKE A LIGHT. ACK. CREAKY, THOUGH!

NOT A *GREAT* BED, THAT'S FOR SURE, BUT IT DID THE TRICK.

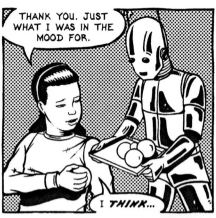

THANK YOU. JUST WHAT I WAS IN THE MOOD FOR.

I *THINK...*

HOW'D YOU GUYS SLEEP, ANYWAY?

MEH. NOT GREAT, BUT OK, I GUESS.

WELL, I THINK WE SHOULD START *WALKING* SOON, RIGHT? 'CUZ WE DON'T REALLY KNOW HOW FAR AWAY THAT TOWER YOU SPOTTED IS.

UH, YEAH, OK. THAT'S A GOOD IDEA. EARLY START AND ALL THAT.

I WOULDN'T EXPECT *YOU* TO BE SAYING WE SHOULD GET GOING, BUT...

I'D JUST LIKE TO GET MOVING.

UH, WHAT DO WE DO ABOUT YOUR LITTLE *FRIEND*, THOUGH? SHOULD WE TAKE IT ALONG WITH US?

CAN WE *TRUST* IT?

YOU KNOW, HE COULD HAVE *HURT* US IN OUR SLEEP, HMM?

AND STOP CALLING HIM "IT." HE'S NOT AN "*IT*" AT ALL!

RIGHT. OK. GOOD POINT.

BESIDES, WE DON'T EVEN KNOW IF HE'LL COME ALONG. IT LOOKS LIKE HE'S BEEN WAITING HERE A *LONG* TIME.

AND IT'S NOT LIKE HE *TALKS* OR ANYTHING, EITHER. WE DON'T EVEN KNOW IF HE UNDERSTANDS US.

HAS HE EVEN MADE A *SOUND?*

NOPE. I GUESS WHOEVER MADE HIM DIDN'T WANT HIM TO CHIT-CHAT.

C'MON, LET'S GET PACKED UP.

I'M GOING TO GO SEE IF THERE'S ANY OTHER FOOD WE CAN TAKE.

GOOD IDEA. LET'S GRAB *EVERYTHING* WE CAN. SOPH, YOU DIDN'T EAT MUCH. NOT HUNGRY?

NO. MAYBE LATER.

'LORA, WHAT ARE WE GONNA DO ABOUT *HIM?*

UH, LOOK, LITTLE GUY. WE GOTTA GO SO...I MEAN, YOU'RE WELCOME TO *JOIN* US, OF COURSE, BUT...

OY...

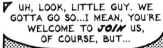

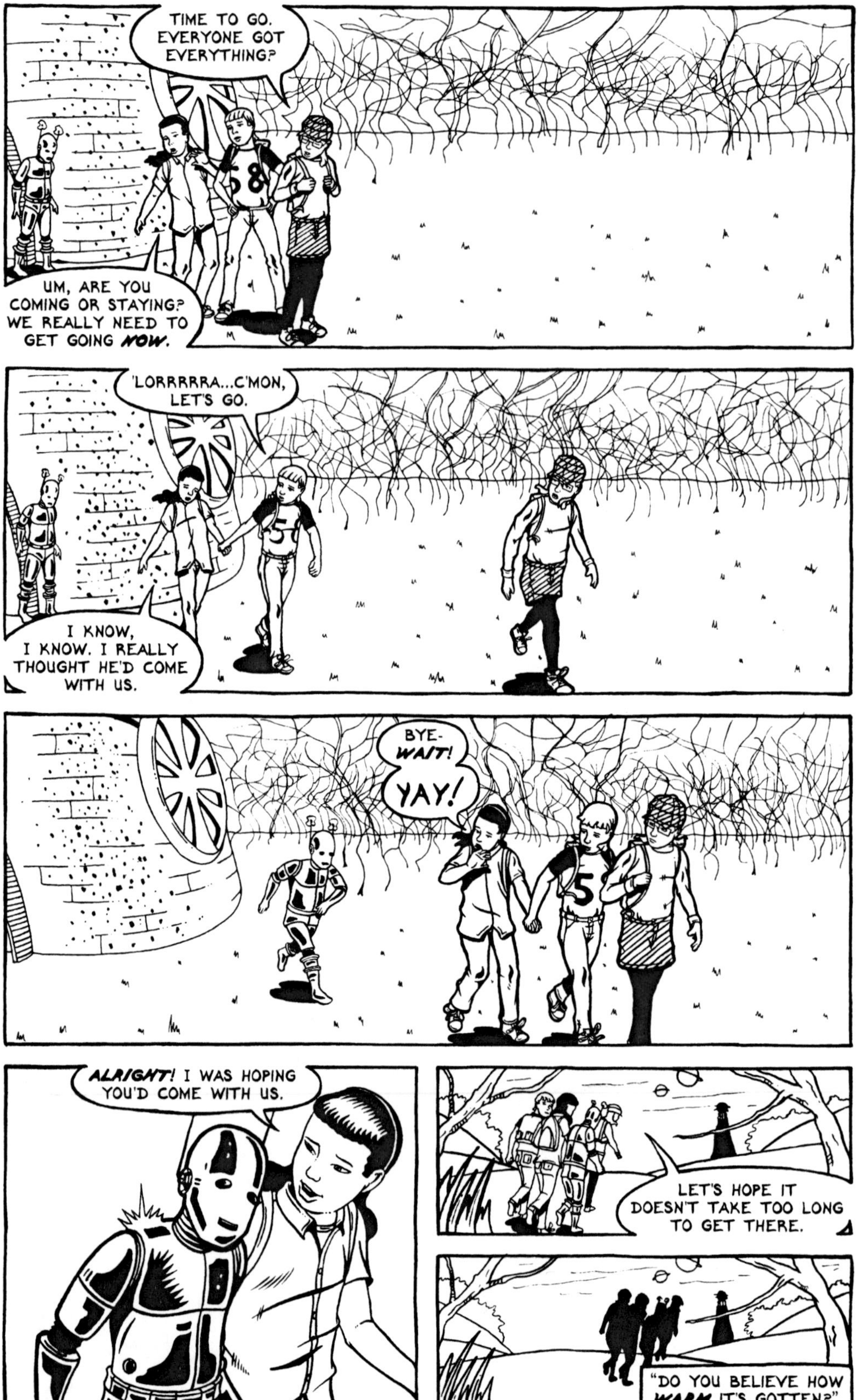
TIME TO GO. EVERYONE GOT EVERYTHING?
UM, ARE YOU COMING OR STAYING? WE REALLY NEED TO GET GOING *NOW*.
'LORRRRRA...C'MON, LET'S GO.
I KNOW, I KNOW. I REALLY THOUGHT HE'D COME WITH US.
BYE-
WAIT!
YAY!
ALRIGHT! I WAS HOPING YOU'D COME WITH US.
LET'S HOPE IT DOESN'T TAKE TOO LONG TO GET THERE.
"DO YOU BELIEVE HOW *WARM* IT'S GOTTEN?"

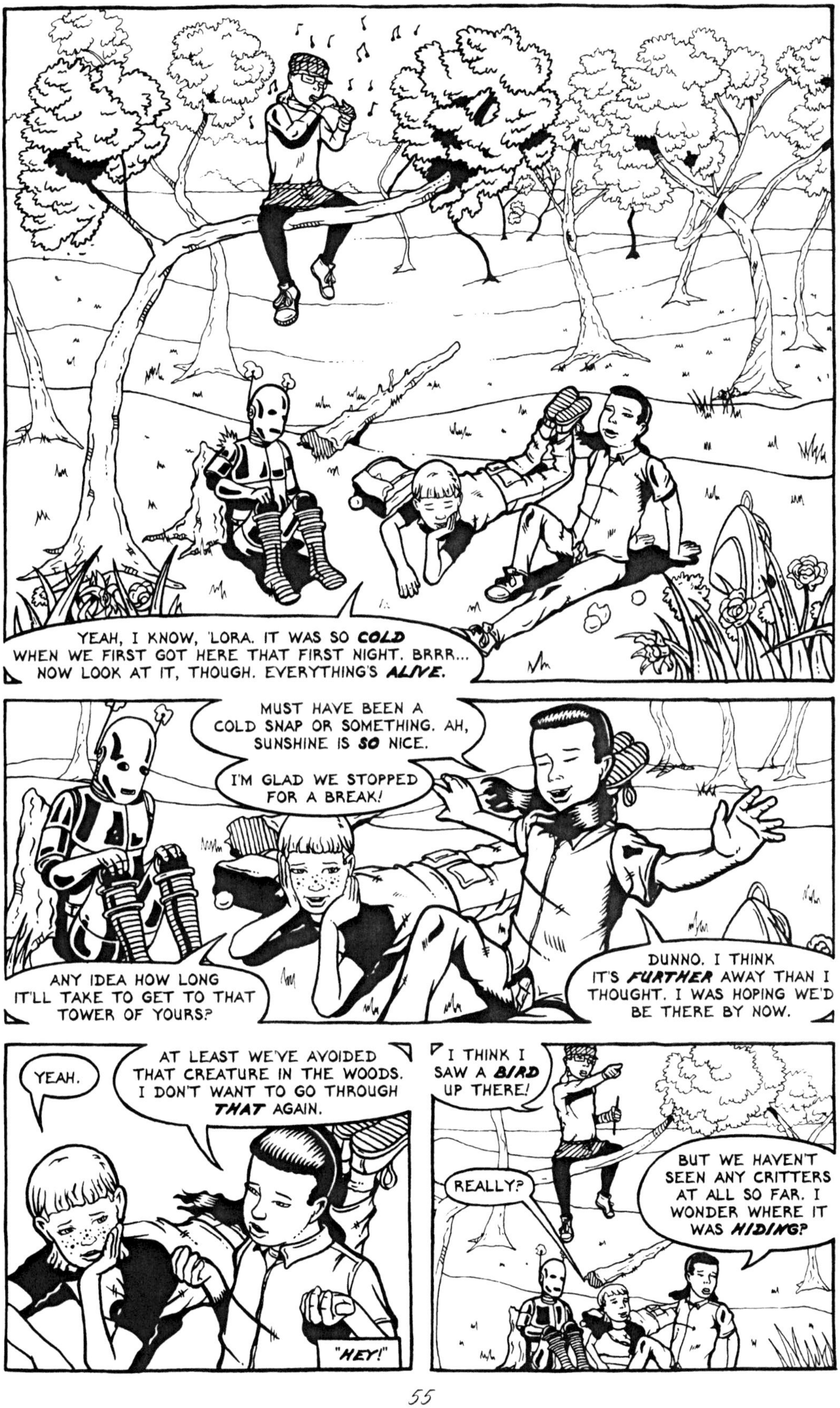
YEAH, I KNOW, 'LORA. IT WAS SO COLD WHEN WE FIRST GOT HERE THAT FIRST NIGHT. BRRR... NOW LOOK AT IT, THOUGH. EVERYTHING'S ALIVE.
MUST HAVE BEEN A COLD SNAP OR SOMETHING. AH, SUNSHINE IS SO NICE.
I'M GLAD WE STOPPED FOR A BREAK!
ANY IDEA HOW LONG IT'LL TAKE TO GET TO THAT TOWER OF YOURS?
DUNNO. I THINK IT'S FURTHER AWAY THAN I THOUGHT. I WAS HOPING WE'D BE THERE BY NOW.
YEAH.
AT LEAST WE'VE AVOIDED THAT CREATURE IN THE WOODS. I DON'T WANT TO GO THROUGH THAT AGAIN.
"HEY!"
I THINK I SAW A BIRD UP THERE!
REALLY?
BUT WE HAVEN'T SEEN ANY CRITTERS AT ALL SO FAR. I WONDER WHERE IT WAS HIDING?

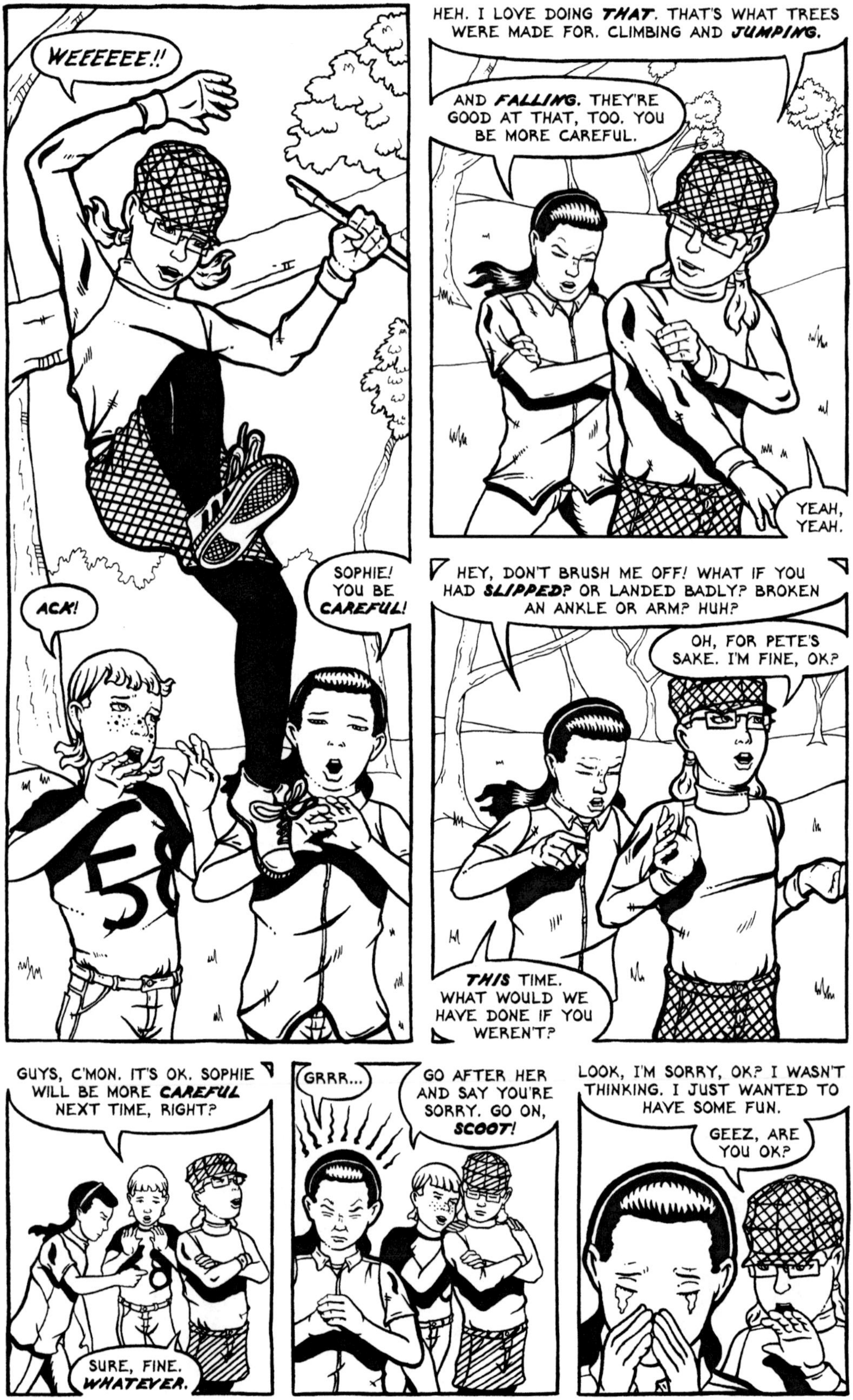
WEEEEEE!!
ACK!
SOPHIE! YOU BE CAREFUL!
HEH. I LOVE DOING THAT. THAT'S WHAT TREES WERE MADE FOR. CLIMBING AND JUMPING.
AND FALLING. THEY'RE GOOD AT THAT, TOO. YOU BE MORE CAREFUL.
YEAH, YEAH.
HEY, DON'T BRUSH ME OFF! WHAT IF YOU HAD SLIPPED? OR LANDED BADLY? BROKEN AN ANKLE OR ARM? HUH?
OH, FOR PETE'S SAKE. I'M FINE, OK?
THIS TIME. WHAT WOULD WE HAVE DONE IF YOU WEREN'T?
GUYS, C'MON. IT'S OK. SOPHIE WILL BE MORE CAREFUL NEXT TIME, RIGHT?
SURE, FINE. WHATEVER.
GRRR...
GO AFTER HER AND SAY YOU'RE SORRY. GO ON, SCOOT!
LOOK, I'M SORRY, OK? I WASN'T THINKING. I JUST WANTED TO HAVE SOME FUN.
GEEZ, ARE YOU OK?

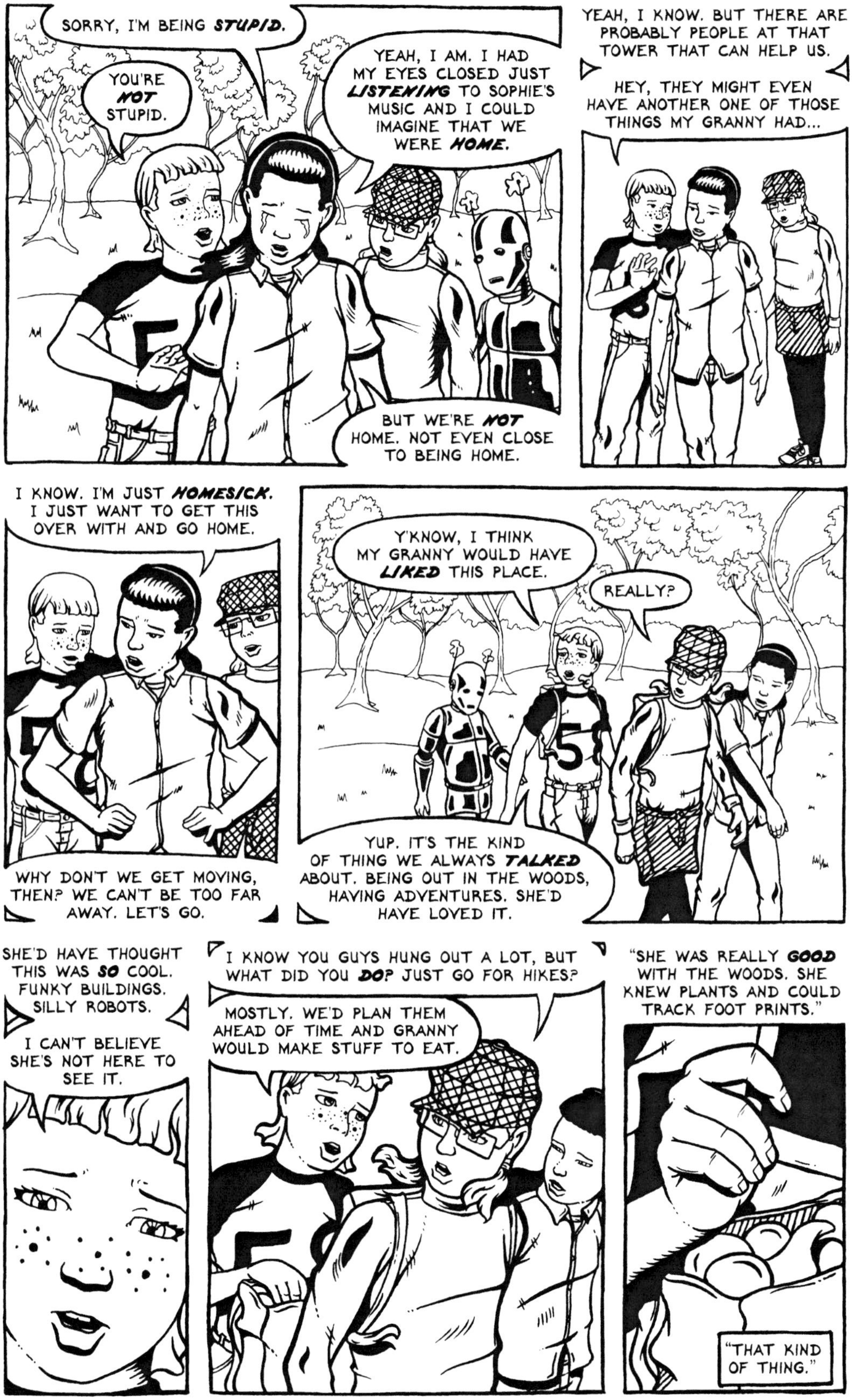
SORRY, I'M BEING STUPID.
YOU'RE NOT STUPID.
YEAH, I AM. I HAD MY EYES CLOSED JUST LISTENING TO SOPHIE'S MUSIC AND I COULD IMAGINE THAT WE WERE HOME.
BUT WE'RE NOT HOME. NOT EVEN CLOSE TO BEING HOME.
YEAH, I KNOW. BUT THERE ARE PROBABLY PEOPLE AT THAT TOWER THAT CAN HELP US.
HEY, THEY MIGHT EVEN HAVE ANOTHER ONE OF THOSE THINGS MY GRANNY HAD...
I KNOW. I'M JUST HOMESICK. I JUST WANT TO GET THIS OVER WITH AND GO HOME.
WHY DON'T WE GET MOVING, THEN? WE CAN'T BE TOO FAR AWAY. LET'S GO.
Y'KNOW, I THINK MY GRANNY WOULD HAVE LIKED THIS PLACE.
REALLY?
YUP. IT'S THE KIND OF THING WE ALWAYS TALKED ABOUT. BEING OUT IN THE WOODS, HAVING ADVENTURES. SHE'D HAVE LOVED IT.
SHE'D HAVE THOUGHT THIS WAS SO COOL. FUNKY BUILDINGS. SILLY ROBOTS.
I CAN'T BELIEVE SHE'S NOT HERE TO SEE IT.
I KNOW YOU GUYS HUNG OUT A LOT, BUT WHAT DID YOU DO? JUST GO FOR HIKES?
MOSTLY. WE'D PLAN THEM AHEAD OF TIME AND GRANNY WOULD MAKE STUFF TO EAT.
"SHE WAS REALLY GOOD WITH THE WOODS. SHE KNEW PLANTS AND COULD TRACK FOOT PRINTS."
"THAT KIND OF THING."

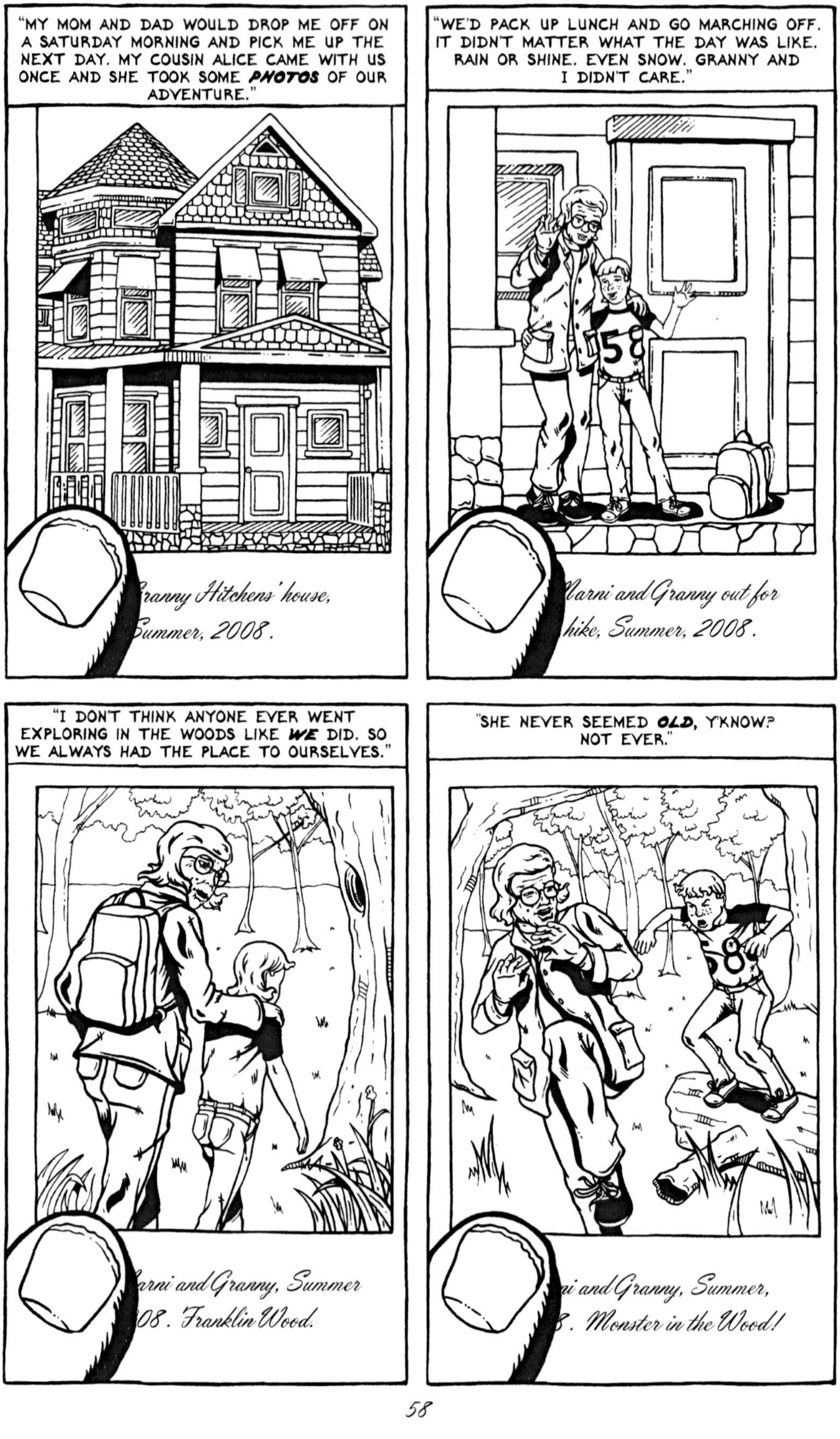
"MY MOM AND DAD WOULD DROP ME OFF ON A SATURDAY MORNING AND PICK ME UP THE NEXT DAY. MY COUSIN ALICE CAME WITH US ONCE AND SHE TOOK SOME **PHOTOS** OF OUR ADVENTURE."
ranny Hitchens' house,
ummer, 2008.
"WE'D PACK UP LUNCH AND GO MARCHING OFF. IT DIDN'T MATTER WHAT THE DAY WAS LIKE. RAIN OR SHINE. EVEN SNOW. GRANNY AND I DIDN'T CARE."
58
arni and Granny out for
hike, Summer, 2008.
"I DON'T THINK ANYONE EVER WENT EXPLORING IN THE WOODS LIKE **WE** DID. SO WE ALWAYS HAD THE PLACE TO OURSELVES."
arni and Granny, Summer
08. Franklin Wood.
"SHE NEVER SEEMED **OLD**, Y'KNOW? NOT EVER."
58
ni and Granny, Summer,
8. Monster in the Wood!

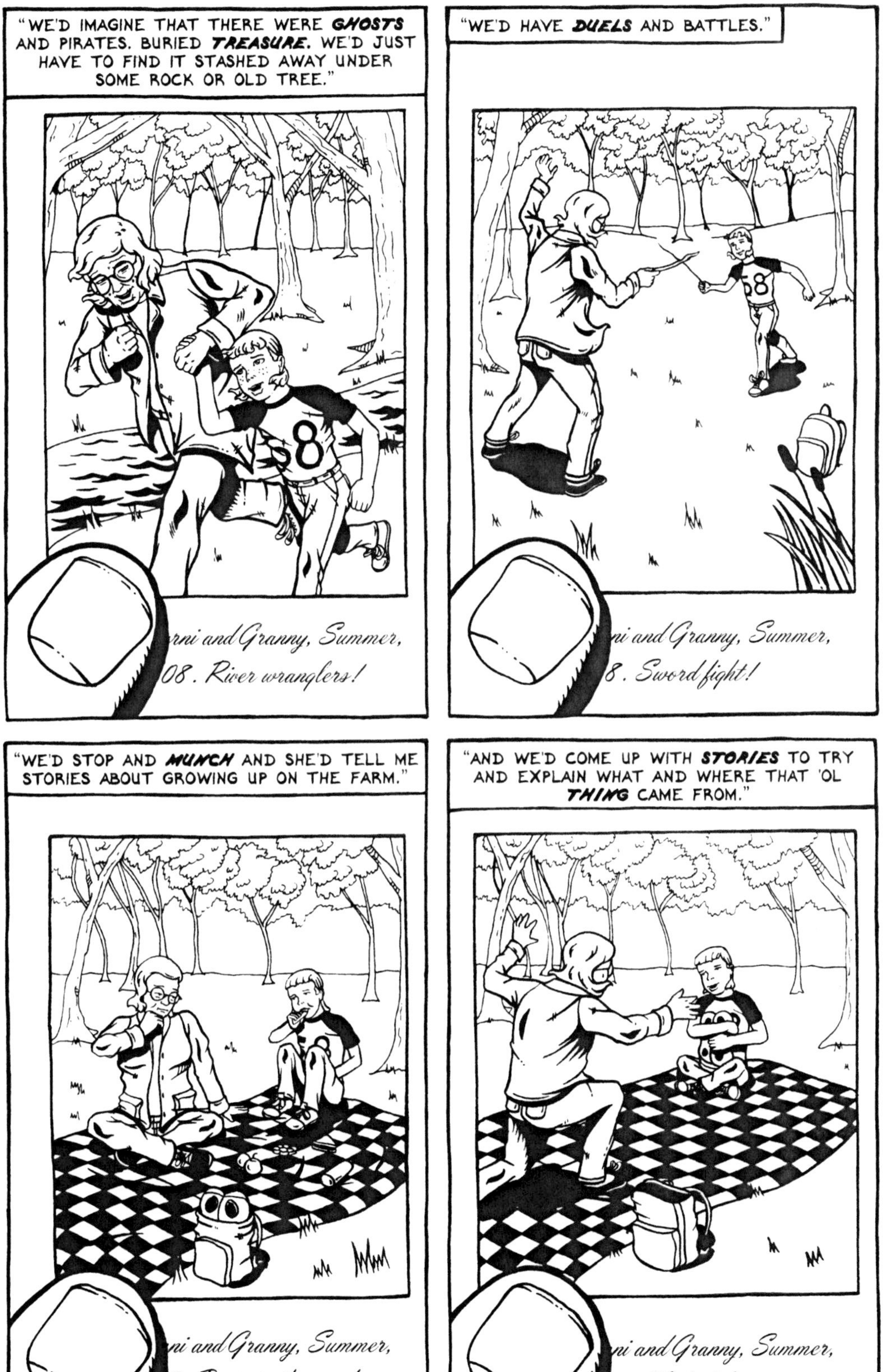
"WE'D IMAGINE THAT THERE WERE **GHOSTS** AND PIRATES. BURIED **TREASURE**. WE'D JUST HAVE TO FIND IT STASHED AWAY UNDER SOME ROCK OR OLD TREE."
rni and Granny, Summer,
08. River wranglers!
"WE'D HAVE **DUELS** AND BATTLES."
ni and Granny, Summer,
8. Sword fight!
"WE'D STOP AND **MUNCH** AND SHE'D TELL ME STORIES ABOUT GROWING UP ON THE FARM."
ni and Granny, Summer,
8. Picnic in the woods.
"AND WE'D COME UP WITH **STORIES** TO TRY AND EXPLAIN WHAT AND WHERE THAT 'OL **THING** CAME FROM."
ni and Granny, Summer,
8. Make believe.

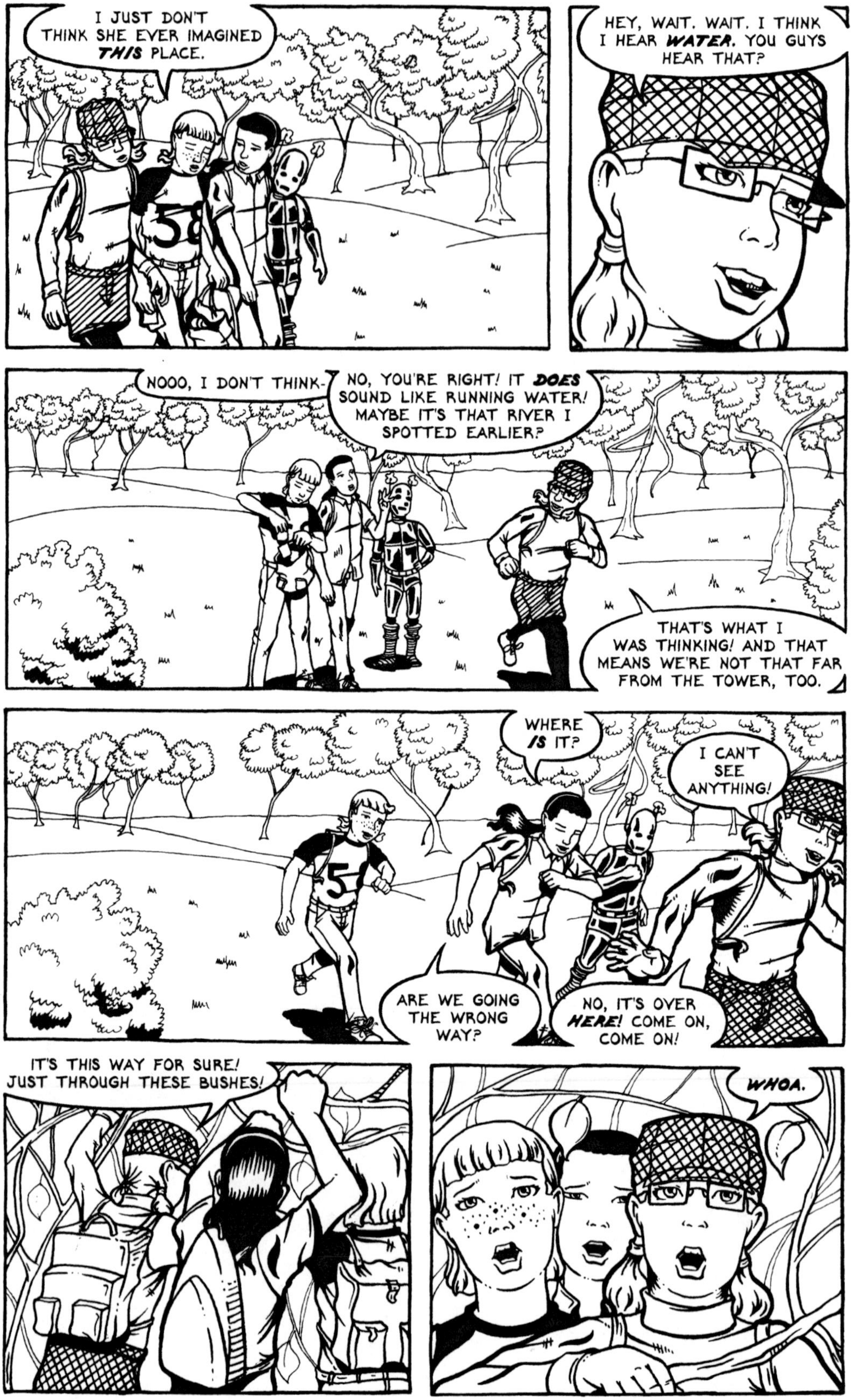
I JUST DON'T THINK SHE EVER IMAGINED *THIS* PLACE.
HEY, WAIT. WAIT. I THINK I HEAR *WATER*. YOU GUYS HEAR THAT?
NOOO, I DON'T THINK-
NO, YOU'RE RIGHT! IT *DOES* SOUND LIKE RUNNING WATER! MAYBE IT'S THAT RIVER I SPOTTED EARLIER?
THAT'S WHAT I WAS THINKING! AND THAT MEANS WE'RE NOT THAT FAR FROM THE TOWER, TOO.
WHERE *IS* IT?
I CAN'T SEE ANYTHING!
ARE WE GOING THE WRONG WAY?
NO, IT'S OVER *HERE*! COME ON, COME ON!
IT'S THIS WAY FOR SURE! JUST THROUGH THESE BUSHES!
WHOA.

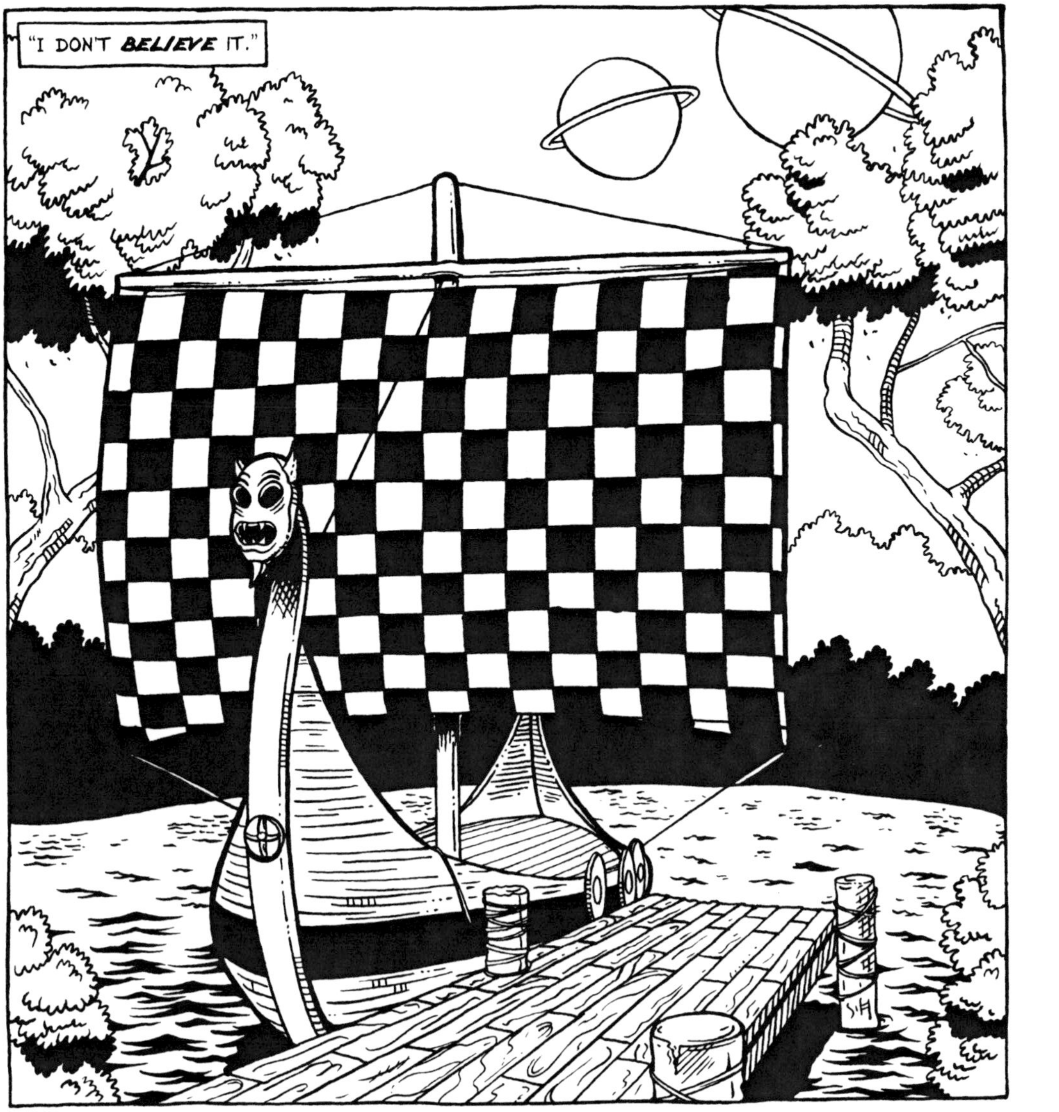
"I DON'T BELIEVE IT."

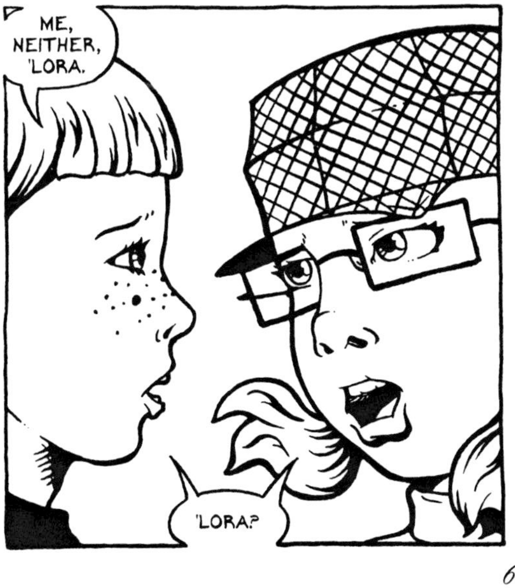
ME, NEITHER, 'LORA.
'LORA?

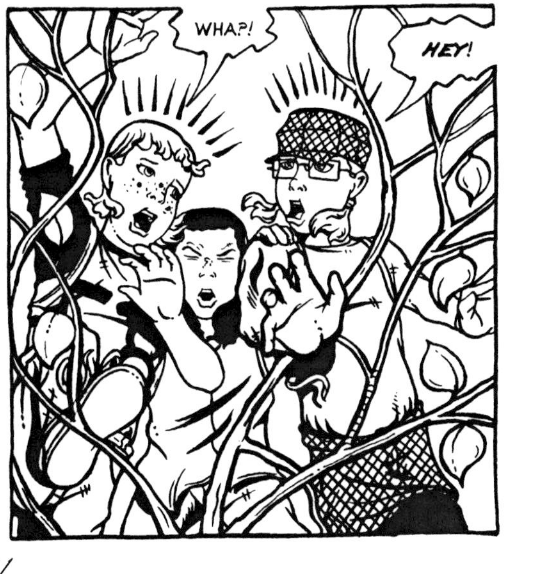
WHA?!
HEY!

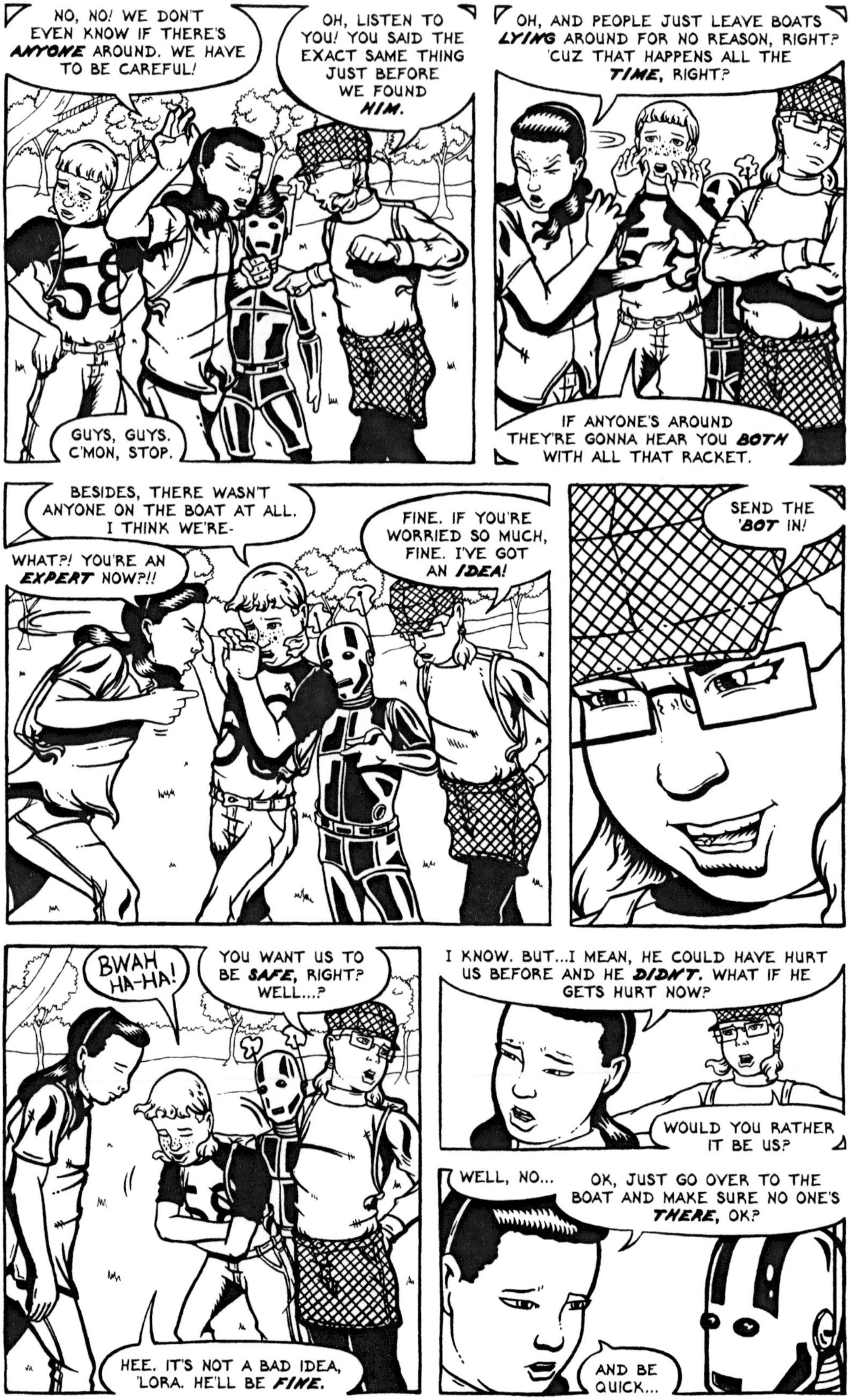
NO, NO! WE DON'T EVEN KNOW IF THERE'S ANYONE AROUND. WE HAVE TO BE CAREFUL!
OH, LISTEN TO YOU! YOU SAID THE EXACT SAME THING JUST BEFORE WE FOUND HIM.
GUYS, GUYS. C'MON, STOP.
OH, AND PEOPLE JUST LEAVE BOATS LYING AROUND FOR NO REASON, RIGHT? 'CUZ THAT HAPPENS ALL THE TIME, RIGHT?
IF ANYONE'S AROUND THEY'RE GONNA HEAR YOU BOTH WITH ALL THAT RACKET.
BESIDES, THERE WASN'T ANYONE ON THE BOAT AT ALL. I THINK WE'RE-
WHAT?! YOU'RE AN EXPERT NOW?!!
FINE. IF YOU'RE WORRIED SO MUCH, FINE. I'VE GOT AN IDEA!
SEND THE 'BOT IN!
BWAH HA-HA!
YOU WANT US TO BE SAFE, RIGHT? WELL...?
HEE. IT'S NOT A BAD IDEA, 'LORA. HE'LL BE FINE.
I KNOW. BUT...I MEAN, HE COULD HAVE HURT US BEFORE AND HE DIDN'T. WHAT IF HE GETS HURT NOW?
WOULD YOU RATHER IT BE US?
WELL, NO...
OK, JUST GO OVER TO THE BOAT AND MAKE SURE NO ONE'S THERE, OK?
AND BE QUICK...

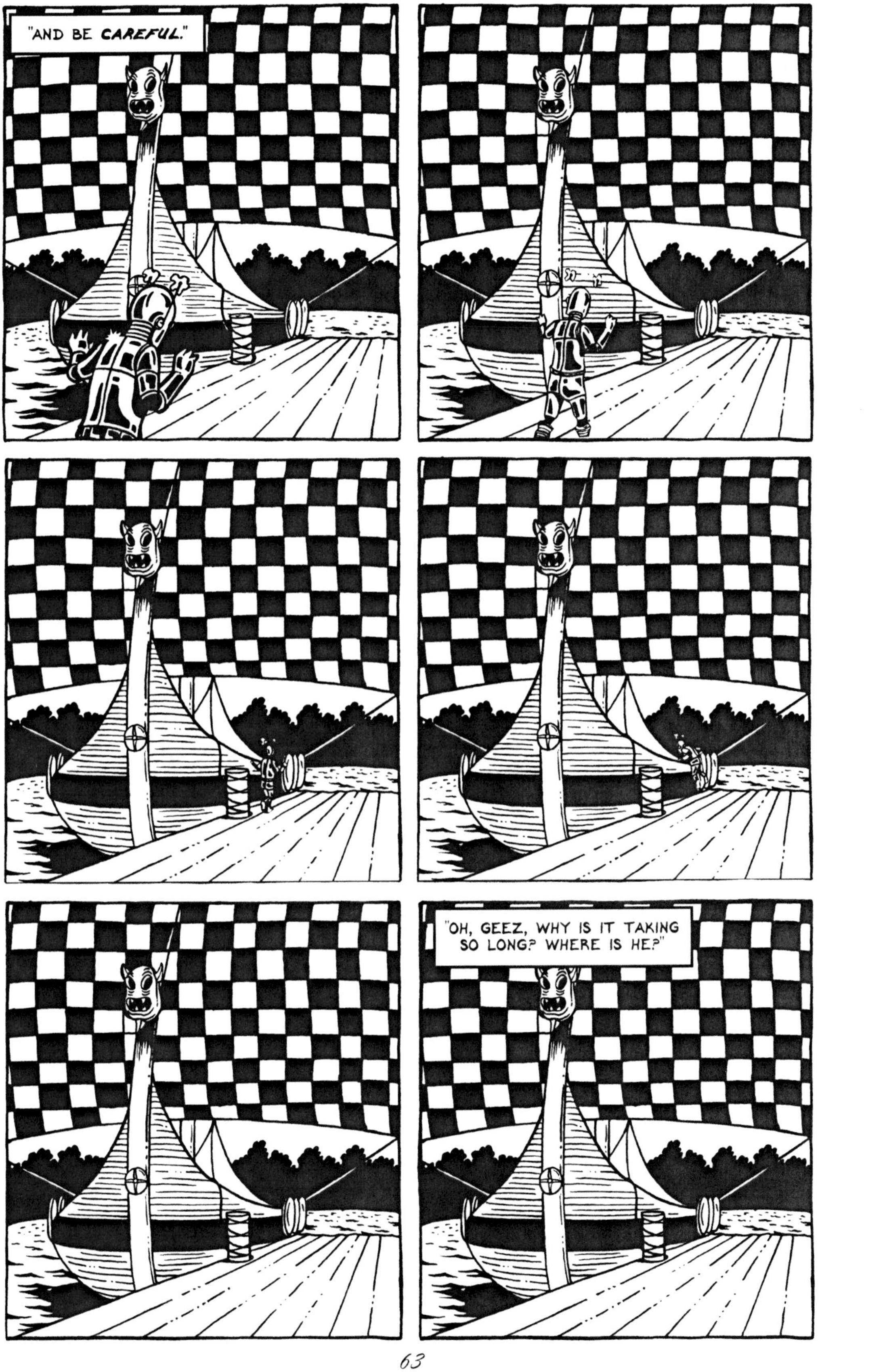
"AND BE CAREFUL."
"OH, GEEZ, WHY IS IT TAKING SO LONG? WHERE IS HE?"

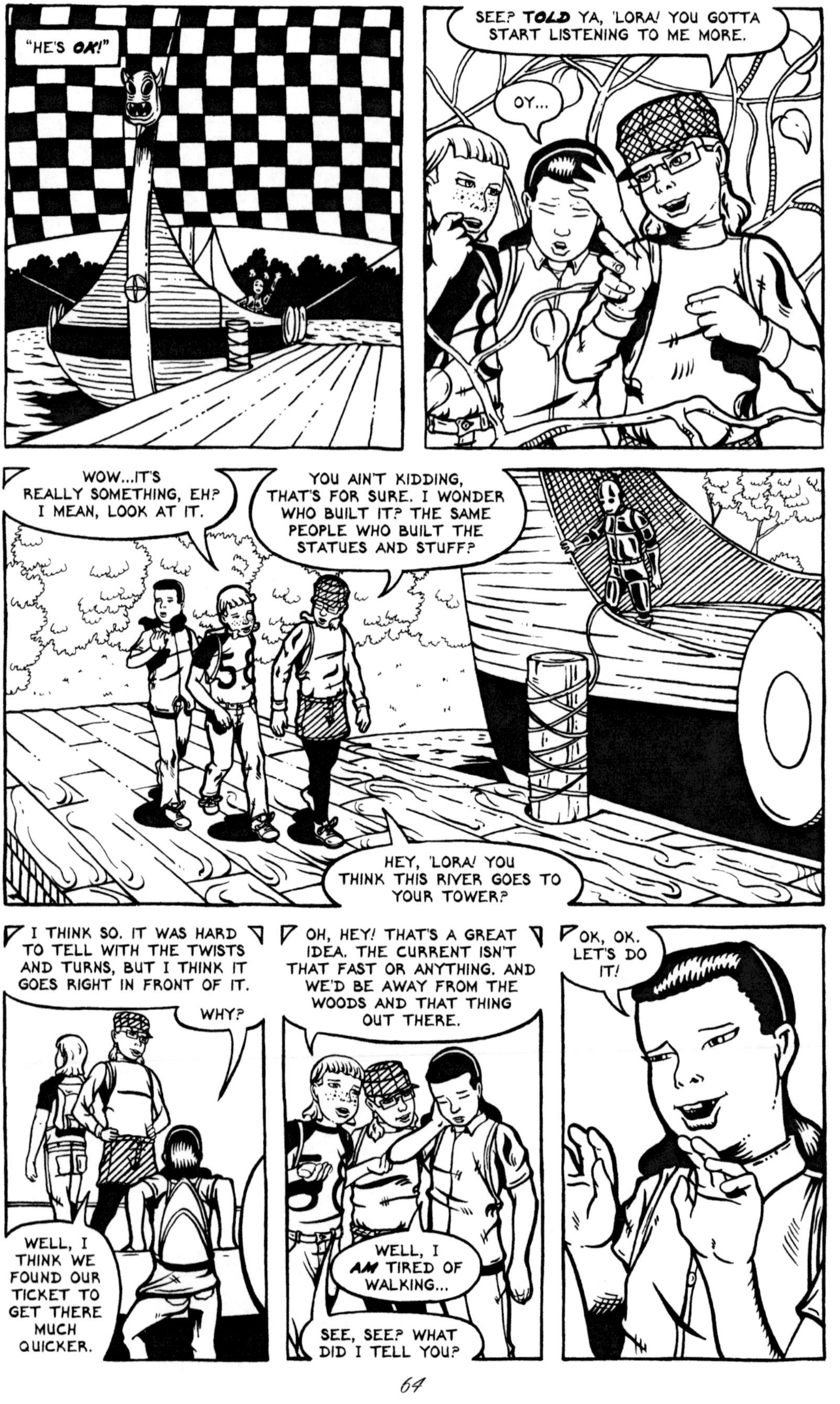
"HE'S OK!"
SEE? TOLD YA, 'LORA! YOU GOTTA START LISTENING TO ME MORE.
OY...
WOW...IT'S REALLY SOMETHING, EH? I MEAN, LOOK AT IT.
YOU AIN'T KIDDING, THAT'S FOR SURE. I WONDER WHO BUILT IT? THE SAME PEOPLE WHO BUILT THE STATUES AND STUFF?
HEY, 'LORA! YOU THINK THIS RIVER GOES TO YOUR TOWER?
I THINK SO. IT WAS HARD TO TELL WITH THE TWISTS AND TURNS, BUT I THINK IT GOES RIGHT IN FRONT OF IT.
WHY?
WELL, I THINK WE FOUND OUR TICKET TO GET THERE MUCH QUICKER.
OH, HEY! THAT'S A GREAT IDEA. THE CURRENT ISN'T THAT FAST OR ANYTHING. AND WE'D BE AWAY FROM THE WOODS AND THAT THING OUT THERE.
WELL, I AM TIRED OF WALKING...
SEE, SEE? WHAT DID I TELL YOU?
OK, OK. LET'S DO IT!

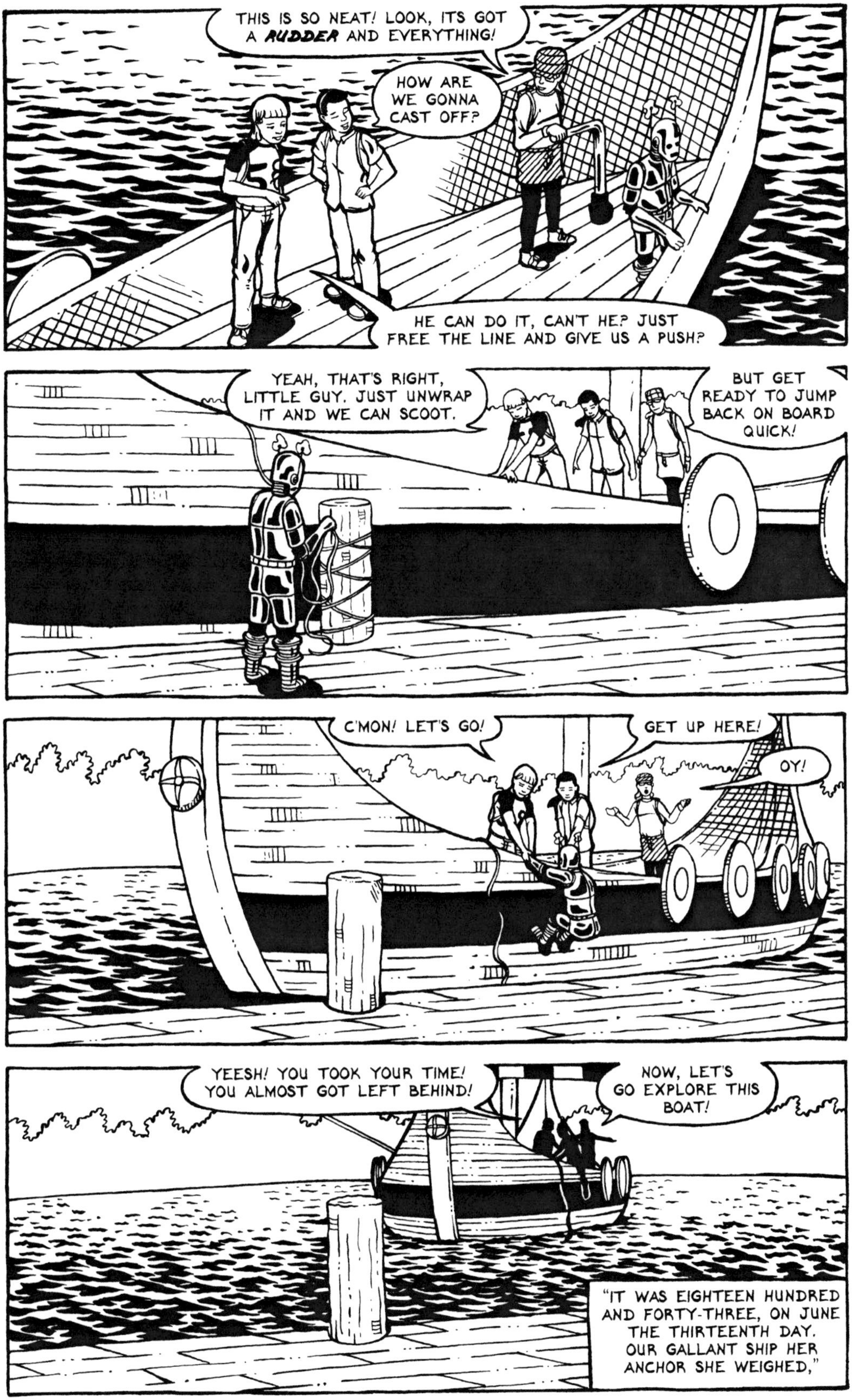
THIS IS SO NEAT! LOOK, ITS GOT A **RUDDER** AND EVERYTHING!
HOW ARE WE GONNA CAST OFF?
HE CAN DO IT, CAN'T HE? JUST FREE THE LINE AND GIVE US A PUSH?
YEAH, THAT'S RIGHT, LITTLE GUY. JUST UNWRAP IT AND WE CAN SCOOT.
BUT GET READY TO JUMP BACK ON BOARD QUICK!
C'MON! LET'S GO!
GET UP HERE!
OY!
YEESH! YOU TOOK YOUR TIME! YOU ALMOST GOT LEFT BEHIND!
NOW, LET'S GO EXPLORE THIS BOAT!
"IT WAS EIGHTEEN HUNDRED AND FORTY-THREE, ON JUNE THE THIRTEENTH DAY. OUR GALLANT SHIP HER ANCHOR SHE WEIGHED,"

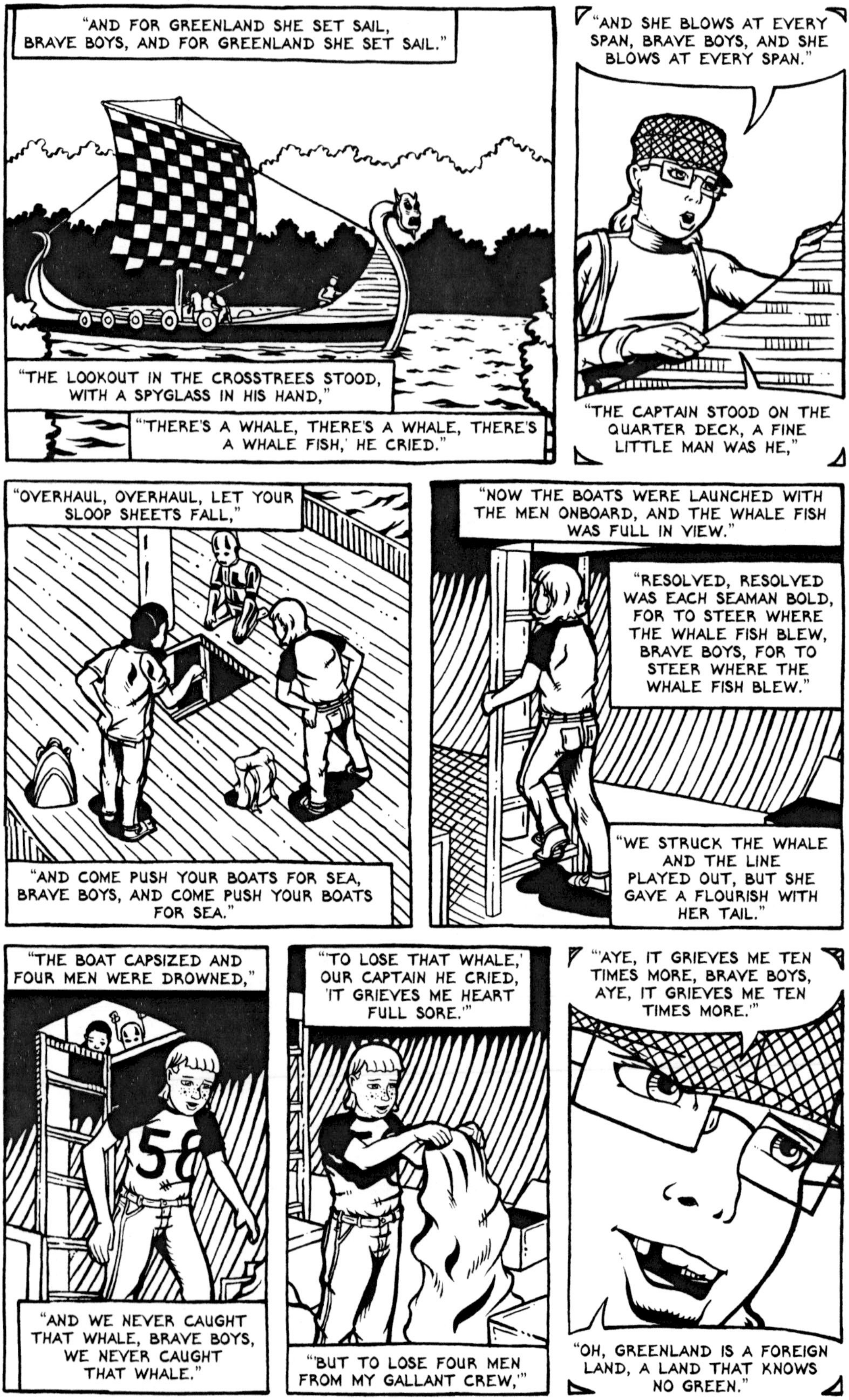
"AND FOR GREENLAND SHE SET SAIL, BRAVE BOYS, AND FOR GREENLAND SHE SET SAIL."
"THE LOOKOUT IN THE CROSSTREES STOOD, WITH A SPYGLASS IN HIS HAND,"
"'THERE'S A WHALE, THERE'S A WHALE, THERE'S A WHALE FISH,' HE CRIED."
"AND SHE BLOWS AT EVERY SPAN, BRAVE BOYS, AND SHE BLOWS AT EVERY SPAN."
"THE CAPTAIN STOOD ON THE QUARTER DECK, A FINE LITTLE MAN WAS HE,"
"OVERHAUL, OVERHAUL, LET YOUR SLOOP SHEETS FALL,"
"AND COME PUSH YOUR BOATS FOR SEA, BRAVE BOYS, AND COME PUSH YOUR BOATS FOR SEA."
"NOW THE BOATS WERE LAUNCHED WITH THE MEN ONBOARD, AND THE WHALE FISH WAS FULL IN VIEW."
"RESOLVED, RESOLVED WAS EACH SEAMAN BOLD, FOR TO STEER WHERE THE WHALE FISH BLEW, BRAVE BOYS, FOR TO STEER WHERE THE WHALE FISH BLEW."
"WE STRUCK THE WHALE AND THE LINE PLAYED OUT, BUT SHE GAVE A FLOURISH WITH HER TAIL."
"THE BOAT CAPSIZED AND FOUR MEN WERE DROWNED,"
58
"AND WE NEVER CAUGHT THAT WHALE, BRAVE BOYS, WE NEVER CAUGHT THAT WHALE."
"'TO LOSE THAT WHALE,' OUR CAPTAIN HE CRIED, 'IT GRIEVES ME HEART FULL SORE.'"
"'BUT TO LOSE FOUR MEN FROM MY GALLANT CREW,'"
"'AYE, IT GRIEVES ME TEN TIMES MORE, BRAVE BOYS, AYE, IT GRIEVES ME TEN TIMES MORE.'"
"OH, GREENLAND IS A FOREIGN LAND, A LAND THAT KNOWS NO GREEN."

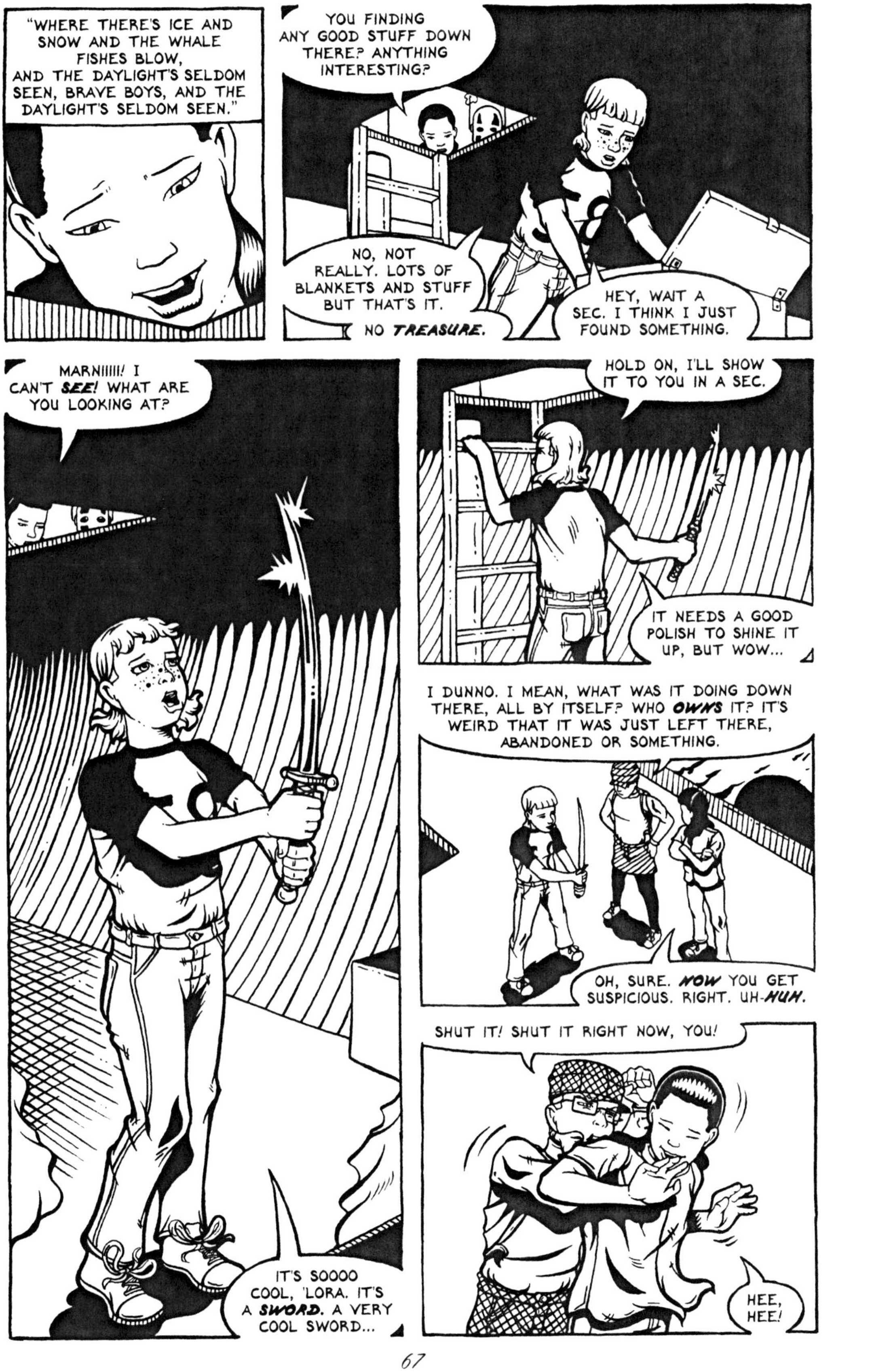
"WHERE THERE'S ICE AND SNOW AND THE WHALE FISHES BLOW, AND THE DAYLIGHT'S SELDOM SEEN, BRAVE BOYS, AND THE DAYLIGHT'S SELDOM SEEN."
YOU FINDING ANY GOOD STUFF DOWN THERE? ANYTHING INTERESTING?
NO, NOT REALLY. LOTS OF BLANKETS AND STUFF BUT THAT'S IT.
NO TREASURE.
HEY, WAIT A SEC. I THINK I JUST FOUND SOMETHING.
MARNIIIII! I CAN'T SEE! WHAT ARE YOU LOOKING AT?
IT'S SOOOO COOL, 'LORA. IT'S A SWORD. A VERY COOL SWORD...
HOLD ON, I'LL SHOW IT TO YOU IN A SEC.
IT NEEDS A GOOD POLISH TO SHINE IT UP, BUT WOW...
I DUNNO. I MEAN, WHAT WAS IT DOING DOWN THERE, ALL BY ITSELF? WHO OWNS IT? IT'S WEIRD THAT IT WAS JUST LEFT THERE, ABANDONED OR SOMETHING.
OH, SURE. NOW YOU GET SUSPICIOUS. RIGHT. UH-HUH.
SHUT IT! SHUT IT RIGHT NOW, YOU!
HEE, HEE!

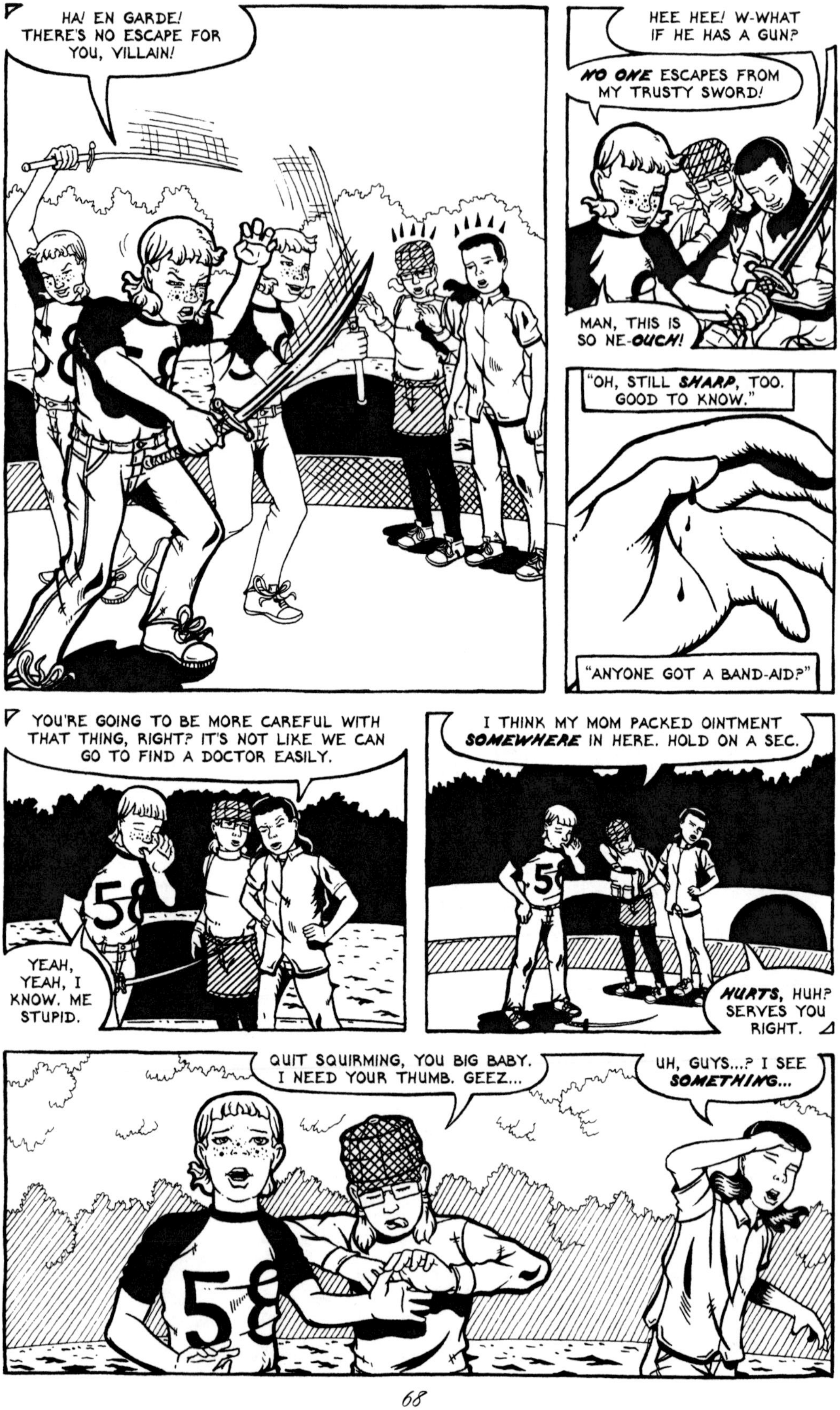
HA! EN GARDE! THERE'S NO ESCAPE FOR YOU, VILLAIN!
HEE HEE! W-WHAT IF HE HAS A GUN?
NO ONE ESCAPES FROM MY TRUSTY SWORD!
MAN, THIS IS SO NE-OUCH!
"OH, STILL SHARP, TOO. GOOD TO KNOW."
"ANYONE GOT A BAND-AID?"
YOU'RE GOING TO BE MORE CAREFUL WITH THAT THING, RIGHT? IT'S NOT LIKE WE CAN GO TO FIND A DOCTOR EASILY.
YEAH, YEAH, I KNOW. ME STUPID.
I THINK MY MOM PACKED OINTMENT SOMEWHERE IN HERE. HOLD ON A SEC.
HURTS, HUH? SERVES YOU RIGHT.
QUIT SQUIRMING, YOU BIG BABY. I NEED YOUR THUMB. GEEZ...
UH, GUYS...? I SEE SOMETHING...

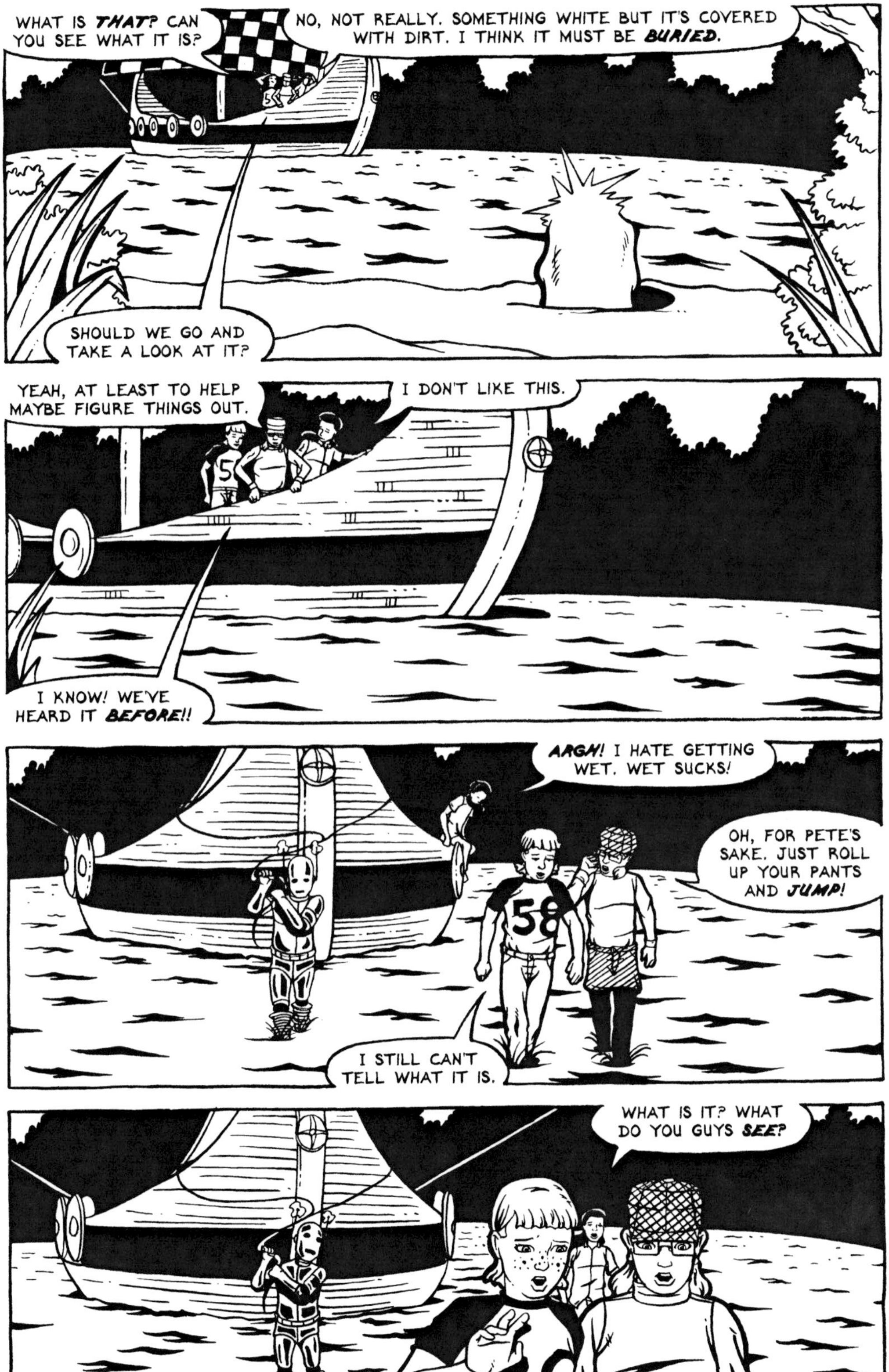
WHAT IS THAT? CAN YOU SEE WHAT IT IS?
NO, NOT REALLY. SOMETHING WHITE BUT IT'S COVERED WITH DIRT. I THINK IT MUST BE BURIED.
SHOULD WE GO AND TAKE A LOOK AT IT?
YEAH, AT LEAST TO HELP MAYBE FIGURE THINGS OUT.
I DON'T LIKE THIS.
I KNOW! WE'VE HEARD IT BEFORE!!
ARGH! I HATE GETTING WET. WET SUCKS!
OH, FOR PETE'S SAKE. JUST ROLL UP YOUR PANTS AND JUMP!
I STILL CAN'T TELL WHAT IT IS.
WHAT IS IT? WHAT DO YOU GUYS SEE?

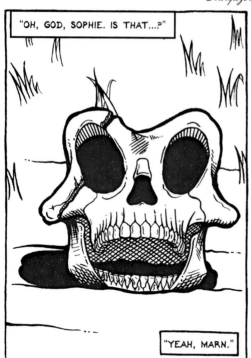

"OH, GOD, SOPHIE. IS THAT....?"

"YEAH, MARN."

I'VE SEEN OLD **BONES** OF SQUIRRELS AND STUFF BEFORE...

GUYS...?

BUT NOTHING LIKE THIS. IT'S STRANGE.

IT LOOKS ANCIENT.

UH-HUH. IT'S REALLY OLD.

I'D...I'D LIKE TO G-GET OUT OF HERE.

IT'S OK. IT'S BEEN HERE FOR A **LONG** WHILE SO WE'RE OK. LOOK HOW IT'S BEEN BURIED BY THE SAND.

I DON'T **CARE!** I'M GOING B-BACK TO THE BOAT!

MAYBE WE SHOULD GO AFTER HER?

IN A SEC. I JUST WANNA CLEAR OFF SOME OF THE DIRT...

WHAT THE-?

L-LET'S GET OUT OF HERE!

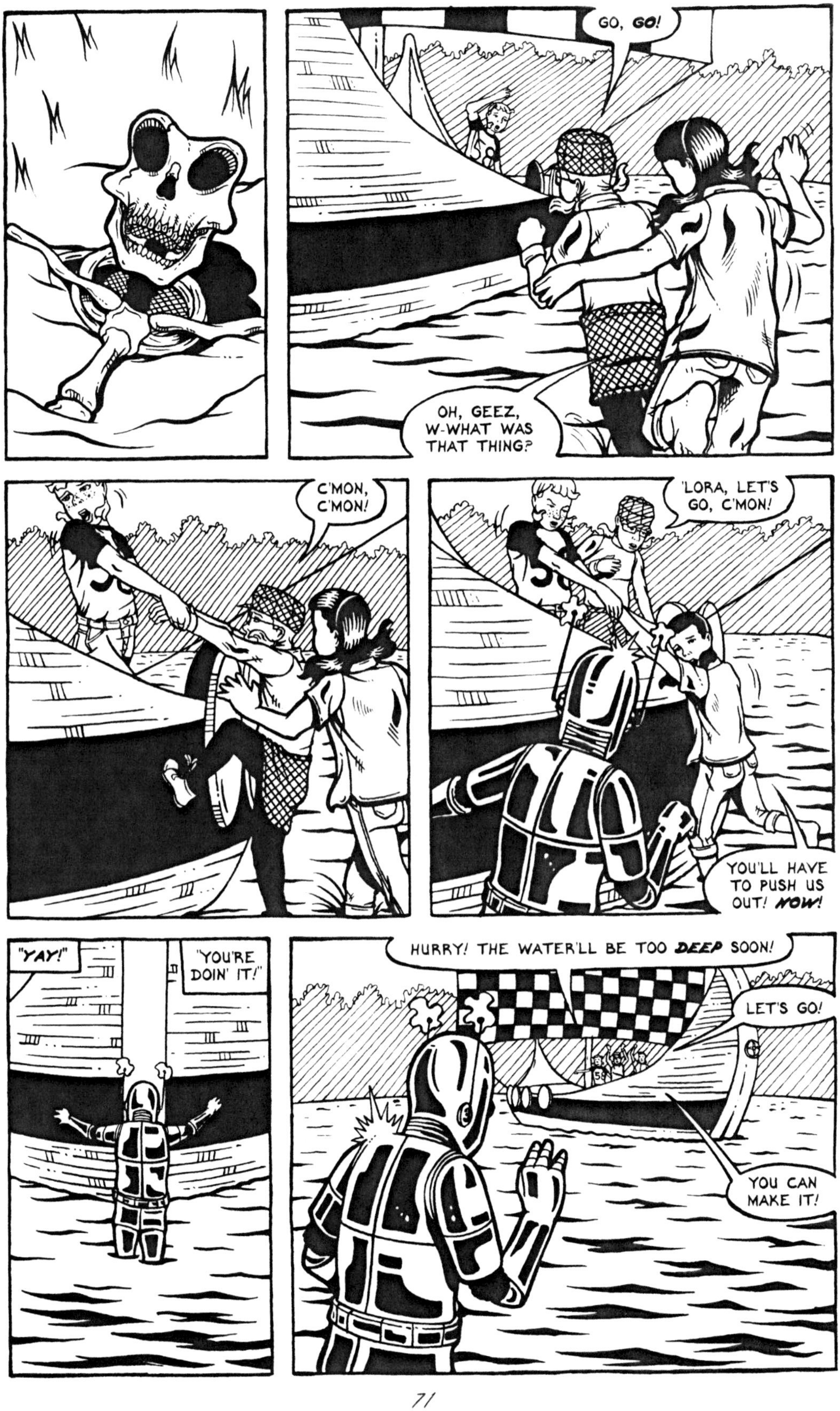
GO, GO!
OH, GEEZ, W-WHAT WAS THAT THING?
C'MON, C'MON!
'LORA, LET'S GO, C'MON!
YOU'LL HAVE TO PUSH US OUT! NOW!
"YAY!"
"YOU'RE DOIN' IT!"
HURRY! THE WATER'LL BE TOO DEEP SOON!
LET'S GO!
YOU CAN MAKE IT!

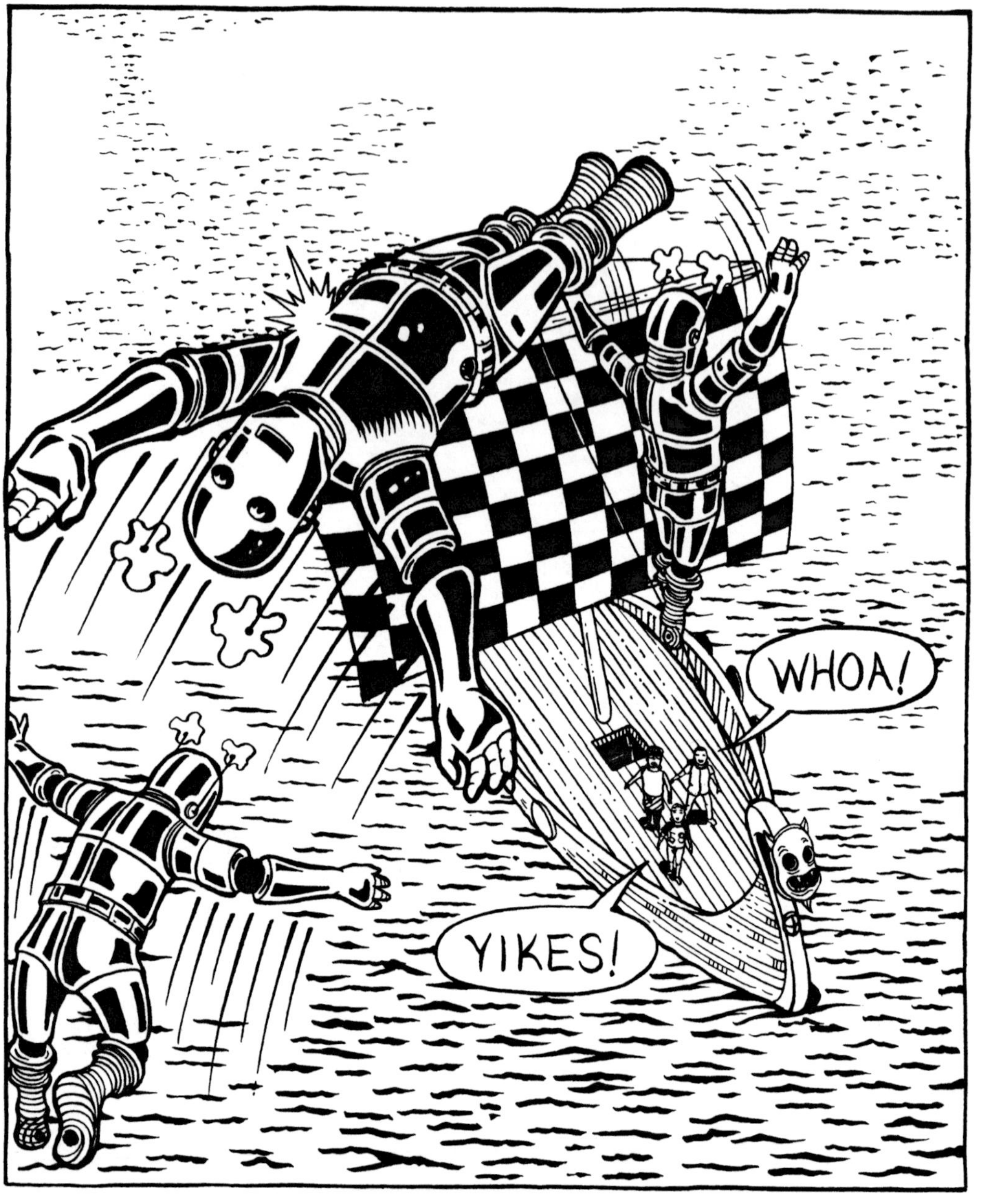
WHOA!
YIKES!

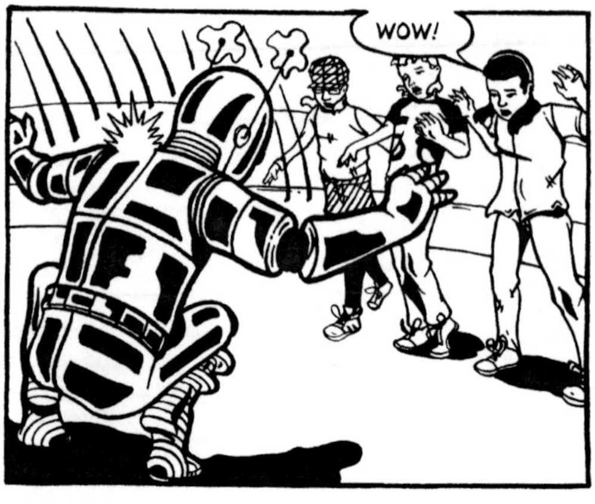
WOW!

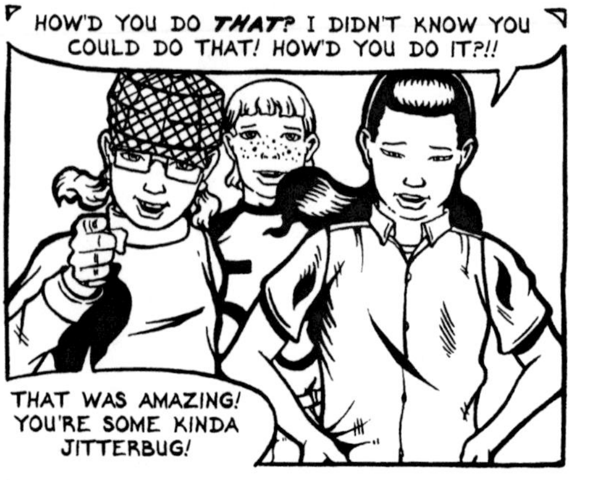
HOW'D YOU DO **THAT?** I DIDN'T KNOW YOU COULD DO THAT! HOW'D YOU DO IT?!!
THAT WAS AMAZING! YOU'RE SOME KINDA JITTERBUG!

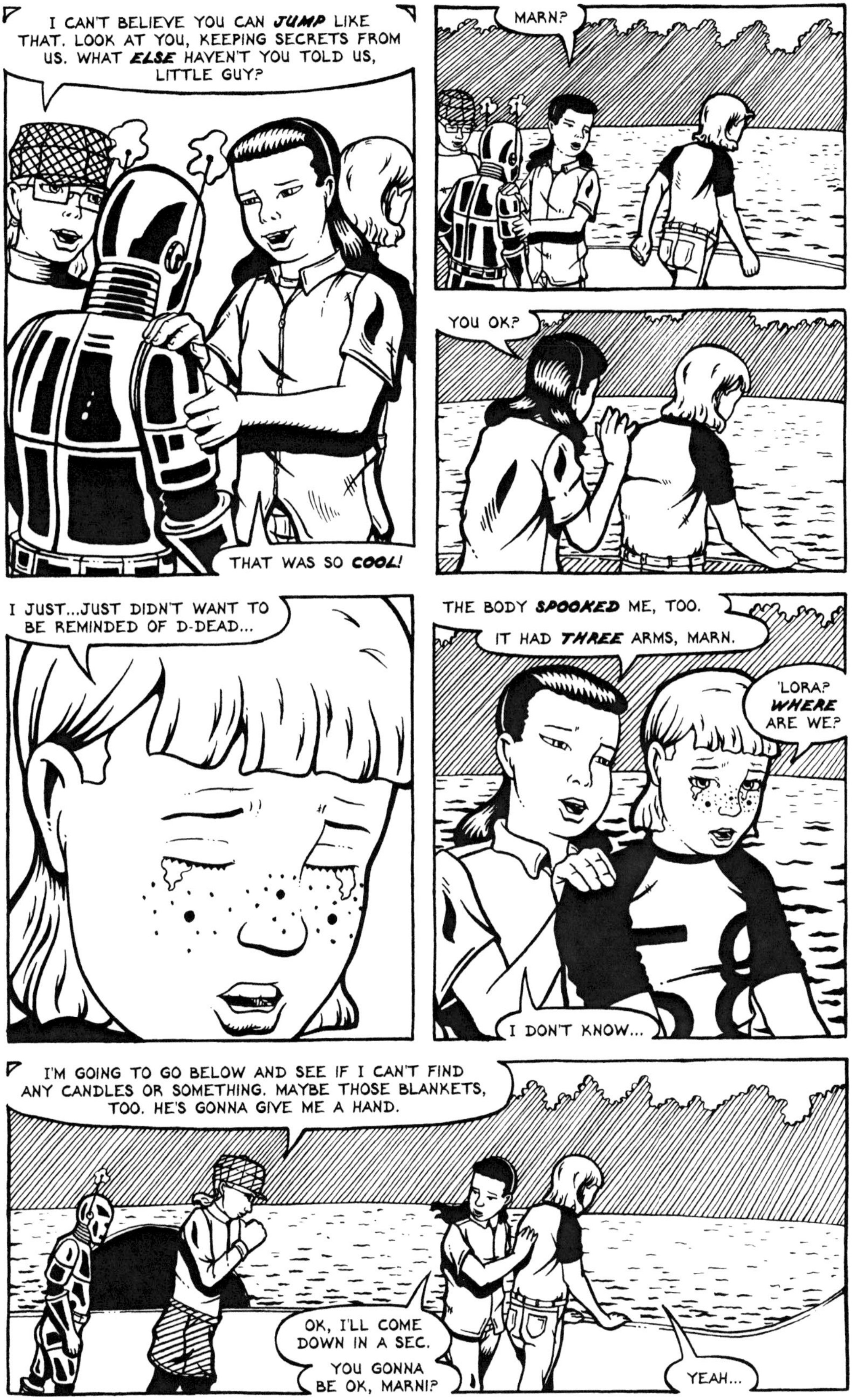
I CAN'T BELIEVE YOU CAN JUMP LIKE THAT. LOOK AT YOU, KEEPING SECRETS FROM US. WHAT ELSE HAVEN'T YOU TOLD US, LITTLE GUY?
THAT WAS SO COOL!
MARN?
YOU OK?
I JUST...JUST DIDN'T WANT TO BE REMINDED OF D-DEAD...
THE BODY SPOOKED ME, TOO.
IT HAD THREE ARMS, MARN.
'LORA? WHERE ARE WE?
I DON'T KNOW...
I'M GOING TO GO BELOW AND SEE IF I CAN'T FIND ANY CANDLES OR SOMETHING. MAYBE THOSE BLANKETS, TOO. HE'S GONNA GIVE ME A HAND.
OK, I'LL COME DOWN IN A SEC.
YOU GONNA BE OK, MARNI?
YEAH...

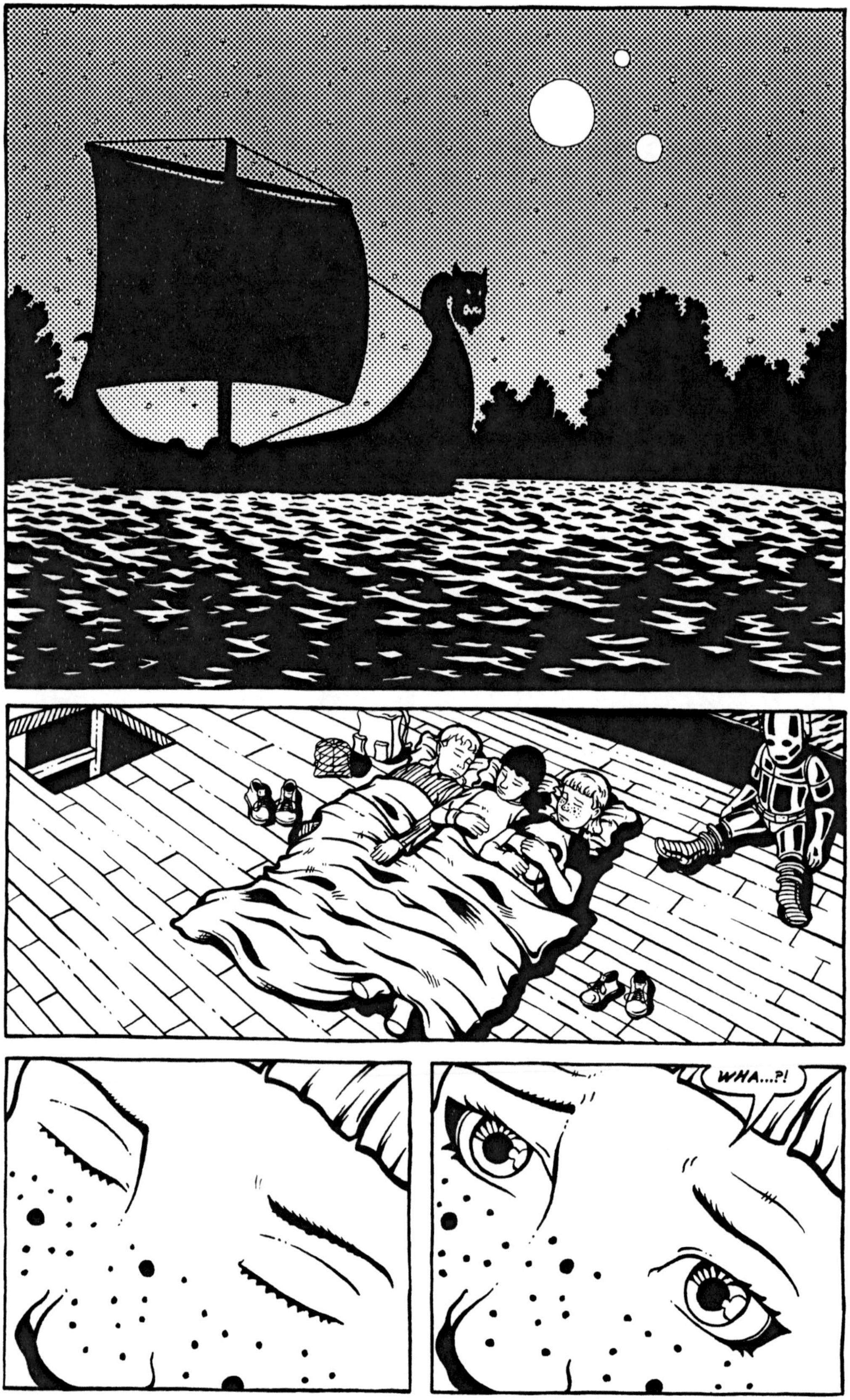
WHA...?!

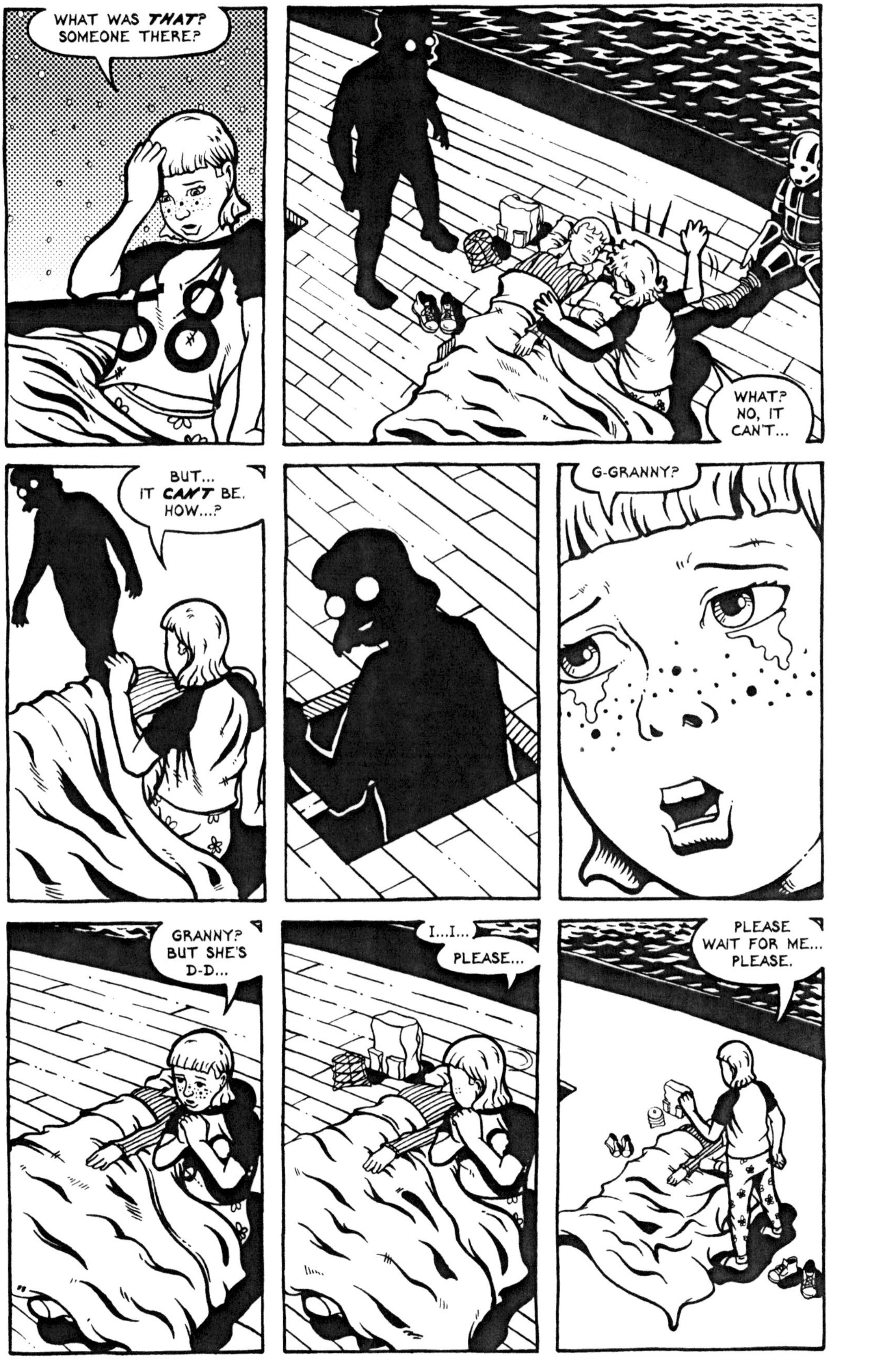
WHAT WAS **THAT**? SOMEONE THERE?
WHAT? NO, IT CAN'T...
BUT... IT **CAN'T** BE. HOW...?
G-GRANNY?
GRANNY? BUT SHE'S D-D...
I...I...
PLEASE...
PLEASE WAIT FOR ME... PLEASE.

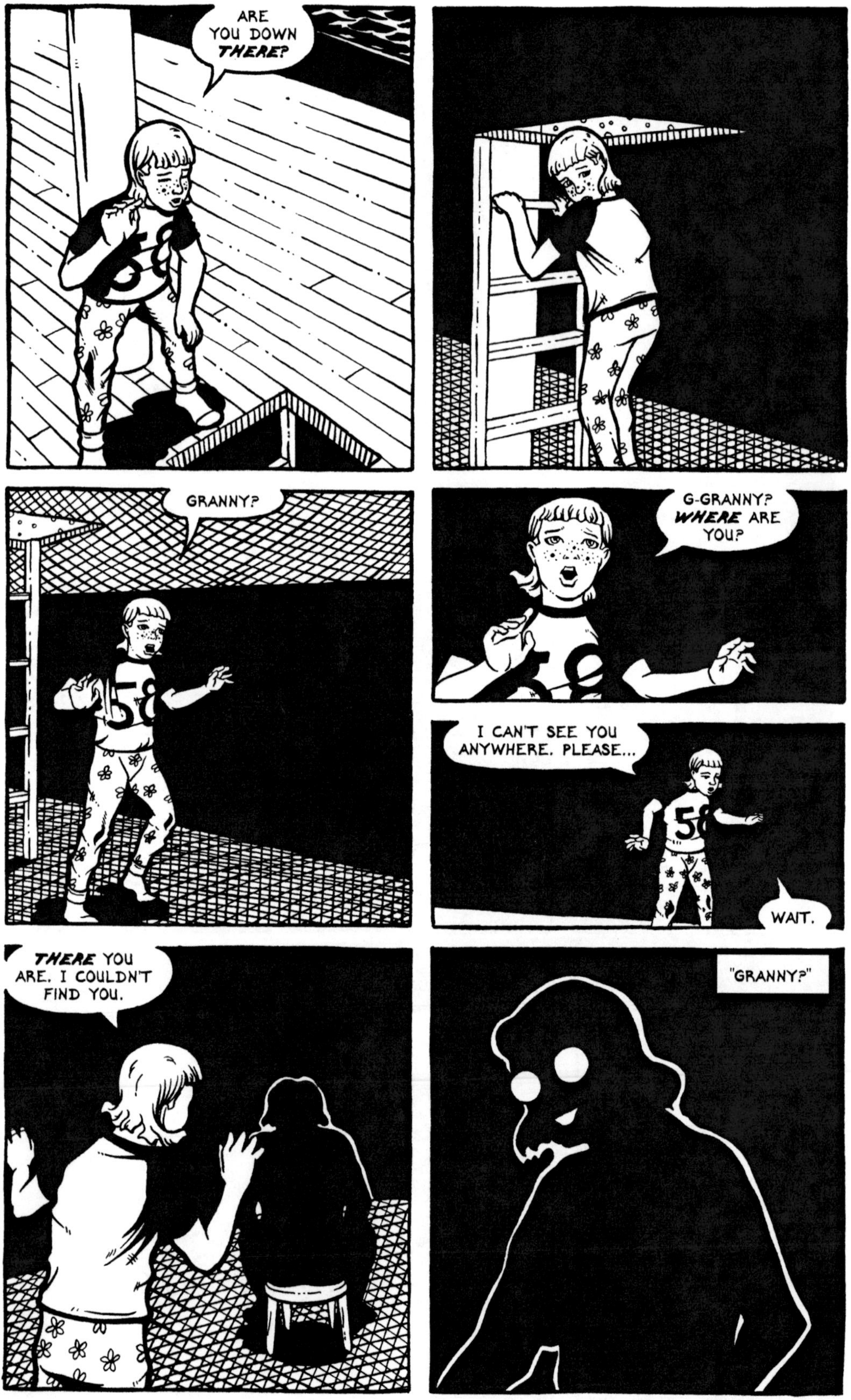
ARE YOU DOWN *THERE?*
GRANNY?
G-GRANNY? *WHERE* ARE YOU?
I CAN'T SEE YOU ANYWHERE. PLEASE...
WAIT.
THERE YOU ARE. I COULDN'T FIND YOU.
"GRANNY?"

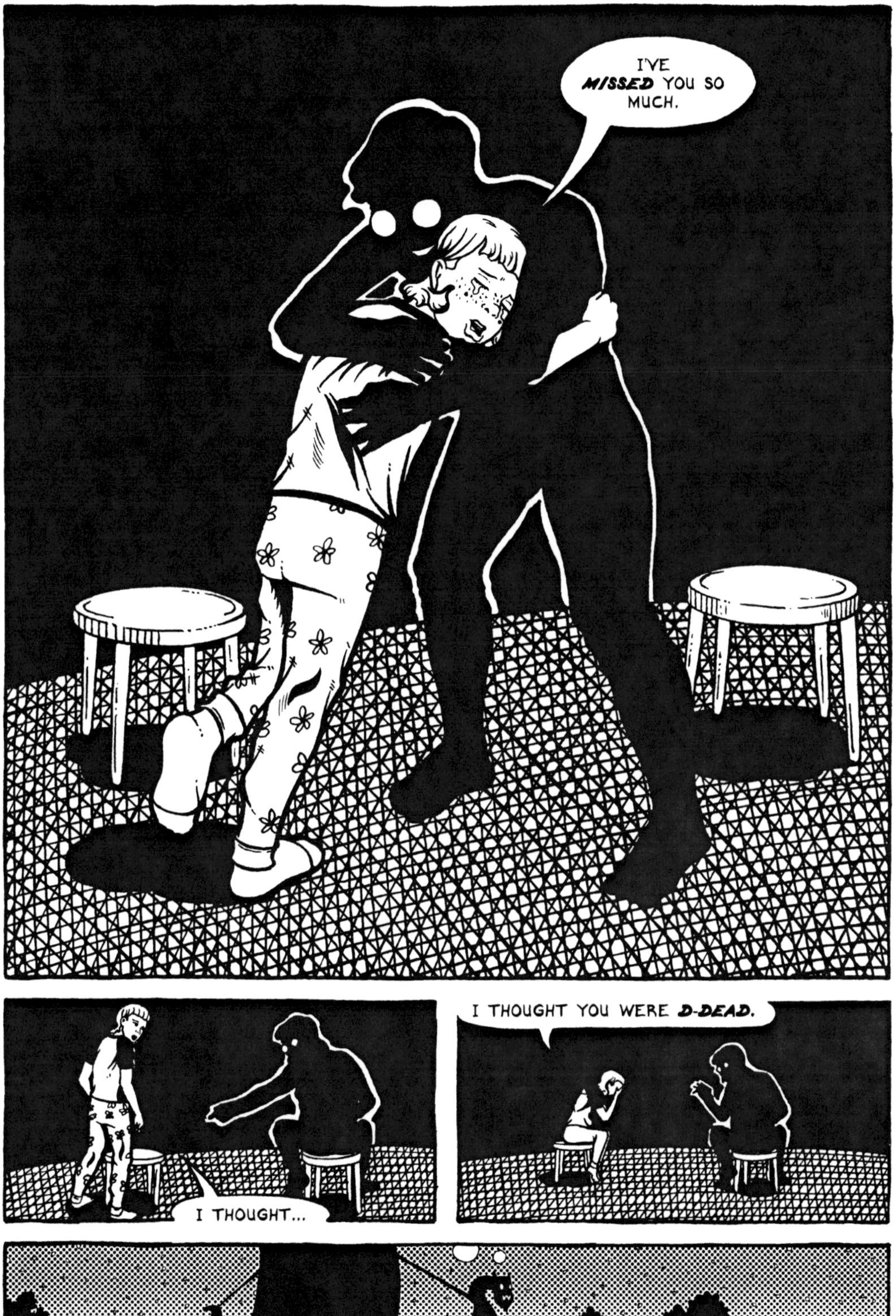
I'VE **MISSED** YOU SO MUCH.
I THOUGHT...
I THOUGHT YOU WERE **D-DEAD.**

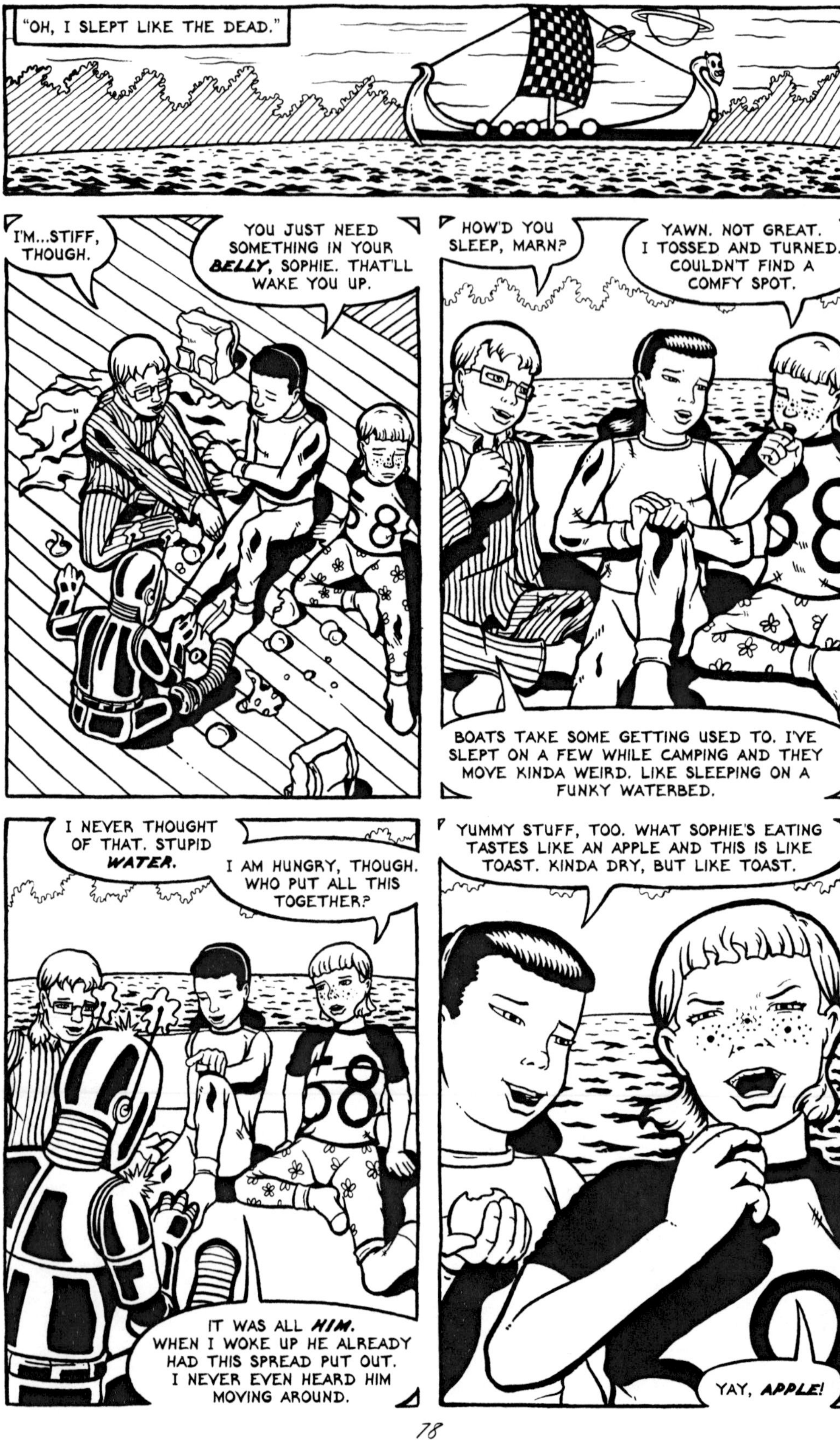
"OH, I SLEPT LIKE THE DEAD."
I'M...STIFF, THOUGH.
YOU JUST NEED SOMETHING IN YOUR BELLY, SOPHIE. THAT'LL WAKE YOU UP.
HOW'D YOU SLEEP, MARN?
YAWN. NOT GREAT. I TOSSED AND TURNED. COULDN'T FIND A COMFY SPOT.
BOATS TAKE SOME GETTING USED TO. I'VE SLEPT ON A FEW WHILE CAMPING AND THEY MOVE KINDA WEIRD. LIKE SLEEPING ON A FUNKY WATERBED.
I NEVER THOUGHT OF THAT. STUPID WATER.
I AM HUNGRY, THOUGH. WHO PUT ALL THIS TOGETHER?
IT WAS ALL HIM. WHEN I WOKE UP HE ALREADY HAD THIS SPREAD PUT OUT. I NEVER EVEN HEARD HIM MOVING AROUND.
YUMMY STUFF, TOO. WHAT SOPHIE'S EATING TASTES LIKE AN APPLE AND THIS IS LIKE TOAST. KINDA DRY, BUT LIKE TOAST.
YAY, APPLE!

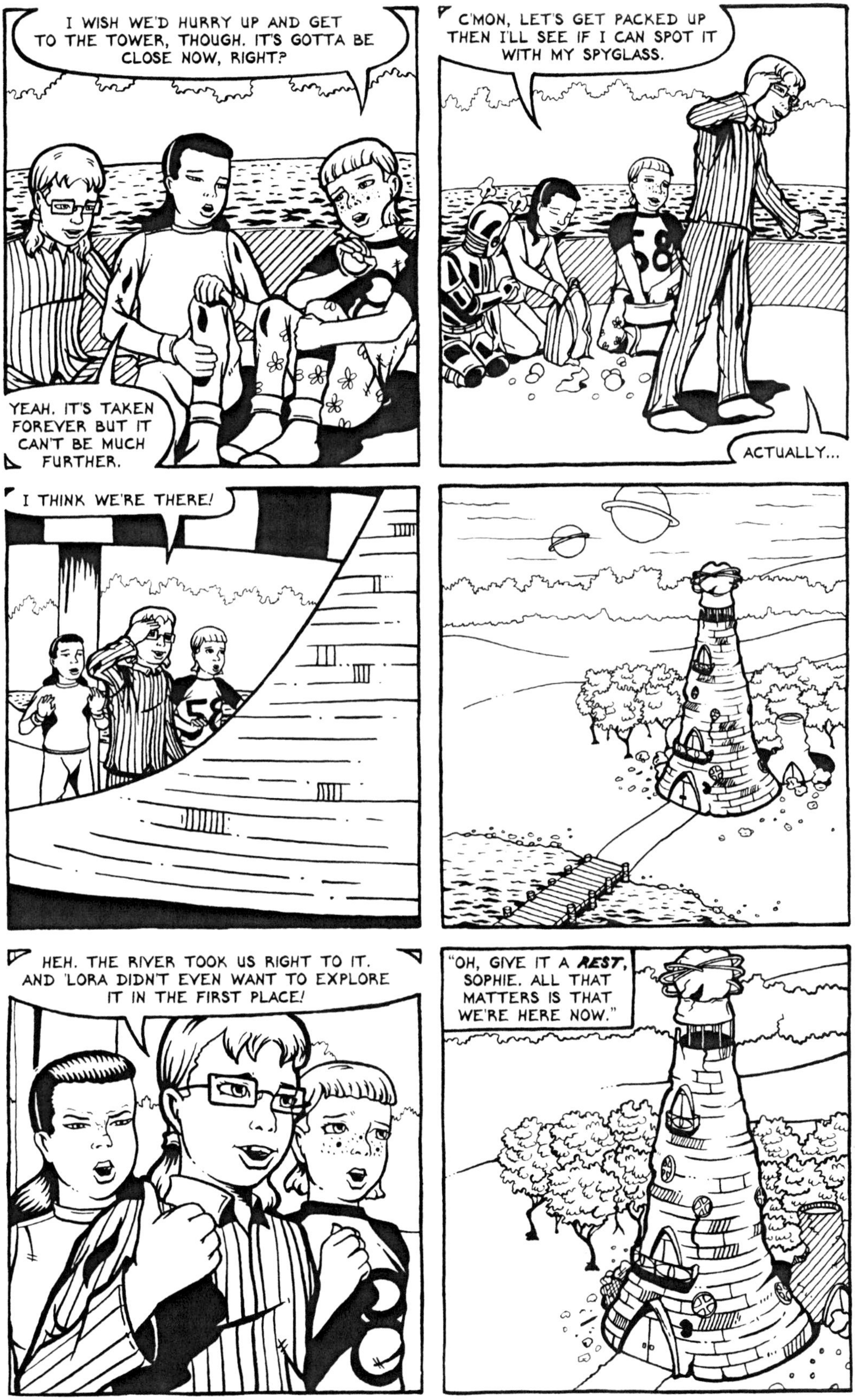
I WISH WE'D HURRY UP AND GET TO THE TOWER, THOUGH. IT'S GOTTA BE CLOSE NOW, RIGHT?
YEAH. IT'S TAKEN FOREVER BUT IT CAN'T BE MUCH FURTHER.
C'MON, LET'S GET PACKED UP THEN I'LL SEE IF I CAN SPOT IT WITH MY SPYGLASS.
ACTUALLY...
I THINK WE'RE THERE!
HEH. THE RIVER TOOK US RIGHT TO IT. AND 'LORA DIDN'T EVEN WANT TO EXPLORE IT IN THE FIRST PLACE!
"OH, GIVE IT A *REST*, SOPHIE. ALL THAT MATTERS IS THAT WE'RE HERE NOW."

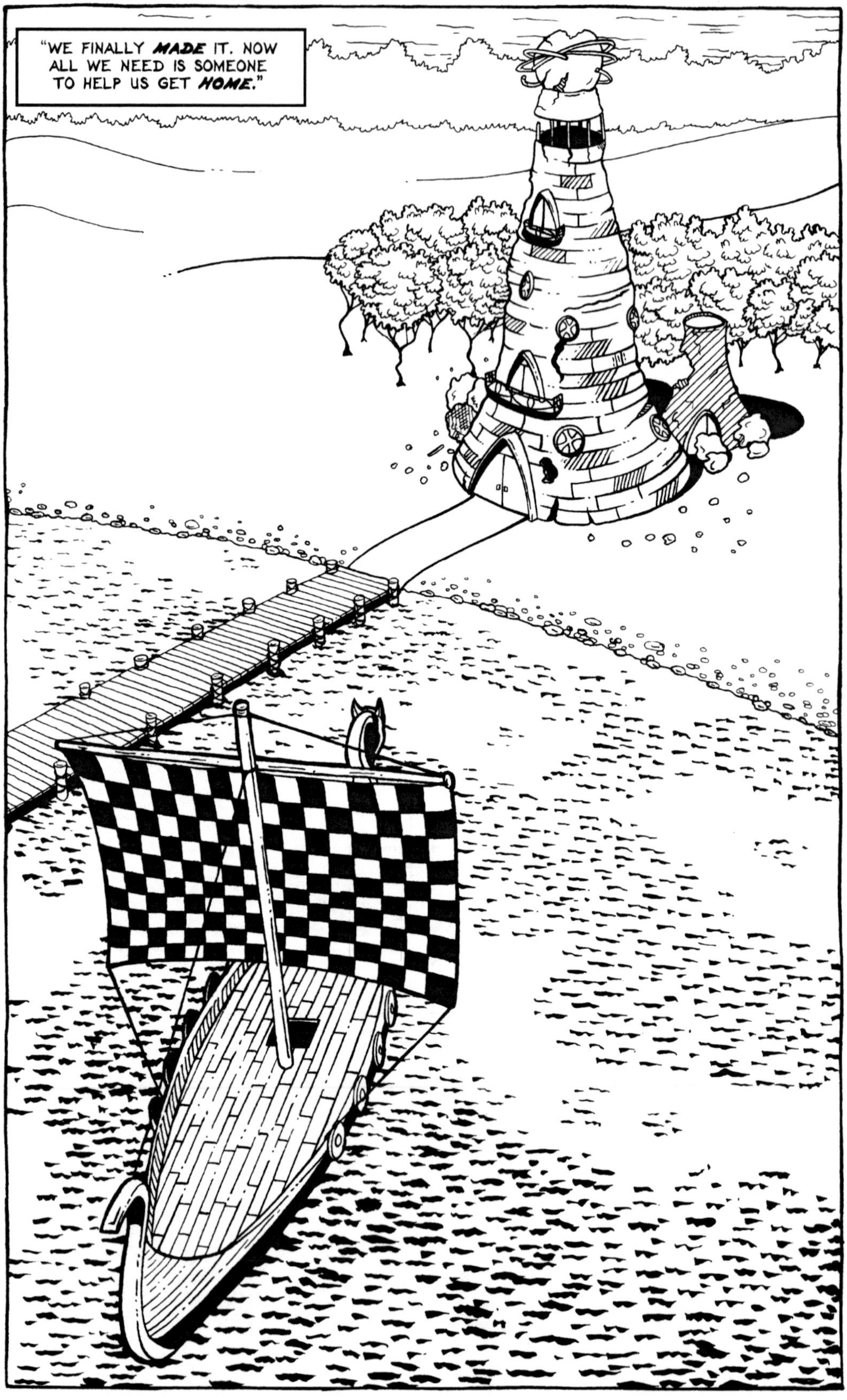
"WE FINALLY MADE IT. NOW ALL WE NEED IS SOMEONE TO HELP US GET HOME."

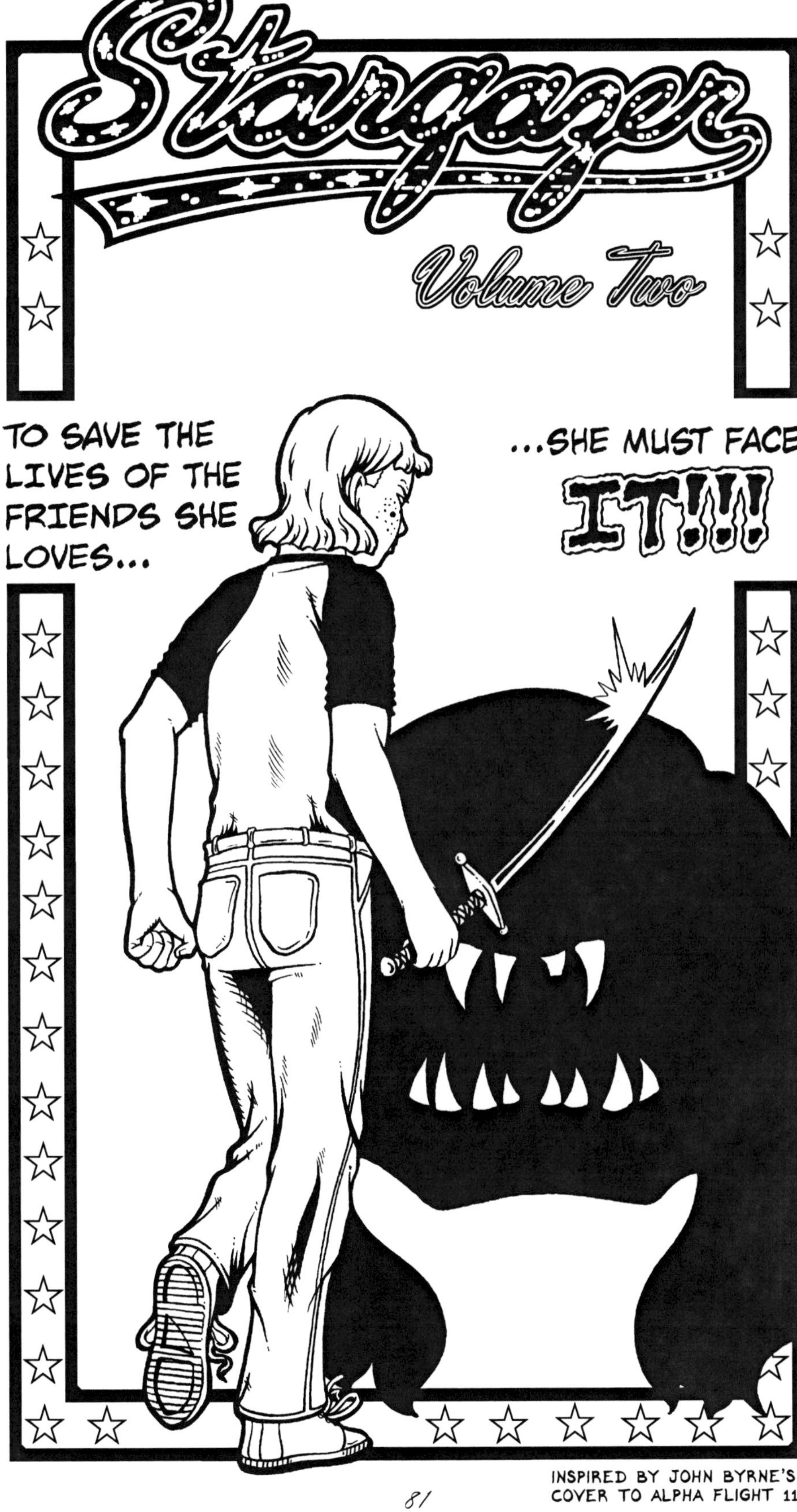
Stargazer
Volume Two
TO SAVE THE LIVES OF THE FRIENDS SHE LOVES...
...SHE MUST FACE
IT!!!

INSPIRED BY JOHN BYRNE'S COVER TO ALPHA FLIGHT 11!

Extras

How I Write

"Where do ideas come from?" is a classic question for almost any writer. And since it's one I've thought of quite a bit myself, I thought it would be interesting to include some of the brainstorming that led to *Stargazer* – mainly because, when I initially sat down to try and figure out what story I wanted to tell, I had no idea what I'd come up with. What follows, then, are a number of my initial thoughts that would eventually lead to the finished script and the illustrated graphic novel. I'm offering these thoughts without a lot of comment mainly so that they stand on their own. I did redact a few things just to keep it spoiler free as much as possible. Hopefully it serves as an overview of the story in broad strokes without revealing anything about the next volume.

I've also included an excerpt from pages twelve through fifteen to try and show how these four pages were specifically put together; this is a very fluid process, though, and it shouldn't be looked as the only way to come up with a final script. It's *my* way, of course, but it's only *one* way. I generally write pretty much full script even though I'm illustrating it myself; which means I don't generally put in as much detail as other writers do in their full scripts – since I'm the artist I like to keep it at least a little bit loose. I'm certainly not afraid, though, of changing things on the fly if I think I can execute a panel or a page in a better way than I initially described. Part of the fun of comics, at least for me, is how different things present themselves at different times. Art is fundamentally problem-solving and a script, even one I've written myself, presents unique problems that have to be continuously solved.

Generally I work out the plot once I have the initial idea and the characters thought out; usually in loose form and often with bullets to define each section. This kind of plot breakdown doesn't concern itself with panels or pages; rather, it's the themes that a scene specifically requires – sometimes even just what scene it should be. Anything goes at this point and I'm certainly not thinking of too many "nitty gritty" details. That comes later.

Once I get that to a point that I'm happy with (usually including lots of revisions), I'll turn it into an outline, which is a more formal structure where I *am* thinking of panels and pages. If a key image strikes me, I'll note it. If a piece of dialogue comes to me, I'll write it down. It doesn't matter how rough it is; I just want to get it on the page. In the case of *Stargazer*, you'll notice that page thirteen of the outline was actually broken up at the final script stage into two pages. This kind of thing happens all the time and is perfectly ok. Again, the outline is a tool to get me where I want to go.

Lastly comes the formal script. I'll take that outline and really block it out, finalizing my thoughts on panel layout, dialogue, and structure. Sometimes I'll really add quite a bit of additional character information, as I did with the character notes for Marni, Sophie and Elora on page 12; other times I'll keep it fairly brief. I suspect if I was writing for another artist I would probably add quite a bit of additional information - writers like Alan Moore and Neil Gaiman are somewhat legendary for doing exactly this, but there really is no one right way.

Concept Art

A lot of sketching, character design, location design and other concept work went into creating the world of *Stargazer* and I've included a number of these initial pieces here. I actually began this process around the time I had finished the brainstorming. Long before I had the script finished or the outline done, I was drawing, trying to crystallize the visuals of the main characters and their world, though a lot of these designs evolved over time.

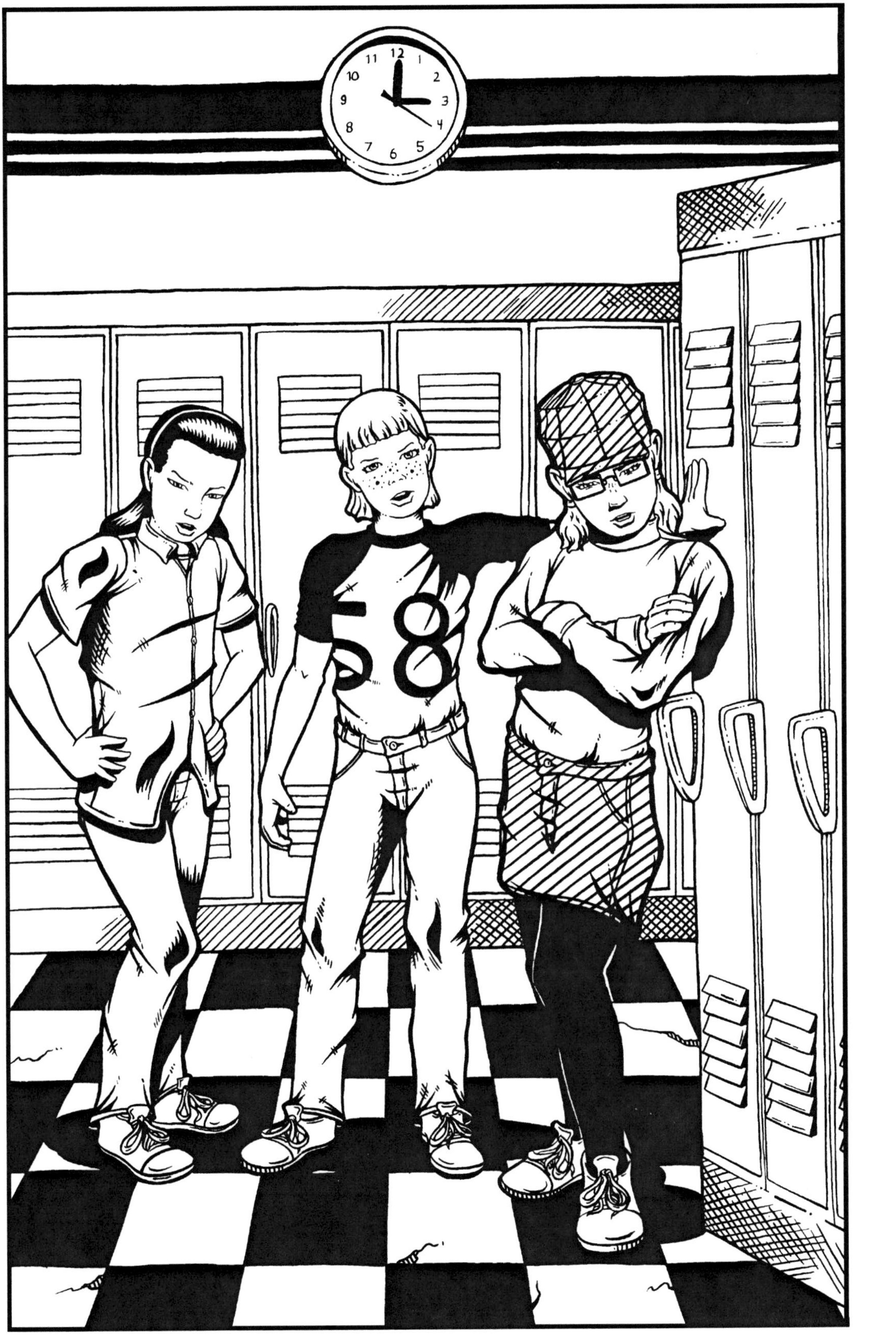
58

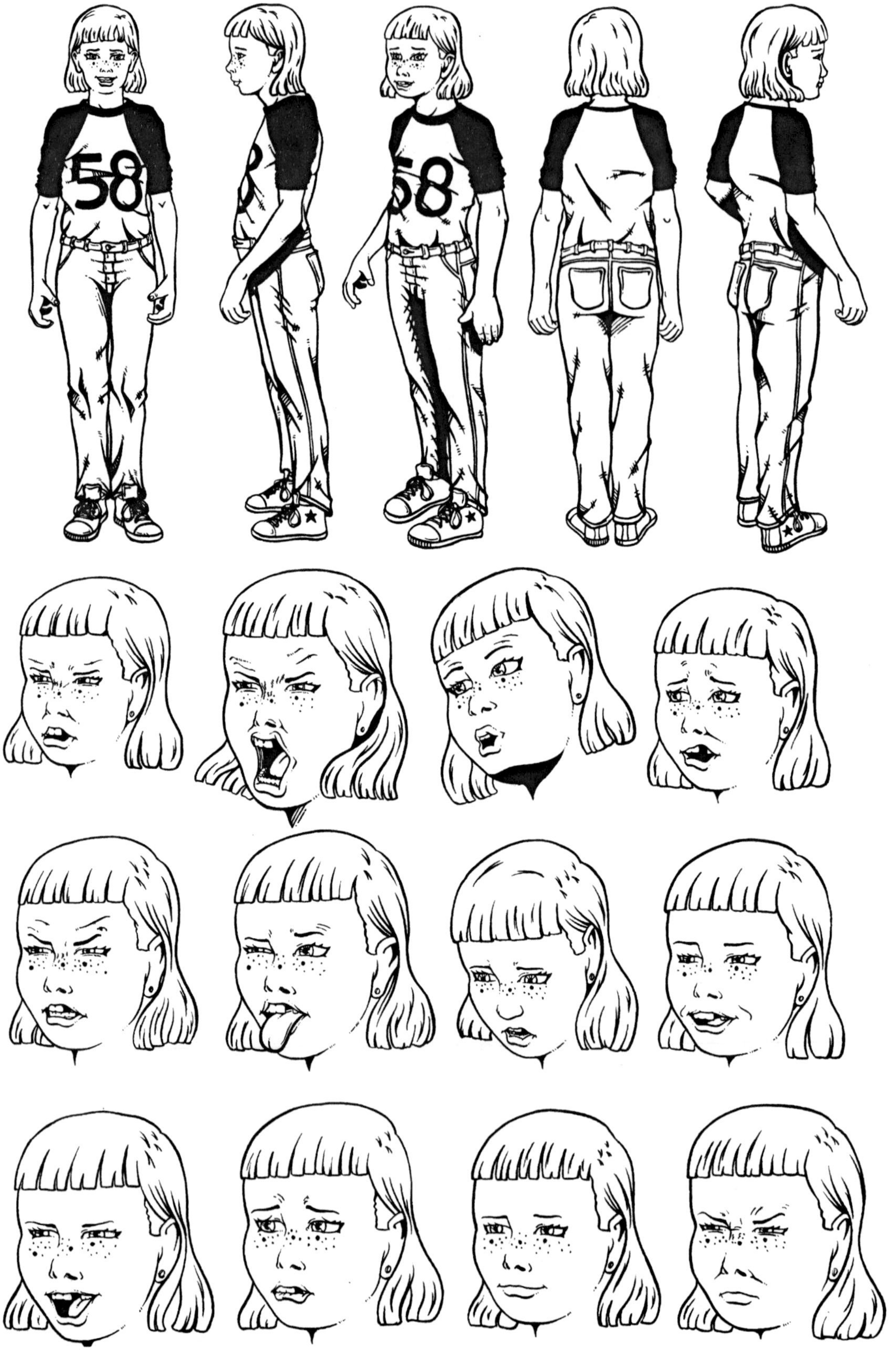
58
58

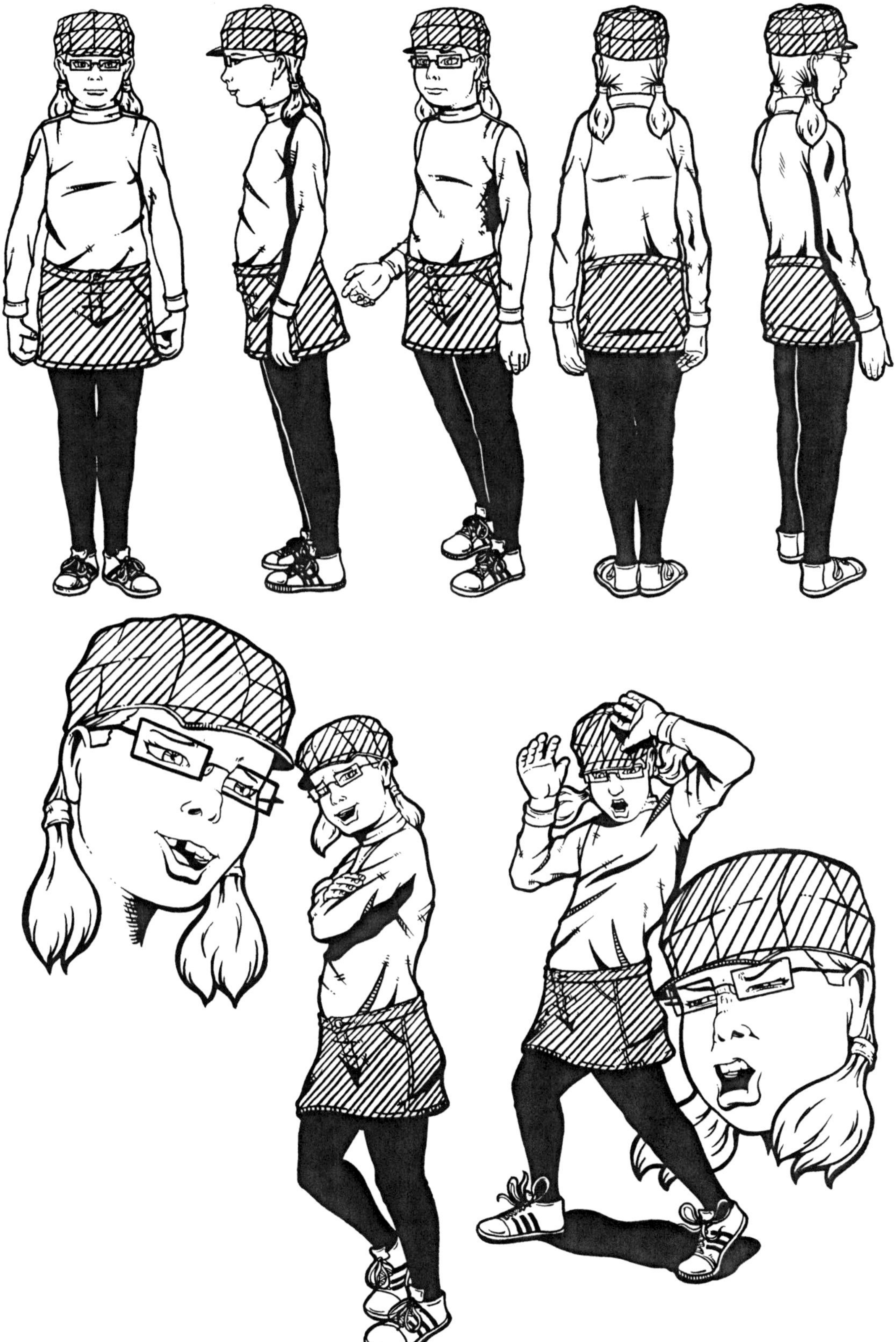

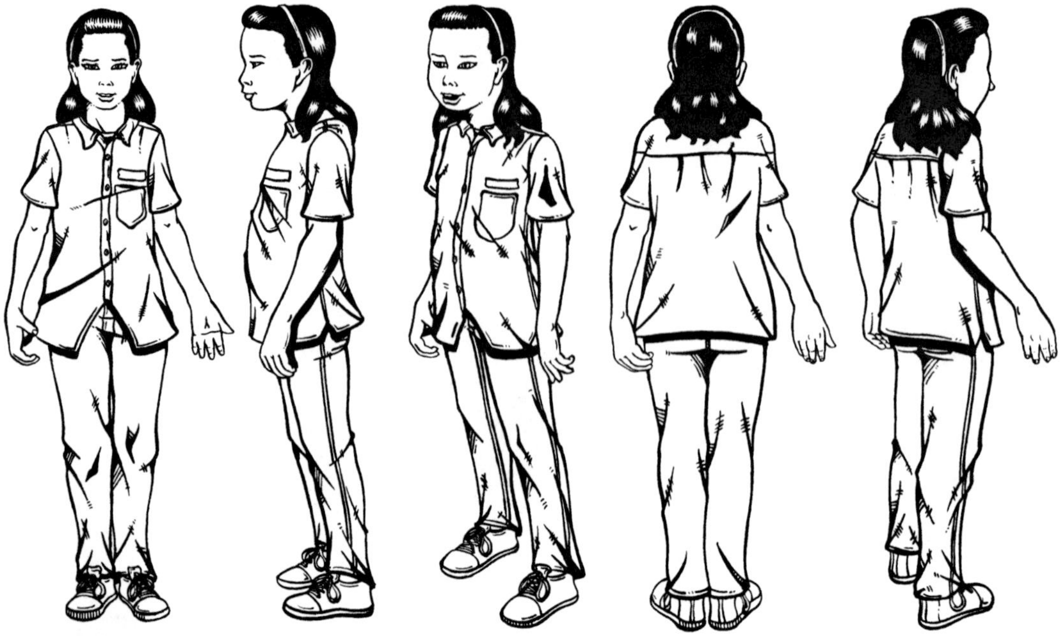

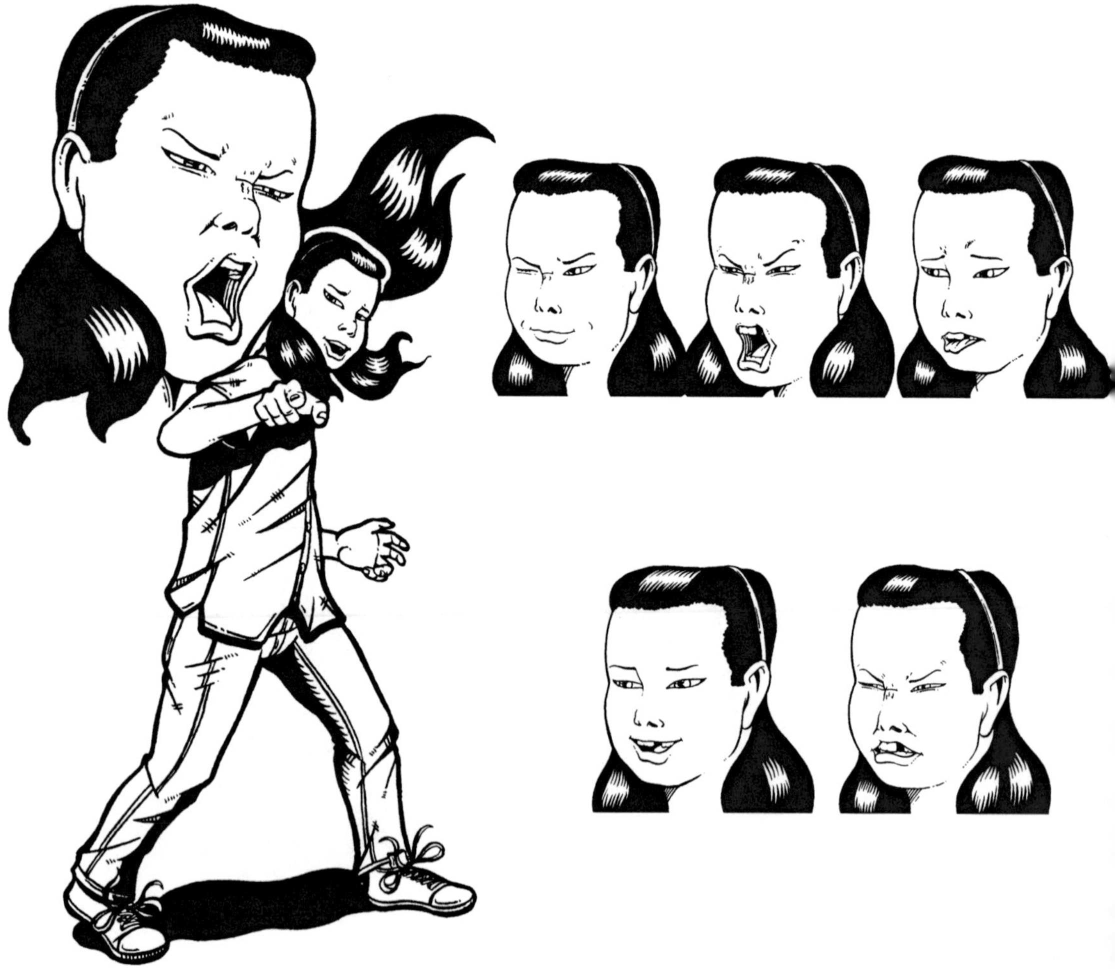

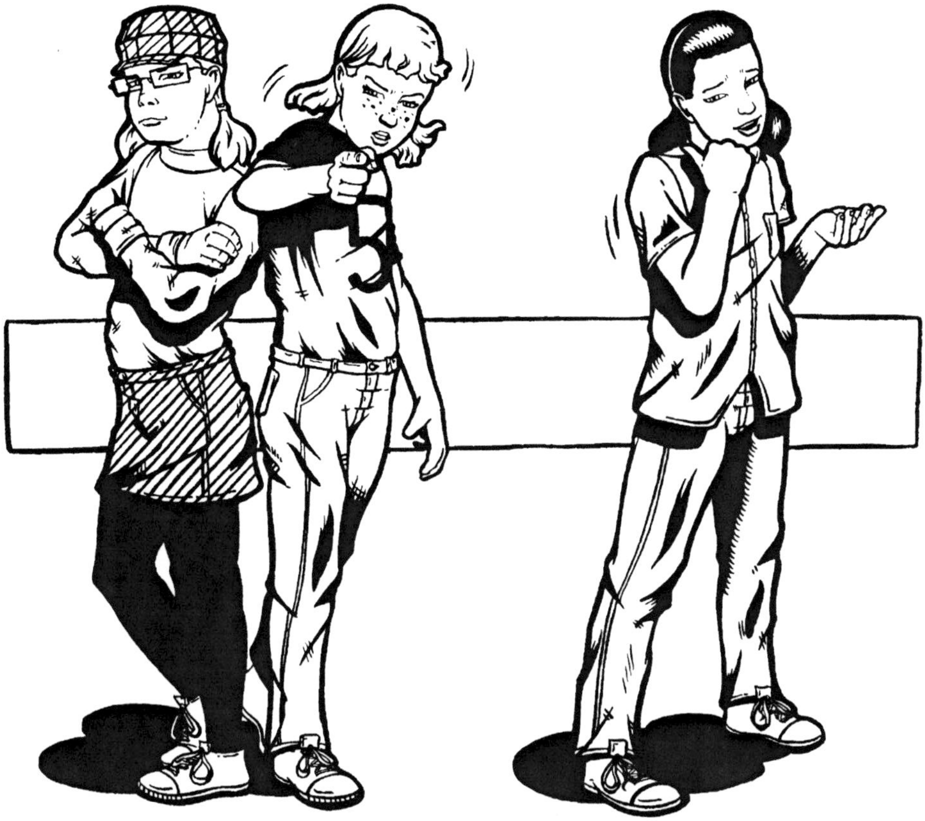

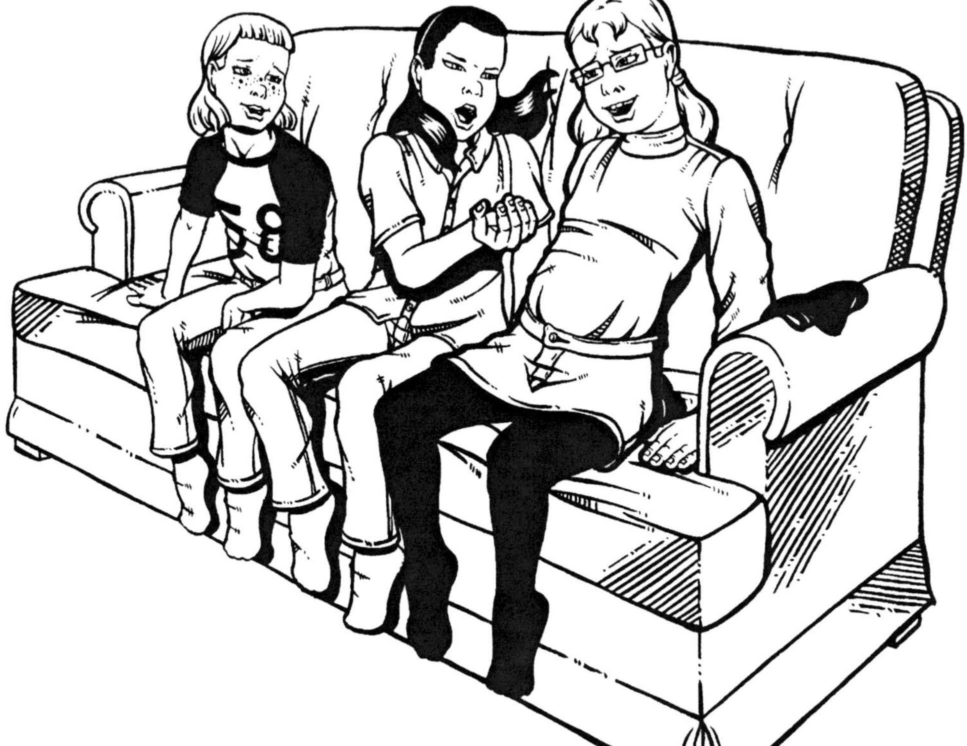

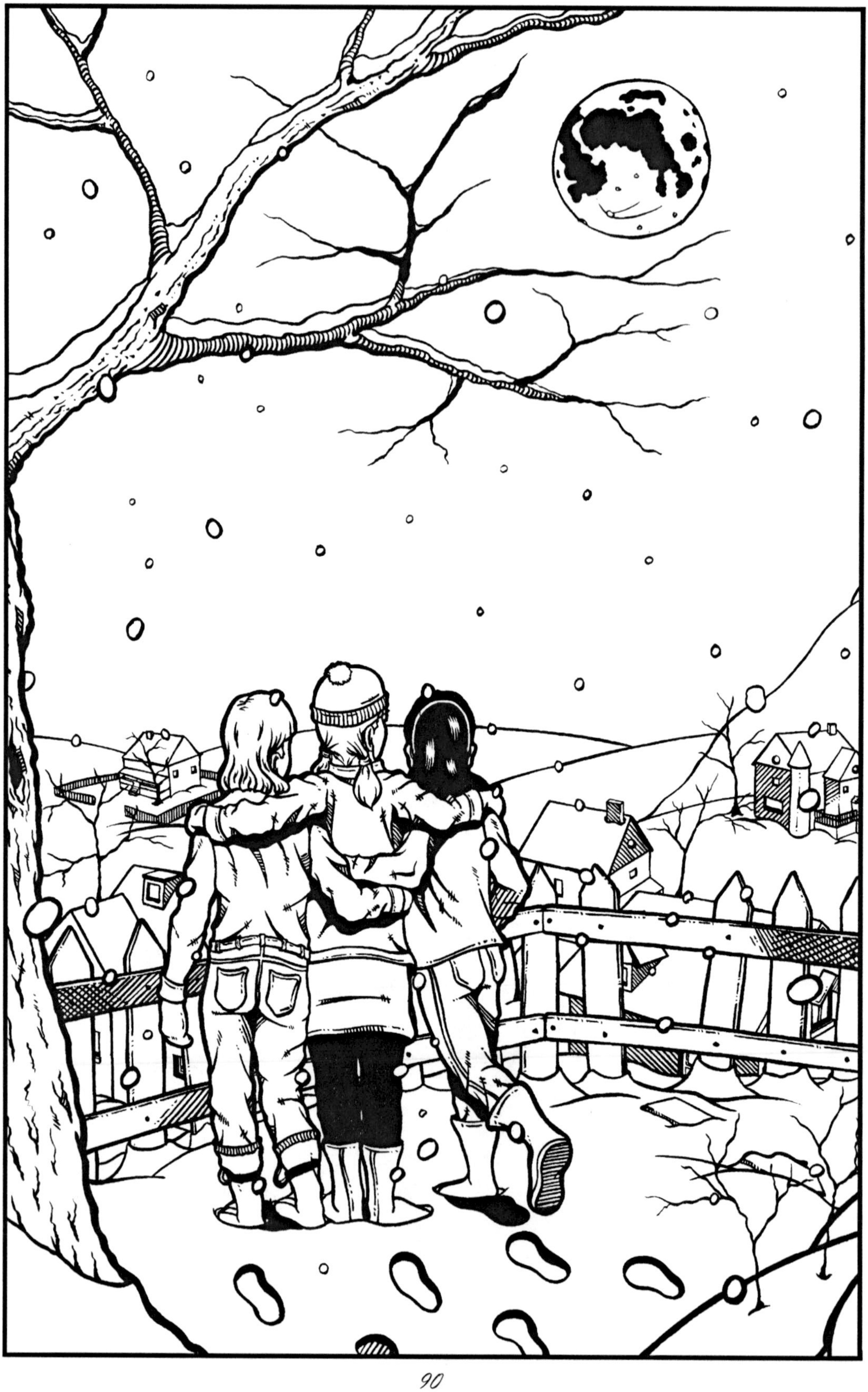

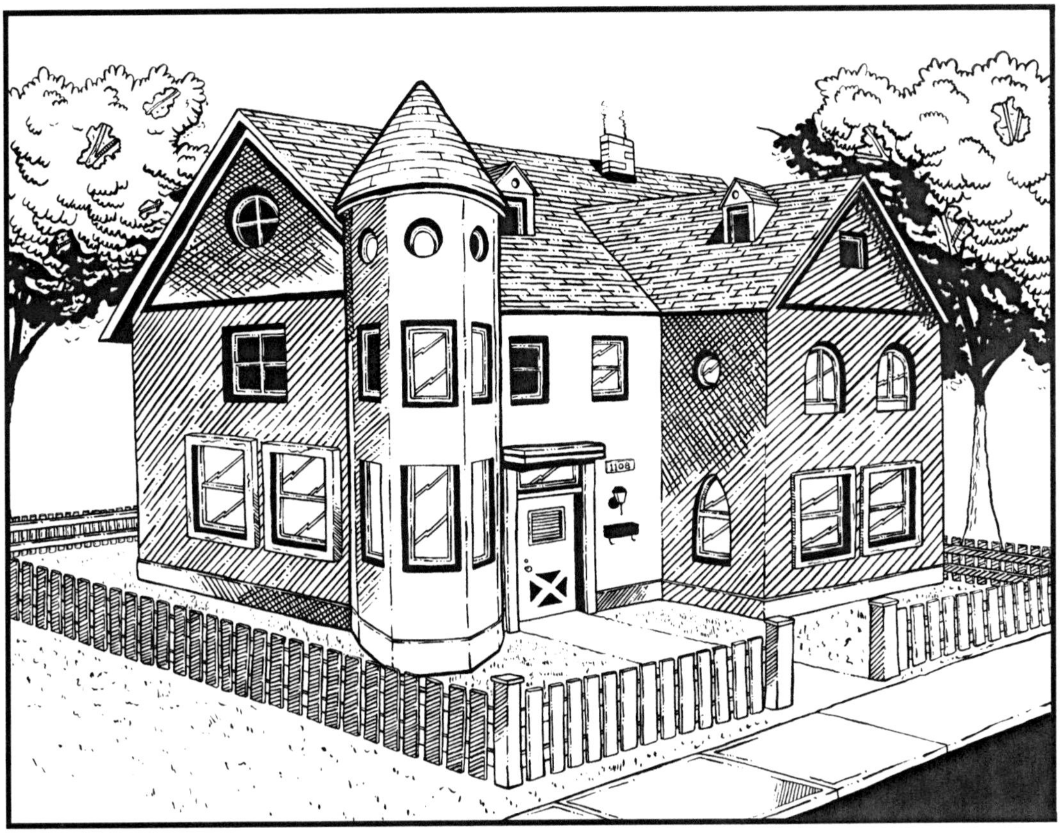
1108

Marni's House - Original Concept

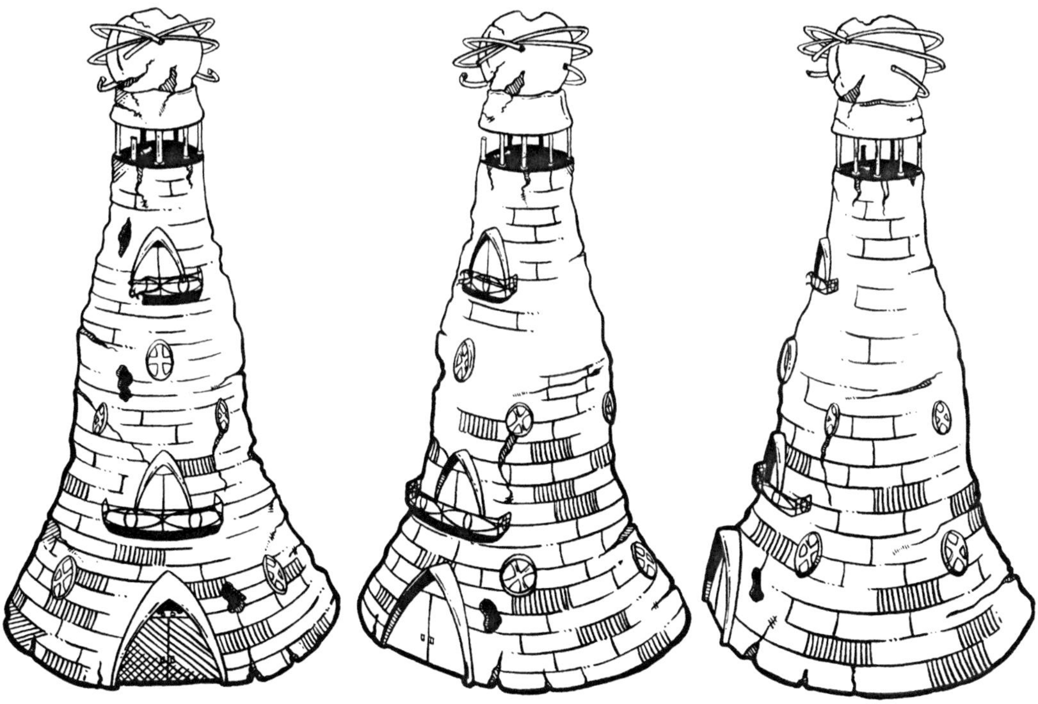

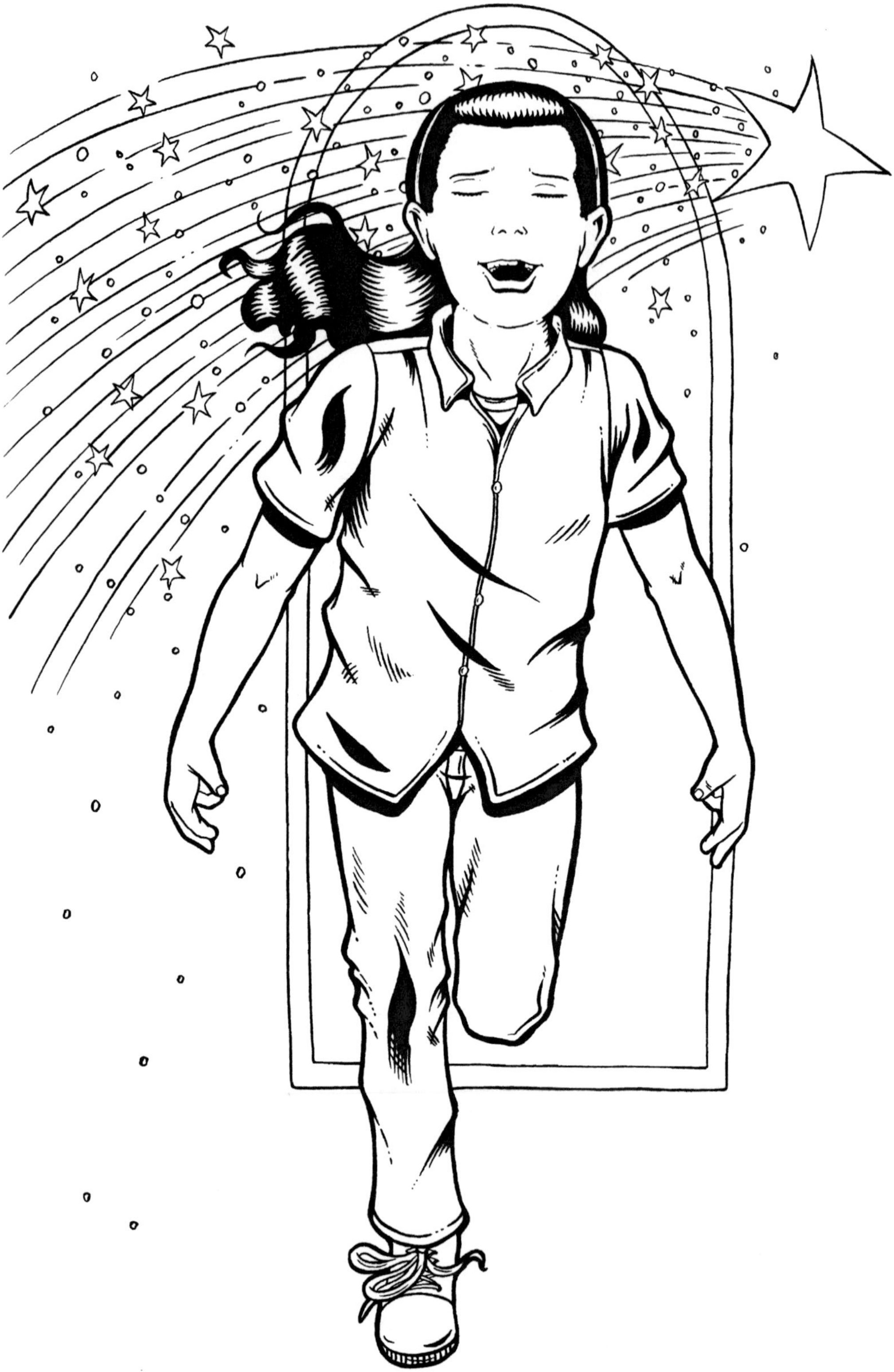

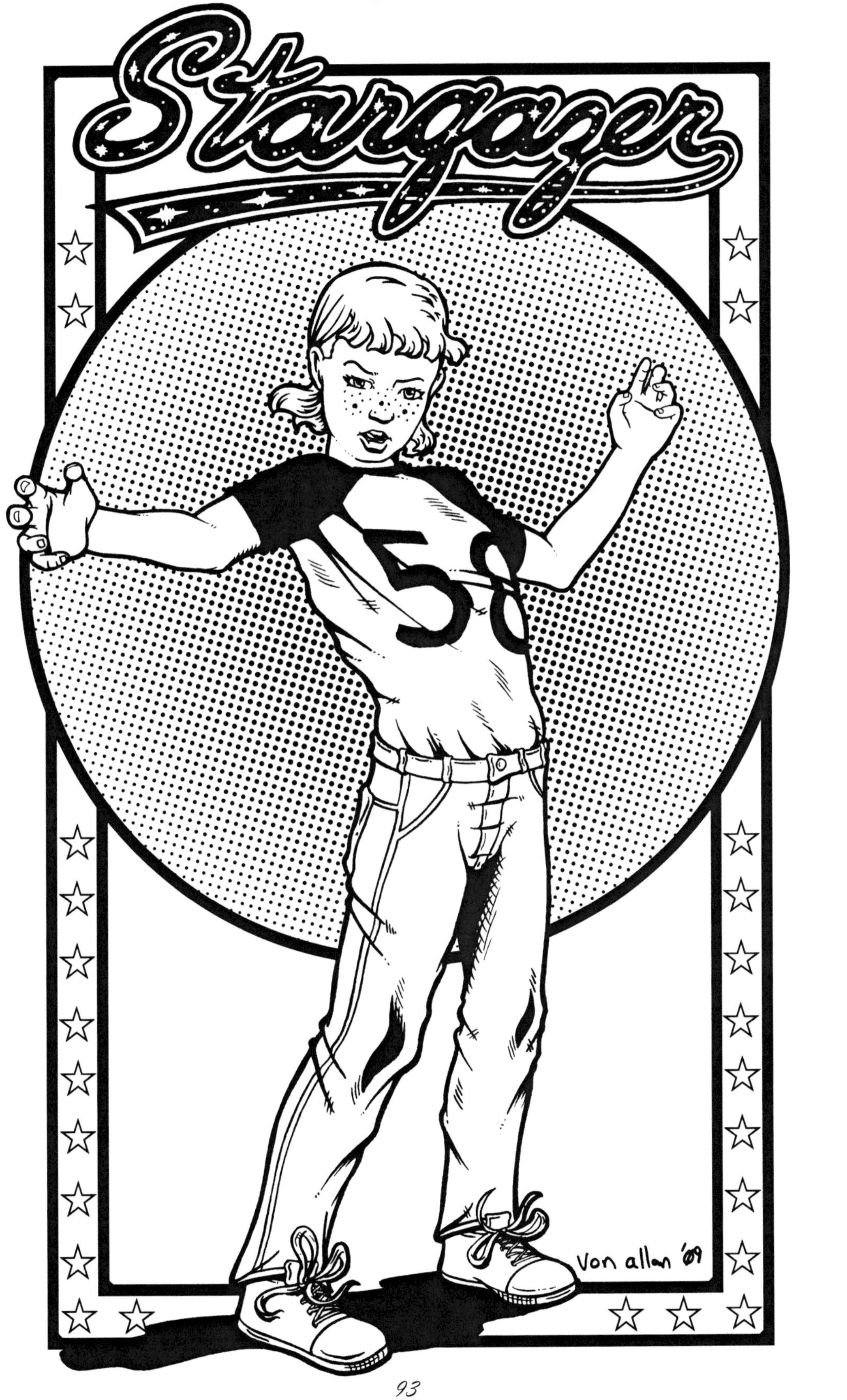
Stargazer
58
Von allan '09

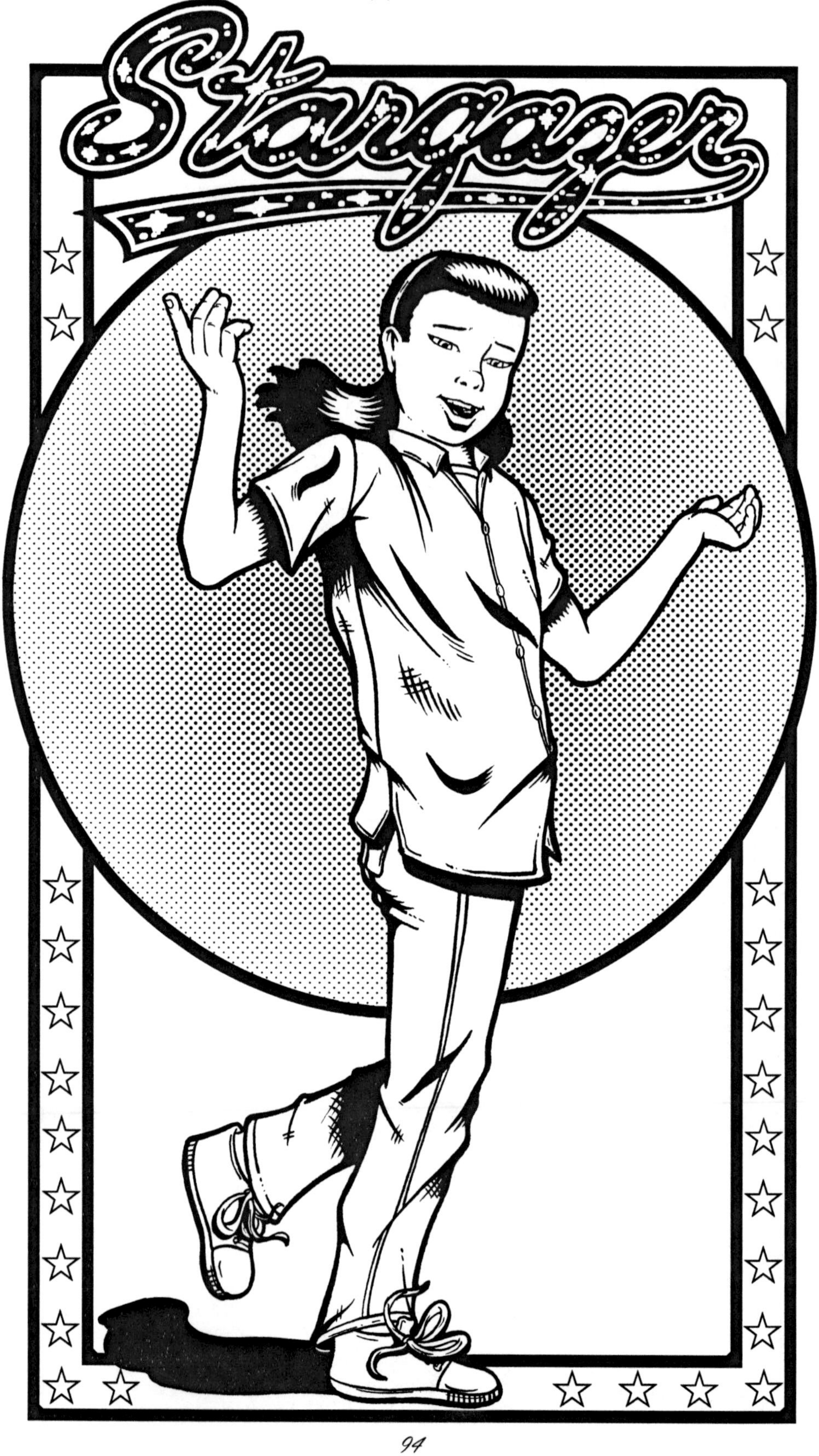
Stargazer

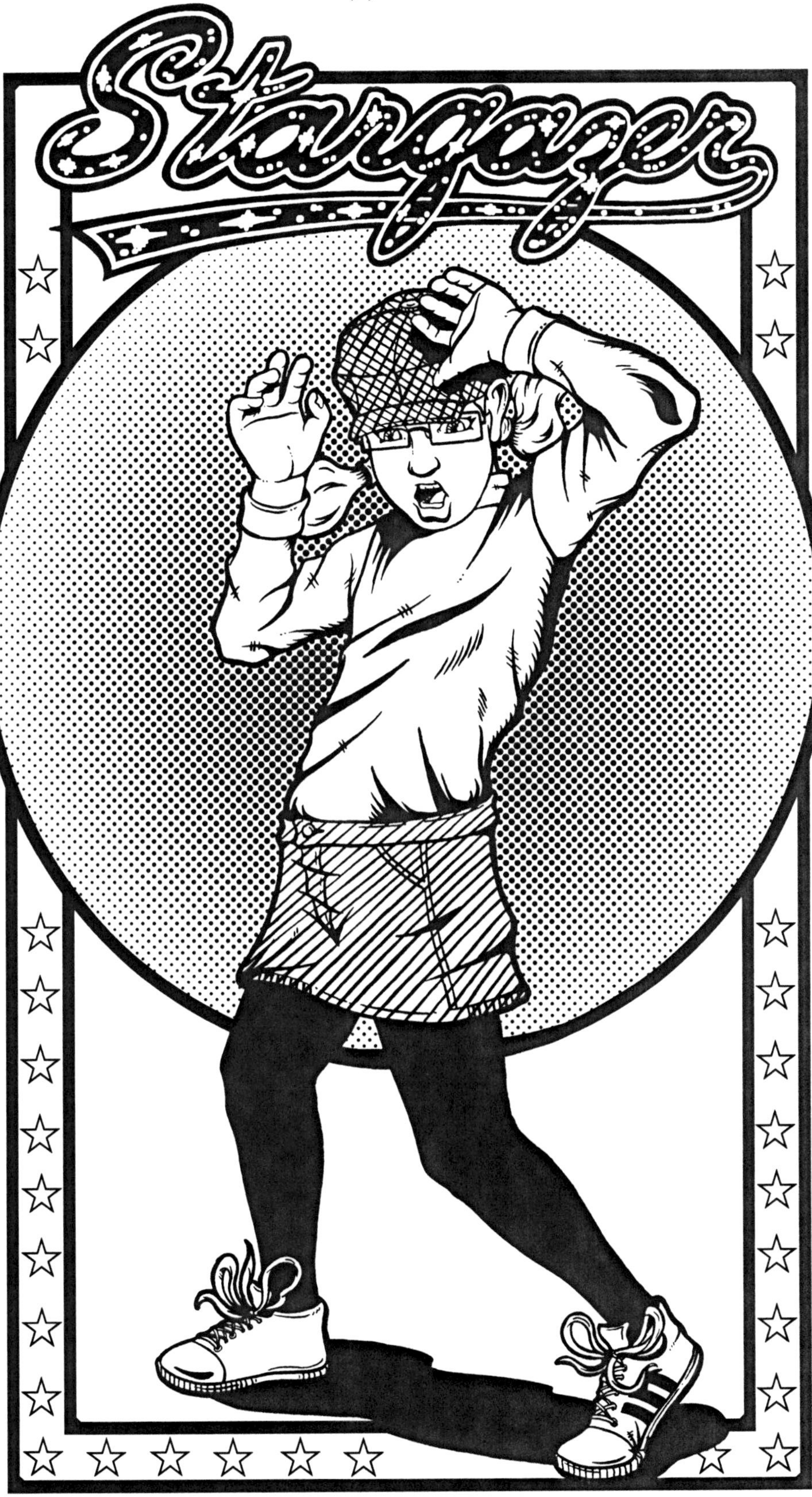
Stargazer

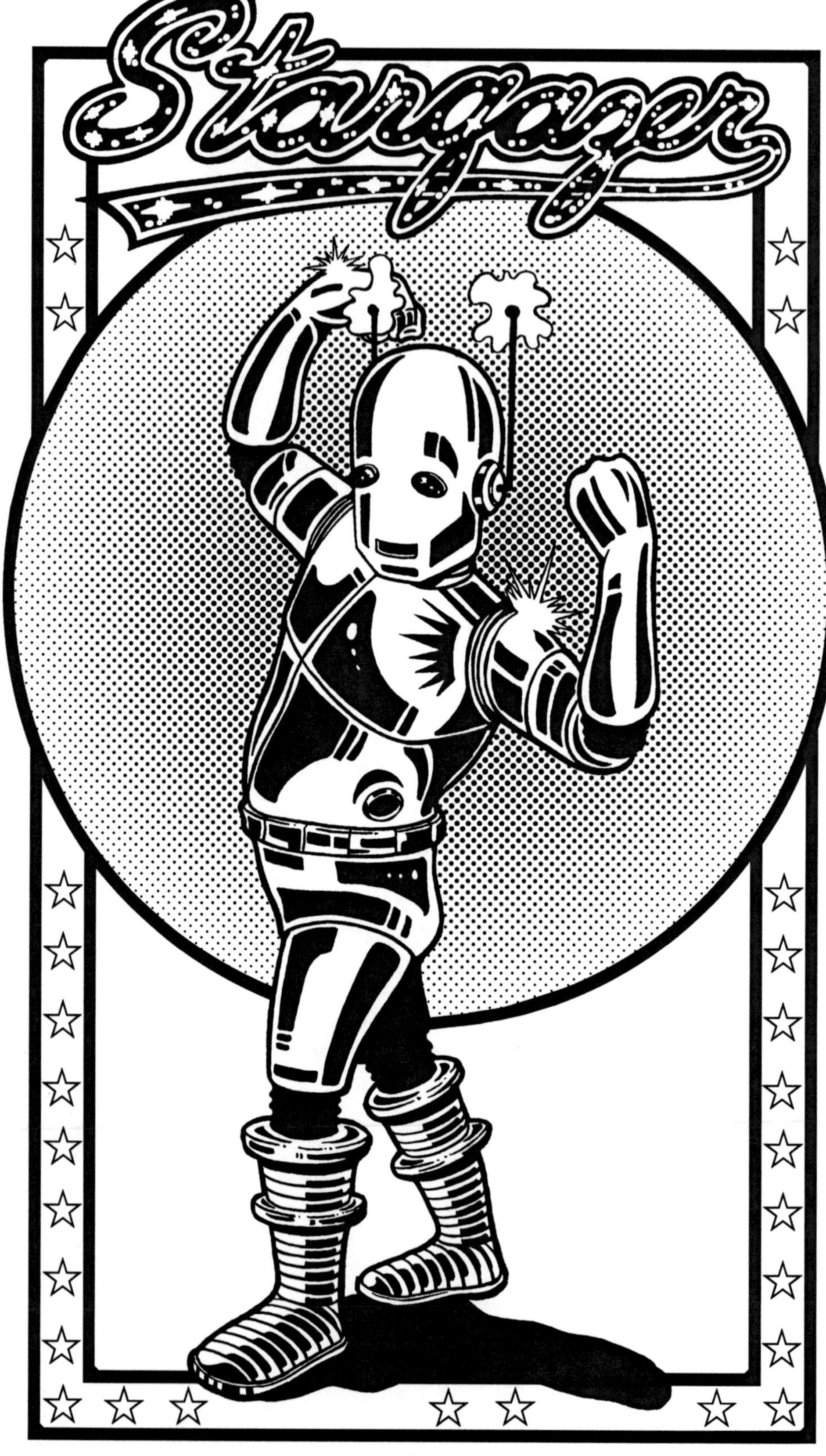
Stargazer

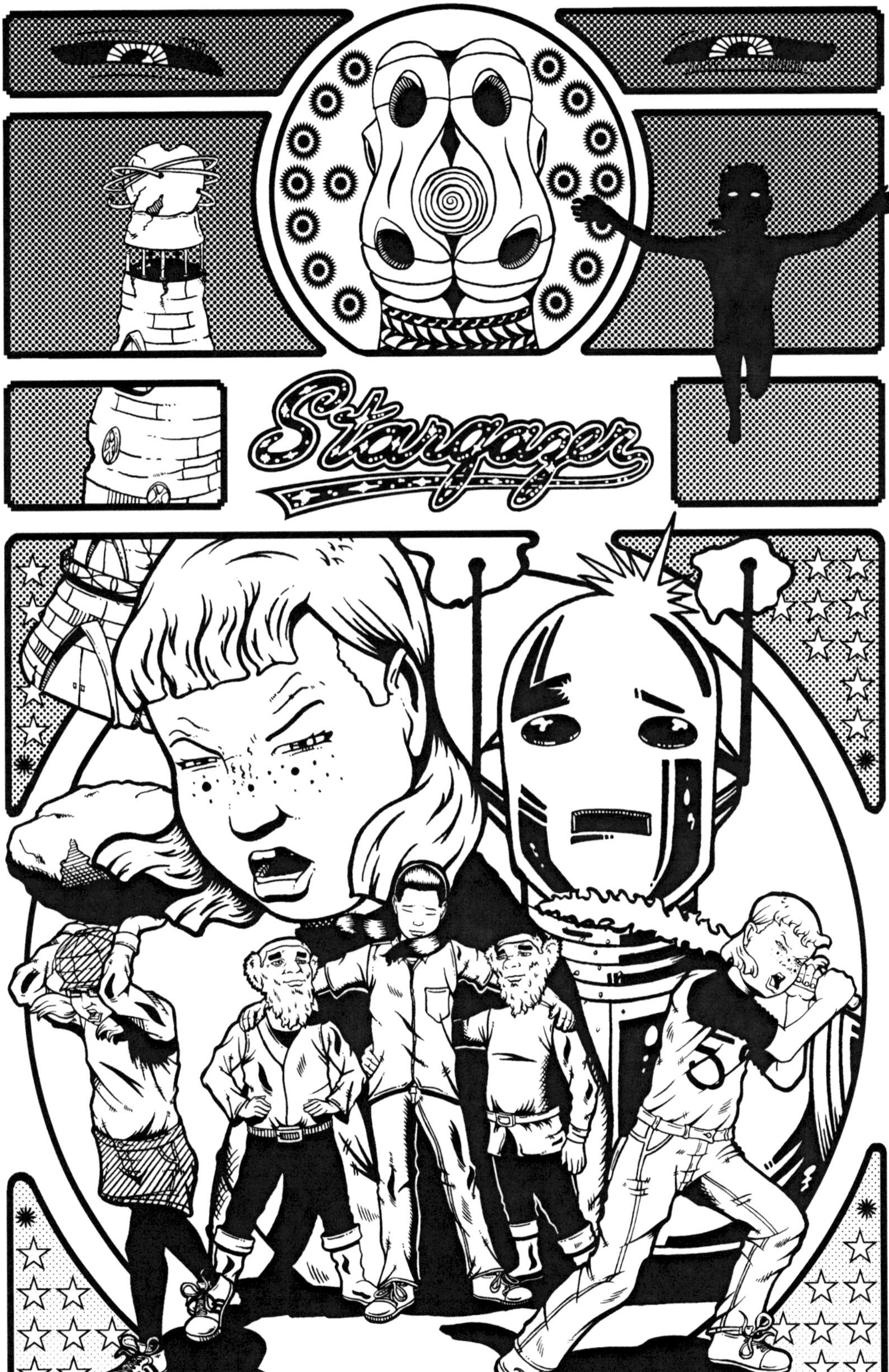
Stargazer

Brainstorming

These are the first few entries in my brainstorming "diary," which are offered without comment and are fairly "rambly." The goal isn't to write well; rather, I'm just trying to get thoughts down as I struggle to come up with *something* to say. You'll see influences that I used as a spark to get things going before I eventually abandon them, and you'll notice false starts as I abandon certain ideas that I initially seemed to embrace. So it goes.

It's written in "entry form" and each entry is separated by a number of days. Mainly to give myself a bit of distance while I thought things over. That happens quite a bit. Anyway! Off we go!

First Entry

I really like the ol' *Star Trek: The Next Generation* episode that featured Scotty appearing in the 24th century and helping the Enterprise escape from an abandoned Dyson Sphere. I think the key thing that I loved was the fact that the Dyson Sphere was completely empty – whoever built it and then inhabited it had long since moved on. The emotional feel was kinda like *Lord of the Rings* (when they do scenes with old statues that have toppled over, or some abandoned tower that used to mark the outer limits of some Empire that's been almost forgotten). I love that.

I've also been really interested in doing something all-ages and I keep coming back to stories like *Narnia*. In a way, doing a contemporary take on *Narnia* would be quite interesting (without, of course, the Christian allegory). Three Earth kids appear on the Sphere and have a number of experiences there. Probably with robots and other fantastical creatures (possibly akin to the Island of Misfit Toys – 'bots whose makers abandoned them when they left the Sphere).

I'm also tempted to make one of the kids (three girls) turn evil or dark as the story progresses.

The Ice Age: I like the idea of the Sphere decaying. The engines that run it (or whatever) are failing and eventually it will be destroyed. Parts of it might be encased in ice and snow while others might be on fire (think of an industrial fire that's as large as North America). In some ways it could be like Norse myths – maybe the world right after Ragnarök.

Second Entry

Just finished up watching *Kiki's Delivery Service* on Monday night while Moggy was in Halifax. I liked it a whole bunch and, as I sit here in Ottawa University's Morriset Library chewing it over, I'm interested in doing something like that for my next book. A lot of this is touched on above, but I'm in a bit of a weird place. I just put brush to paper for the final page of *the road to god knows...* and there's all kinds of uncertainty with what will happen next. Not so much in the immediate future (there are corrections and other editing to do, not to mention the grey washes that are still ahead of me) but I have no idea how that book will do over the next year. Will there even be a chance for a next book? Who knows?

What I do know is that I'd like the next story to be different. *Road* hit themes that were very important to me personally and were really cool to talk about in the pages of a comic book. I'd like the next story to be different and perhaps more accessible, too. I like the idea of writing something that a kid could pickup. I also like the idea of doing something all-ages that doesn't dumb things down at all. Just because it's approachable to kids doesn't mean it has to be *unapproachable* for adults. I also think it might open a few more doors for me commercially than *road* will. Not sure about that one, but I'm speculating here so what the hell.

In some ways, doing a thematic sequel to *road* could be interesting, too. One of the things that always struck me about the Norse myths is how fatalistic they are; they live life to the fullest since it could all be over tomorrow. Even the gods die and, further, they know they are fated to die (at Ragnarök, the twilight of the gods). That knowledge gives them a tremendous freedom for they know that the world itself doesn't end at Ragnarök; it's fated to go on.

Marie's struggle in *road* is really one of control – there's very little she can do to affect what's going on in the world around her. She also knows that things can't stay the same way for her Mom: if Betty doesn't change or cannot change, she will be consumed by her demons; they'll kill her. Marie can't do anything with this knowledge, though; she can't even communicate that to her Mom at all. Doing a story where the "letting go" is dealt with as a major theme or idea could be quite fascinating. And doing it in the pages of an all-ages book is more interesting, too. The trick is how will the "letting go" be portrayed?

Thinking back to *Kiki's*, one of the things that struck me about that story was how the world just accepted that there were witches. The macguffin (and I think I'm using that right!) that the story hinged on was the fact that witches really *do* exist. The world wound up being an amalgam of different time periods (the 30s mixed in with the 50s and so on) but it didn't matter; that was really subtext for the story. All you need to believe is that in this world witches exist. Hand in hand with that, though, is that her powers don't make her that special. Kiki screws up and makes mistakes. She's poor (well, relatively) and doesn't dress like the cool kids. She can do things that no one else can (talk with a cat and fly) but most of these come from her strength of will. Like the comic *St. George*, when she loses her confidence and focus she also loses her powers.

How to deal with magic, then? I know that I want the story to take place in another world and not on Earth. I don't want to have to explain loads of things, either. If I do go the Dyson Sphere route, the question becomes: how to the characters get there? *Narnia* and *Alice in Wonderland* have already hit the other worldly element, though. Hmmm…I don't want to go the mad professor route (besides, that's what Lewis did with *Narnia* anyway) and I'm not sure I want it to be a coincidence. Though…do I want the story to focus on random kids or have them be somehow connected? See, I think I prefer the randomness of it. The idea that it was these kids *only* because they stumbled across something today, but if it had been tomorrow or yesterday, it would have been someone else entirely. I don't want to get too hung up on this, though. One simple option would be just have something from the Dyson Sphere hit the Earth and the kids discover it. Another, better option might be for them to uncover something someone else already found, so instead of being the first on the scene, they're the first to activate it. The "thing" (whatever it is) could have been sitting on someone's shelf for years and no one managed to figure it out.

How 'bout this? Years ago, a young girl found an object in the woods. The object, whatever it is, is a transporter of some sort. A key to the Dyson Sphere, perhaps dropped long ago by a visitor to Earth. Or perhaps by someone who fled the Sphere. Doesn't matter. The object has odd markings etched on its surface that no one can figure out; as the girl grew older, she lost interest in it. Maybe the girl left it on a shelf or in a trunk. As she grew older still and had a family of her own, she forgot about it. Until one day her granddaughter, full of spunk and imagination, stumbled across it (on a shelf, in a trunk…) and became fascinated by it. The granddaughter wanted it but had been taught not to ask, so she'd look at it when she was visiting but always put it back. One day, the grandmother died. And the object, whatever it was, was given (in the will, in a letter…) to the little girl. And somehow, that little girl figured out how to make it work. When she did, she and those around her (say in her bedroom or maybe on a camping trip in the back yard) vanished from Earth and appeared on the Dyson Sphere.

I could actually open the story with the funeral service and go from there. Funky way to start an all-ages story but I think it might work. I'll need to figure out more about the device and more about why this one girl figured it out. It could still have been anyone (and maybe I should mention in the narrative that a lot of other kids have tried? Maybe the granny babysat or taught art to local kids or something?) but really it comes down to who stumbled across it first (the granny as a kid) and then who figured it out. I'm kinda thinking right now that it could be a code; but, if so, I'll need some help making it some type of artistic or mythological code. I also like the idea that it could have been dropped many many years ago, subtly implying (without ever going into details) that maybe the survivors of the Sphere travelled to Earth and populated it.

One thing I do know is that I don't want the kids to develop super powers by accident. Rather, I'd like the Dyson Sphere to be full of wonderful stuff that gives them abilities we don't have on Earth. But those abilities are finite and they come from something else. With the Dyson Sphere both in ruins and quite futuristic, I want the kids to interact with all kinds of fantastic creatures both alive and mechanical. I love the idea of little clockwork robots running about. And that'll work doubly well since it will aid language and communication amongst the characters (maybe starting as translators before the 'bots learn English). I should also see if I can dig up that "extinct mammal" book just to get ideas for sketching very different types of animals than what's currently on the planet. I like the idea of starting the Dyson Sphere out in a ruined town (I'll need to create a map) and have the characters move slowly to larger and larger cities.

Thinking of *Star Trek*, I also really love that 1st season episode *The Last Outpost* where the Enterprise encounters the remnant from the "Dkon" Empire. An automated portal that comes alive and challenges the crew (in particular Riker). That type of obstacle would be cool to touch on and it would also be nifty to add characters like this in strong supporting roles; I mean, the tragedy of a guardian that realizes all that it guards are dead is an intriguing concept.

I suppose it's time to chew over the idea of having some type of antagonist in the story. But I dunno. I'm not really keen on having them discover some heavy (a Ming the Merciless type) and I think the obstacles should be more primal (just survival at first and then dealing with the oddities of the Dyson Sphere itself). The goal should be for the kids to try and get home, at least at first, and this might be the key plot of the story. The first part should be fear and wonder, all mixed together, especially as they realize they are witnessing some great civilization laid low by time. The emptiness should be haunting – and then, of course, the realization that the kids aren't alone. I'm wondering, though, if I could have one kid slowly go mad over the course of the story, perhaps as they discover great power or face the realization that if they go home none of it will work (that will have to be really developed). If I structure the story from the point of view of them all wanting to come home and then create conflict in that, it might work quite well. Especially if, for whatever reason, transporting them back to Earth doesn't work without all of 'em. Seems like a bit of a cliché but it might do the trick..

All this said, when I think back to *Kiki's*, one of the things I really enjoyed about it was the lack of a heavy. Kiki's problems weren't as a result of an antagonist; they were a result of her own fears and insecurities, and doubts and lack of focus. Instead of having any character "go bad," it might work really well just to have the insecurities pull and push the group in different directions. Dealing with each other and dealing with survival might just be enough to make the story work.

I also need to chew over who the inhabitants of the sphere were. Part of the trick with this is that they can't be so far advanced to be completely unrecognizable. In some ways, I'm kinda chewing almost making them superheroes or, rather, technological supermen almost like the Silver-Aged version of Krypton. Or what some of the better stories that showcased the *Legion of Superheroes* had. Anti-gravity devices. Ray beams. That sort of thing. There needs to be a cool factor in the visuals and also a cool factor in the concepts. Some place that we'd all want to go. I could also really stretch myself with some of the designs (think Gaudi here with all kinds of parabolic arches and the like).

Another thing I could explore would be ghosts and the like; having a girl standing on a grassy plain, looking out at the heavens and seeing a fire that burns across half the sky is really cool. Having her realize she's surrounded by ghosts at the same time is quite intriguing.

Third Entry

Just re-reading the above while listening to a variety of tunes on Real Player (especially in the mood for *Final Fantasy* and *The Stars* for some reason). Been doing a lot of touch-ups on *road* this week, too. Plus a photo shoot today for *Sandy Hill Image* and figuring out the Small Press Expo next week.

It's funny. I like the narrative possibilities of the above quite a bit; the sense of loss and characters having to choose between letting things go (or not) could be a theme that constantly runs through the entire story. And what's nice about it is that it can be a subtle thing (letting go of a favourite toy) to a major thing (letting go of the entire Dyson Sphere itself).

What I need to start figuring out is a little bit more about the three protagonists and also a bit more about what the Dyson Sphere allows them to do. I certainly want to avoid the randomness of classic superhero stuff (no mutagenic gene or splashing of some elixir here!) and it certainly can't be anything that's replicable on Earth. It has to be unique to the inhabitants of the Sphere but something that wouldn't overwhelm kids.

I'm wondering here if I could draw on myths and legends here but make it more plausible. Some of the Norse myths drew on mystical objects (Mjnollnir or Odin's spear) while others were more subtle (the knowledge runes that Odin gained); there should be a sense of wonder with everything, too. I'm thinking here of how well Morrison and Quitely have captured Superman in *All-Star Superman* – that beautiful Silver Age feel. Kirby did something similar in the pages of *Thor* that only Walt Simonson was able to capture later and I like that sense of awesomeness. I know I want to avoid unexplainable powers, but some things could be tied to objects of great wonder.

What I need to be careful of is having too much. There's no point in having all kinds of objects kicking around; the temptation would be to tell a 'smash-up' story instead of focusing on character. Any items that the characters find should be limited and they should have consequences. One other thing that I need to keep in mind is who the Dyson people were. If I want them to be basically humans, it's not so much of an issue. But if I want them to be more alien, then the items the kids find should reflect that. No point to have magic rings if the Dysons don't have fingers. Same goes for weird activation rituals and the like (if you need 12 fingers to punch in a code, for example).

It shouldn't be like the kids are lost in a magic shop, though; it should be stuff they stumble across. Stuff that can help them, sure, but not stuff they find every day. Part of what I need to figure out, then, is just how the kids stay alive. And not by just subsisting – they need to survive. What do they eat? Where do they sleep? Where do they go to the bathroom? That kind of thing. All the basics of survival has to be fairly obvious and also something that I should address. It's part of the reason I like the idea of 'bots and critters – some of 'em could be set-up to care for visitors. Actually, that could be something I play up; a 'bot that follows them, observing in the shadows as it absorbs their language, learning before it finally reveals itself. I don't want the robots to be C-3PO, though, so it might be better to keep a lot of it non-verbal, at least at first. That'll work if I make the 'bot more afraid of the girls then they are of him.

The Kids: I want to start chewing over who these girls are. I've already got names for them (I'm going to use some ol' favourites) but I still need to learn a bit more about who they are. The three characters are Marni, Elora, and Sophie and they range in ages from about 9-11. I have to be careful here because if there's too big of an age gap it wouldn't make sense that they'd be friends. And I think I want to avoid them being family; we pick our friends but we don't choose our family. The ties of friendship will also serve them well in the early part of the story, helping them deal with their initial fear. Thinking back to what I wrote before, I like the idea of having them doing a sleepover in the backyard shortly after the grandmother's funeral. Marni, the granddaughter, is finally given the Dyson doohickey by her parents just before her friends come over. And then the three of them, together, manage to unlock the gateway (or whatever it is) that brings them to the Dyson sphere. One advantage of this is that I can bring the whole tent (and everything inside of it) with them, too.

Character-wise, Marni should be the dreamer. She was the one that was always attracted to the gadget; it filled her with wonder and imagination and she'd have long talks with her granny about it (actually, that begs the point: do I want to do *Lost* type flashbacks or just keep it in the present. Hmmm…). A bit of a tom-boy, Marni is quite happy tramping in the woods, exploring. She's probably a bit of a builder, too. Maybe constructing a milk carton boat to plop in some stream somewhere. Dirty blonde with shoulder length hair. Maybe some freckles sprinkled over her nose. Elora is a brunette with longish hair that she often wraps with a bandana. Somewhat bookish but not shy. Sophie should have longish hair that she keeps in a pony tail behind her head. Probably the youngest of the group and a little shy. Her voice shouldn't be too prominent; she lets the other two girls do most of the talking. That might be a bit too close to Emma from *road*, though, so I may have to chew that over a bit. There'll probably be a few comparisons, but I really want to go for a strong triumvirate with the three instead of just two main players and a supporting character.

Fourth Entry

This story has possibilities and I like where it's going. But I need to start figuring out who these kids are a bit more. I touched on it above but fleshing them out is fairly important. One thing I was chewing over was making Elora more of a practical character. I was kinda thinking of making her more of a scientist then the other two. More down to earth but not in a curmudgeonly way. I don't want her to be lecturing or otherwise correcting the other two; aside from anything else, these are all friends. And Sophie and Marni wouldn't hang out with her if she was being a bitch all the time. So I'm thinking more she'd correct them quietly and softly but with authority ("no, the stars are different. I don't recognize any of the stars or constellations."). I really like the idea of her being a budding astronomer, hanging out with her granddad at a cottage and looking at the stars for hours on end, drinking hot chocolate and eating rice crispy squares on an autumn night. It might be fun to make her dad a mechanic and have her be pretty comfortable with machinery. Not so much electronics (she ain't a 'puter nerd) but just things mechanical. If I do something with clockwork 'bots then she'd be a natural to fall for him, just fascinated with what they are and what makes 'em tick.

Sophie is still somewhat tricky. If Marni is the myth-loving dreamer and storyteller and Elora is more of an astronomer, I'd like Sophie to be something in-between. One thing that might work would be to make her a musician. It could be tricky to show (but then again, check out *Wahoo Morris*) but having her play something abstract and non-vocal would work well. So wind-powered, huh? Then a flute or perhaps something Celtic (what the leader of *The Chieftains* plays?). It needs to be small so a flute would work best since she could always have it on her; in a back pocket or whatever. What's neat about this is that she just doesn't have to play the flute; a lot of other things could be open to her but the flute is what she always has with her. But drums (*The Honeycombs*!) or whatnot could be fun, too. And the musical element echoes, at least a little bit, that *Star Trek: The Next Generation* episode where Picard lives another complete life and learns to play the flute. Depending how I structure the world of the Dyson sphere, music could play a large part in their culture. I'm kinda chewing over having that flute be something that's special to her in a bit of a different way then the other two girls. Marni had a close bond with her grandma that just ended sadly, but while Elora's granddad is still alive Sophie never knew her grandfather, the musician in their family, and her memories of her grandmother are sad ones; the old lady never recovered from the loss of her lover and Sophie never got to know her very well as a result. She couldn't cross the distance that the pain had created. So Sophie's probably been a little jealous of her two friends; not in a really negative way, but envious of the fact that they've had something that she doesn't and never will have.

One of the struggles this story will present is how to deal with emotions and fears, along with the bare bones of just survival. Bathroom breaks and starvation, y'know? So I'll need to have an "intervener" of some sort fairly early on in the story to help them out. Some of this I've addressed above (maybe a robot) but it's something to keep in mind as I construct the story. That said, one of the things I found marvelous about *Kiki's* was that the fable did work – you believe that there are witches out there and that they exist. I think that as long as I keep things somewhat believable I won't need to worry about too much of the down and gritty. And, as I touched on above, as long as I have a robot intervene fairly early and then have the girls led to some type of storehouse I'll be ok. And keep in mind that this is supposed to be a futuristic society – I can come up with all kinds of food and water pills to cut down on the bulk of what they carry. Let things be fantastic.

That's actually something I still really need to play with: the fantastic. These kids are walking in a *Legion of Super-heroes* comic without realizing it. The reader won't really get that in the beginning, either. The story feel should be somewhat evocative of *The Wizard of Oz* – out in the sticks with the knowledge that things are different but not really seeing the hows or whys 'til later on in the journey. So there should be hints sprinkled along early enough. There should also be a sense of loss. It's one of the nifty things that Jackson got right about *Lord of the Rings*. It felt like it was in twilight; that a real "thinning" was occurring. In some ways the thinning has already occurred and the world is slowly crumbling apart.

I may actually need to bring some books with me next time I'm here, too. I have a loose idea of what I want (that Silver Age DC feel) but I want to tie it in with some myths and legends, too. Some of it should be like that classic Arthur C. Clarke quote ("any significantly advanced technology will seem like magic to a primitive person" – I'm paraphrasing!) but I want something behind it, too. Figuring out what that something is should be part of the story.

Plot Breakdown

A few days go by and Sophie and Elora are introduced to the reader, which is a smidgen awkward. Maybe they're both in Marni's bedroom while she "sucks it up" in the hallway before entering her room and seeing them. I almost wonder if I could do this as a "split panel" thing. So a panel divided in half (the "wall") as the two groups of girls go through the tension of seeing each other for the first time post-funeral. All three girls are a little unsure of themselves. What does one say when death is in the air? So body language is key and the dialogue should be really soft spoken (Sophie: "I'm really sorry about your grandma…").

Outline

Page 12

First panel has all three of the the girls in Marni's bedroom with the door closed. The room has been cleaned up since the last time (so no clothes everywhere!). Marni is sitting on her bed while Elora and Sophie are standing a little ways away (again with the physical separation). Good bird's eye shot for this one. All the girls are awkward: Marni is sitting holding the card and flowers fairly rigidly while the other two standing awkwardly (maybe holding an arm or something). Any bags haven't been put down yet. M: "T-Thanks for the c-card and flowers, guys. I-I…" S: "I'm r-really sorry about your granny, Marn…" Panel two has Marni bent over, crying, while both Elora and Sophie are to either side of her, holding her. The card and flowers are still on Marni's lap while the bags that Elora and Sophie brought with them have been forgotten on the floor where they were standing. Panel three is a close up (maybe worm's eye?) of the three of them with Elora whispering a worried, "you ok?" Panel four is a similar angle shot with Marni rubbing her nose with the back of her hand (very unladylike!) and saying a very shaky, "yeah…" Panel five is the first real sense of the maturity of them all. Sophie, leaning back on the bed, is smiling ruefully. S: "How have yer mom and dad treated with all of this? I mean, when my granddad died my parents just clammed up. Totally. They just dropped me off a lot more at the Folklore Centre. Yeeesh…"

Page 13

Close up on Marni smiling despite herself. M: "Well, y'know. My mom bailed while my dad tried to talk a bit…they were ok, I guess. I dunno." Panel two is a pull back shot again to establish all of them. Sophie is scowling at this. S: "Man, parents…they get on my nerves." Elora is watching the exchange mainly because she doesn't have anything to add to it. Instead, she's holding the Artifact, examining it quizzically. E: "Hey, this is that thing you were talking about, right? It's really cool…" Panel three has Marni watching Elora and Sophie while the latter two both touch the Artifact. Sophie is sitting up. M: "Yeah, it is. My granny had it forever but I guess it's mine now…" S: "Well, some of these markings remind me of the ol' tattoos that some of my teachers have at the Centre. At least a bit. I can see why you were always so keen on it. Where did yer granny get it again?" Panel four has Marni smiling and half turned towards Elora. Sophie has turned to face them both. They're all in a semi-circle around the Artifact. M: "I dunno. She said she found it when she was really little. There're photos of her with it from around that time so who knows?" Sophie: "Does it do anything?" Marni: "No, we never could figure anything out about it. My dad kinda liked it when he was young but I guess he lost interest." Sophie interjects with a snarky, "Boys." M: "Heh. Well, I guess nobody ever came looking for it or anything, either." Panel five is a pull back shot of the three of them, all sitting cross legged on the bed in a circle chatting and talking away. S: "Well, I brought some stuff for the camping trip. I'm hungry. Are we eating first or later or what?" M: "My dad said something about pizza."

Page 14

Panel one should be a cute shot of both Elora and Sophie, together, shouting "pizza" in a big font! Panel two has Elora going off on a pouty tangent. E: "I like noodles, but my mom is all traditional when it comes to food. All the time. I never get pizza. Even if friends come over, it's all traditional Chinese desserts and stuff. No pizza. Not fair." Panel three has Marni clocking her with a pillow while Sophie is bent over laughing. Elora has her arms all up in the air. M: "'Nuff complaining! You're going to get pizza tonight so shut up!"

One Page - Two Panels

PAGE 12

PANEL ONE

This is a splash with some hopefully interesting design elements. This first panel is a small one at the top left corner of the page, establishing Marni back in her room. The Artifact is on her bed beside her and she's reading a small book. She's not focusing on the book, though; she's looking up towards her closed bedroom door as she listen to her mom's dialogue (out of panel).

1. Mom (out of panel): Marni! Your friends are HERE! I'm sending them up to your room!

PANEL TWO

This panel makes up most of the page. I want the wall between Marni's bedroom and the hall to act as a dividing point between the characters – both physically and a bit emotionally, too. This might work best with an angle to the page just to give me a bit more room for everything. I need to have the dividing wall "read" as a wall, so I'll probably make it thicker and hatch it. Maybe with a shot of the door frame to really bring home what we're seeing. On the left side is Marni, standing awkwardly facing her door. Her hand is close to the door knob but she's not touching it. She should seem unsure of herself. Hesitant.

On the right side of the wall are Elora and Sophie, standing just as awkwardly, nervous about meeting their friend. Each girl is carrying an overnight bag or backpack. Elora is also holding a large, oversized card and maybe a small bouquet of flowers. The card should be obviously big. Way bigger than a normal birthday or greeting card. There's no real way to clearly show that this is the first time that they've seen each other since Granny Hitchins died; but I hope it comes across. As a result, they are both nervous as well and are hesitating before knocking. Perhaps looking at one another, biting their lips.

I'm going to take a moment and describe both Elora and Sophie, since both of them are so key to the rest of the story. Elora is a brunette with longish hair that she often wraps with a bandana. Somewhat bookish, but not shy. One thing I was chewing over was making Elora more of a practical character. down to earth, but not in a curmudgeonly way. I don't want her to be lecturing or otherwise correcting the other two; aside from anything else, they are all friends. And Sophie and Marni wouldn't hang out with her if she was being a bitch all the time. So I'm thinking more she'd correct them quietly and softly but with authority.

I really like the idea of her being a budding astronomer, hanging out with her granddad at a cottage and looking at the stars for hours on end, drinking hot chocolate and eating rice crispy squares on an autumn night. It might be fun to make her dad a mechanic and have her be pretty comfortable with machinery. Not so much electronics (she ain't a 'puter nerd) but just things mechanical. If I do something with clockwork 'bots then she'd be a natural to fall for 'em, just fascinated with what they are and what makes 'em tick.

Elora isn't prone to boasts or really speaking about things that she knows nothing about. She'll keep her mouth shut at those times. But when it comes to something she does know a thing or two about, everything changes. She'll speak her mind, often bluntly, and she doesn't brook much argument on these points. She's quite eager to learn, though, and she doesn't restrict herself to just a few simple interests. Probably a bit like *Star Trek's* Spock in this case – a bit of a sponge, absorbing quite a bit of everything around her. Her real interests, though, are in astronomy and mechanics.

Unlike Marni, Elora is really close to both her dad and her grandfather. She's similar to both men; there's a strong practical streak that runs through all of them and it helps keep all of them grounded. Both of her main interests come from the two of them. Her granddad founded a mechanic shop years ago (probably in the 1950s, and he still proudly proclaims the Edsel as the greatest car ever built) and passed that on to his son when he wanted to retire. His retirement allowed him to pursue his other great love, stargazing, and he shared that love with his granddaughter when she got old enough to really comprehend it. Quite often she spends weekends with him at his winterized cottage, watching the skies from a large patio. Her other great love is cars, especially older ones that aren't "fouled up" by computers. That mechanical streak binds all of the family together and keeps them connected. The drawback is that her dad does work quite a bit and she's left to her own devices quite often at night. While she does hang out at the shop with dad after school, and also spends quite a bit of time with her granddad, she's left on her own quite a bit. Elora isn't a loner by nature so it's no surprise that she often chooses to spend her time with her Marni and Sophie instead.

Clothing-wise, I really like the idea of her long black hair held up in a bandana. I wouldn't mind her wearing plaid but I think that might be too close to *road*. So, what I need is something that she'll wear that's kinda practical…well, duh. The easiest solution would be a mechanics shirt. Could be long sleeved or not, but it could easily have the name of the shop embroidered on it. Good grey shop shirt, green combats, black shoes, and a plain t-shirt. Not bad. Maybe toss in a necklace or something "spacey."

Sophie is quite the burgeoning musician and really into a lot of Celtic tunes. Her granddad was the main songsmith and music maker in her family but she never really got much of a chance to know him before he died. His death, a suicide, became a kind of open wound that no one in her family would talk much about. It devastated her grandmother (who was never the same after it) and her mom didn't deal with it that well, either. She is reasonably close to her mom but this is subject matter that just isn't discussed. That makes things a bit tricky when it comes to Sophie's music; she's clearly talented, but the memory of her father's suicide prevents her mom from really connecting with her on it. So, it's the case of Sophie being dropped off at various folklore-type places and left to develop pretty much on her own. That's left Sophie pretty independent and fairly feisty when it comes to doing things her way. A strong stubborn streak runs through her. It's also left her more experienced then her two friends. She's made connections at her various music classes with people, typically a bit older, who have opened her eyes to all kinds of different music. Her first love is Celtic, though, and her introduction to the Pogues started a love affair that'll probably be lifelong. She, like Marni, has explored the woods and done a reasonable amount of camping.

She's more experimental then most in her age group, too. She's not afraid to try new things since the results have been pretty good so far. And she's not afraid to challenge taboos. She would ask questions at inopportune times (say at a funeral, "how'd they make the body look like that, anyway?"). That could get her into trouble down the road but it's not something she's really aware of right now. So she's stubborn and has a major zest for life. That zest really comes from what happened to her granddad; she doesn't really realize it, but it struck her hard, too. She just deals with it in a very different way then either her mom or grandma. Those two women turned away from it, never wanting to deal with the suicide and certainly never wanting to talk about it. Sophie's reaction was to live a little more and enjoy life. To try new things and never get stuck in the same way she thinks her granddad became stuck. In a way, out of the three of 'em, she's the one who enjoys the forthcoming adventure the most.

Appearance-wise, she's gotta have glasses since that will help separate her from the other two. I went with big glasses with Marie in road, though, so these should be pretty modern and sleek. Maybe small rectangles? A poor boy hat, too? I don't wanna get too folkie, though. Maybe a green army surplus jacket, then? Jeans and an army surplus ain't a bad way to go. Converse runners complete her look.

One Page - Five Panels

PAGE 13

PANEL ONE

Good bird's eye shot of all three girls are back in Marni's bedroom with the door closed. The room has been cleaned up since the last time (so no clothes everywhere!). Marni is sitting on her bed while Elora and Sophie are standing a little ways away (again with the physical separation). All the girls are awkward. Marni is sitting holding the card and flowers fairly rigidly while the other two standing awkwardly (maybe holding an arm or something). They haven't put their backpacks down yet.

1. Marni: T-Thanks for the c-card and flowers, guys. I-I…

2. Sophie: I'm r-really sorry about your GRANNY, Marn.

PANEL TWO

Marni has bent over as she starts to cry, hard. Action lines around her to show that she's shuddering. Elora and Sophie are on either side of her, each with an arm over her shoulder. The card and flowers are still on Marni's lap while the bags that Elora and Sophie brought with them have been forgotten on the floor where they were standing. Medium shot of the three of them.

3. Elora: Oh, Marni.

PANEL THREE

Same shot as the previous panel. Possibly as a worm's eye or I could just replicate the exact same angle.

4. Elora: You ok?

PANEL FOUR

A good close-up on Marni rubbing her nose with the back of her hand (very unladylike!). Her eyes should look raw and sore.

5. Marni: I g-guess.

PANEL FIVE

This repeats the shot of panel two. Marni is looking at the card more carefully now and Elora is pointing at something inside of it. Sophie is leaning back on the bed, supported on her elbows and is smiling ruefully. She's looking at Marni and Elora with a slight scowl.

6. Sophie: How have yer mom and dad TREATED you with all of this? I mean, when my granddad died my parents just clammed up. Totally shut right up.

7. Sophie: They just DROPPED me off a lot more at the Folklore Centre. Yeeesh…

One Page - Five Panels

PAGE 14

PANEL ONE

Close up on Marni smiling despite herself. Her eyes should look quite a bit better now.

1.Marni: Well, y'know. My mom bailed while my dad tried to talk a bit…they were ok, I guess. I dunno.

PANEL TWO

Pull back shot to see all of them. Marni hasn't moved but Sophie is lying down on the bed, resting on her side, her head supported by one hand. She's scowling even more. Elora, still sitting beside Marni, isn't looking at either girl. Instead, she's holding the Artifact, examining it quizzically.

2. Sophie: Man, parents…they get on my NERVES.

3. Elora: Hey, this is that thing you were talking about, right? It's really COOL. I don't know what it is, but it looks neat. So smooth and kinda COLD…

PANEL THREE

Sophie has sat up and both her and Elora are crowding around Marni as they look at it more closely. Marni is watching the two of them slightly amused. Elora is still touching it carefully.

4. Marni: Yup, that's it.

5. Sophie: Well, some of these markings remind me of the ol' tattoos that some of my teachers have at the Centre. At least a bit. I can see why you were always so KEEN on it.

6. Sophie: Where did yer granny get it again?

PANEL FOUR

The girls are now sitting fully on the bed in a semi-circle around the Artifact. Marni is actually smiling and she and Elora are both looking at Sophie. Sophie has turned to face them both and is now holding the Artifact, looking at it closely.

7. Marni: I dunno. She said she found it when she was really little. There're photos of her with it but I don't think she really remembered.

8. Sophie: Does it DO anything?

9. Marni: Nope. It's just DIFFERENT. My dad kinda liked it when he was young but I guess he lost interest.

10. Sophie: BOYS!

PANEL FIVE

Similar shot as panel four. The key thing here is to show that Marni, for the first time since we've been introduced to her, is relaxed. So smiling and leaning back in a very easy going kinda way. The other girls are the same in their own way. Sophie is still holding the Artifact and Elora is grinning.

11. Marni: Heh. Well, nobody ever came LOOKING for it or anything, either.

12. Sophie: Well, I brought some stuff for our camping trip out back, but I haven't had supper yet.

13. Elora: Me, neither! I'm HUNGRY!

14. Sophie: So are we eating first or later or what?

15. Marni: My dad said something about pizza.

One Page - Three Panels

PAGE 15

PANEL ONE

This should be a cute close-up on both Elora and Sophie as they shout out together (big font)

1. Sophie and Elora together: PIZZA!!!

PANEL TWO

Pull back to see all of them. Both Marni and Sophie are smiling ruefully at Elora. Maybe rolling their eyes as they look at one another. Elora has crossed her arms across her chest and is looking quite pouty.

2. Elora: Look, I like NOODLES, but my mom is all traditional when it comes to food. ALL the time.

3. Elora: I never get pizza. Even if friends come over, it's all traditional Chinese desserts and stuff. No pizza.

4. Elora: Not FAIR.

PANEL THREE

This is a large panel and should fill the rest of the page. Sophie has clocked Elora with a pillow. So she's in a full follow-through with it while Elora is falling over in the background, arms flung out in space. Marni is bent over laughing hard.

5. Sophie: 'Nuff complaining! You're going to get pizza tonight so SHUT UP!

Von Allan was born red-headed and freckled in Arnprior, Ontario, just in time for *Star Wars: A New Hope*. Von currently lives in Ottawa, Canada, with his writer/editor geek wife, Moggy; a husky dog, Rowen; and two feisty cats, Bonny and Reilly.

Von loves to hear from people who've read and (hopefully!) enjoyed his work. Feel free to write him at von@vonallan.com.

Von's website is at http://www.vonallan.com and is the best place to go for updates, art, essays and the like. There's a dedicated website for *Stargazer* at http://stargazer.vonallan.com. Von can also be found online in the following places:

Twitter at http://twitter.com/vonallan

Facebook at http://www.facebook.com/von.allan

CPSIA information can be obtained at www.ICGtesting.com
Printed in the USA
LVOW131356061111

253722LV00005BA/16/P